Sports

~~4.95~~
.29

ONE STEP FROM GLORY

On the Fringe of Professional Sports

SKIP ROZIN

SIMON AND SCHUSTER
NEW YORK

Published by Simon and Schuster
A Division of Gulf & Western Corporation
Simon & Schuster Building
Rockefeller Center
1230 Avenue of the Americas
New York, New York 10020
Designed by Stanley S. Drate
Manufactured in the United States of America
Printed by The Murray Printing Company
Bound by The Book Press, Inc.
1 2 3 4 5 6 7 8 9 10
Library of Congress Cataloging in Publication Data
Rozin, Skip.
One step from glory.
Includes index.
1. Professional sports—United States. 2. Athletes —United States. I. Title.
GV583.R69 796 .0973 78-31342
ISBN 0-671-23069-7

Acknowledgments

That this book exists at all is due, largely, to the efforts of James Oliver Brown, my agent, who believed in it.

Research for the project would have been impossible without the help of professional athletic organizations throughout the country. It was through their cooperation that I was able to gain access to the players I interviewed. While all the teams I approached were receptive, I wish especially to thank the New York Yankees, the Giants, the Knicks and the Jets for their repeated assistance.

In collecting information on any subject, it is always wise to seek out established experts. The experts here are the journalists and writers charged with the responsibility of covering sports, and they could not have been more helpful to me. My special thanks to Howie Evans, Phil Pepe, Nick Acocella, Bob Kesling, Michael Katz, Howard Balzer, Jonathan Rand, Ron Martz, John Jeansonne, and Bill Verigan.

But most important, I want to thank the more than two hundred athletes who gave so generously of their time and energy. In particular, there are a number of athletes—Tony LaRussa, Lou Piccone, George Mira, Tom Shopay, Joe Lis and others—whose stories never made it to the final draft, but who nevertheless made solid contributions. Had it not been for the willingness of all of the people to talk with me, candidly and at length, in darkened ball parks, damp locker rooms and noisy bars, I would have had no story to tell.

The importance of that effort was re-emphasized while I was collecting photographs to supplement the text. Along with one picture came a note urging me to return it when I was finished. "After all," said the sender, "it's all I have to prove I was really there."

To all of you for whom being "there" was so important, I thank you for trusting me with your story.

For My Father

Contents

Author's Note

This book started out to be a portrait of the marginal athlete, an old and personal fascination of mine. As a baseball fan in Cincinnati in the early 1950s, I knew few other kinds. Jim Greengrass and Bud Podbielan, Corky Valentine and Lloyd Merriman, I watched them toil from the Sun Deck—called the Moon Deck at night—in old Crosley Field, or listened to their itineracies, described by Waite Hoyt, the Reds' radio announcer. While there were stars—Ted Kluszewski and Ewell Blackwell being the brightest—it was the fringe players who held my interest. They would appear on the club, stay for a season or two, then vanish. From where and to where was always a mystery. They also seemed to represent the true nature of those Cincinnati teams. Their presence mirrored the Reds' quest for the first division of the National League: strong in June, wavering in July, both faded badly in September.

Once into this project, however, meeting and talking with over two hundred athletes, it became clear that the plight of the marginal player is, at one time or another, shared by all but the biggest superstars. That plight—having to convince someone else that you're good enough to play and maintaining your self-confidence in the face of repeated rejections—is universal in sports. John Unitas, The Quarterback in the NFL in the 1960s, came to the Baltimore Colts as a rookie nobody wanted. Tommy Davis, a star and two-time batting champion with the Dodgers, was sold or released by four different teams in his last two seasons. They knew stardom, but they also knew what it was to hang on to the edge of their sport.

And so, while the main focus is still survival in professional athletics, that focus has broadened to cover more than would normally be considered fringe players. The real story of this book is the life outside the spotlight—the men who exist there and why they hold on so tenaciously.

That is why the book is primarily concerned with baseball, football, and basketball. They are the American team sports. This is an American story, the story of the pursuit of that portion of the American Dream that pictures an athlete standing beside his teammates in victory.

The individuals whose lives are touched upon here are introduced at specific times in their lives and their careers because something has happened at this point that is of value to our story. But since these are people whom we will get to know and, hopefully, care about, an epilogue is provided at the end which updates the life of each person as of the writing of this note.

Skip Rozin

June 1, 1978

AN OPENING SCENE

The place is Tampa, Florida, known for its cigars and the frequency of its thunderstorms. Storm clouds gather quickly here. A single wisp of haze, floating lazily across a clear blue sky, will suddenly grow, darken, and spread until it blocks out all evidence of the sun. Thunder will shake the earth, and jagged rips of lightning will stagger across the blackened sky. And then rain, hard rain, will gush down in torrents. It is the way here, at almost any time during the summer. Yet on this particular day, the sixth of July, only hot, glaring sunlight drenches the cities and towns around Tampa Bay. The long holiday weekend commemorating the nation's two hundredth birthday has ended. Natives are back in air-conditioned offices and air-conditioned homes, or are traveling from one to the other in air-conditioned automobiles. Tourists are staked out by their pools, or lie greased and prostrate at the beaches of neighboring Clearwater, Dunedin, and St. Petersburg.

And on a large patch of ground just to the southwest, a professional football team is about to be born. For the Tampa Bay Buccaneers, newest entry in the National Football League, this is the first day of life.

From the outside, the five-acre complex appears to be a painting. There is no visible movement, no audible sound. The parallel practice fields, grass freshly sprigged and bright green, still await the first imprint of a cleat. The goal posts, straight and silver, shine in the sun. Off to the left are the new blocking sleds, one blue and white and the other red and black, and neither has been hit in anger. The thirty-eight-foot photography tower at the rear of the lot has never been used. No fan has yet pressed against the encircling fence, peering at the drama within.

It is perfect, without a flaw, the product of scientific design and efficient planning culled from fifty years of professional football. But it is all decoration. Strip away the newly painted metal and concrete and what remains is an element that has become the hallmark of every newborn professional team. That element—worn and scarred from use, gray with age—is the desire of grown men to live a boy's game. It is at the core of all professional sports, and is as present in the locker room of the Super Bowl champion Pittsburgh Steelers as it is on the rocky playing field of semipro football's Jersey Oaks. It is only more evident here, easier to observe. At a time when superstars and their multimillion-dollar contracts dominate the sports pages, expansion brings together athletes delighted to be offered any contract to sign and any uniform to wear. Winning and stardom and championship checks are eventual goals, but for now belonging is enough. It is the crucial ingredient—that necessary first step. One must be on a team before he can play; he must get into the game before he can play brilliantly.

Look for no unassailed egos here. Of the eighty veterans reporting to camp, almost all have been dropped from at least one team. Cut. Fired. For most, it has happened more than once. Now they focus on survival. Their dreams, tilted toward pure glory as rookies, are now edged in desperation. They know if they cannot make it here, they are not likely to get another chance. In the great mandala of sports, this is the final stop.

It is close to two o'clock. Players have been coming into the locker room and training room since noon, preparing for the opening practice an hour away. While the mind of this sophisticated organization whirs on in the other side of the building—coaching staff and ticket people, public relations department and business section, carrying on their various functions—the arms and legs are being attended to by Dave Kendall and his staff of trainers. Men, all sizes and ages, from the 5-feet-7-inch kick returner to the 6-feet-8-inch tackle, from the youngest rookie to the ten-year veterans, wait to have ankles taped and special attention given to whatever physical problems have accumulated during their careers in football. As each finishes he takes up a position in front of his locker, or stretches out on the floor or in the corridor that leads to the field, and he waits.

Even in the coolness of the air conditioning there is the stale scent of anxiety. And with reason. Ninety-six men have reported to today's first practice; forty-three will be carried on the active roster during the season. That is the normal formula of an opening camp, but the uncertainty is more pronounced here. No one has tenure. One or two high-priced veterans traded from established teams seem reasonably safe, as do the club's top draft choices, but they are the only ones. For most of these men their continued presence here is moment to moment, and they know it. Looking down the rows of new, wood-grained lockers is a study in frustrated ambition. Charlie Evans sits on the floor and looks down at his hands. They, like him, are broad and strong, and abused from four hard years of clinging to professional football. A fourteenth-round draft selection from the University of Southern California, he had been released by the New York Giants and Washington Redskins before signing with Tampa Bay. Nearby is Steve Chomyszak, a huge tackle who had played on five different teams in three leagues before being cut by the Cincinnati Bengals and coming here. Getting a drink of water is Brad Watson, a smiling, round-faced schoolteacher from Kentucky who was signed by the Redskins at a free agent tryout camp, then cut in two successive tries to make that team. Inside the trainer's room, sitting on the table getting taped, is Bill Cappleman, who looks and talks more like a southern businessman than a journeyman quarterback. After setting thirteen passing records at Florida State he spent three frustrating years as a backup quarterback at Minnesota and Detroit, then played in the World Football League before retiring to the magazine business in south Florida. Until the Bucs were formed. Then back he came.

There are others who have made the rounds, playing on different teams in different leagues, for as much as $90,000 a season and as little as $10 a game. Endless names on an ever changing roster. Most of the men have come here as free agents, which means they were not playing on any team when Tampa Bay signed them. Some, like Cappleman, had not played for a season or more. But they are football players, not salesmen or businessmen or teachers or anything else. That is why they are here, hoping for "a shot," as the players put it, a chance to show what they can do. They walk around in the neatly carpeted rooms in their stockinged feet—no cleats permitted inside—and drink soda from the large, lighted dispensers. There is little conversation. Those who talk do so quietly. No one laughs. They just sit, listening to the recorded music that seeps in through the acoustical ceiling, and wait for three o'clock and the beginning of practice.

For each of these men this is a critical test. The pattern and quality of his life—where he will live and what he will be doing—will be determined by what happens in the following days and weeks. In most occupations that would amount to a unique crisis, but not here. It has all happened before, over and over since the beginning of professional athletics. And especially in the past twenty years. With the rush of new leagues and expanded old ones, thousands of athletes have paraded through dozens of first camps, each reaching for a piece of the magic they can find no place else. So it was with the beginning of the American Football League and then the World Football League, and at various stages of expansion of the NFL. It is an unending drama, which has been played out across the country, from Boston to San Diego, from Birmingham to Denver.

In the relatively brief history of professional football, that drama has even played before in central Florida. It opened first across the bay from here in St. Petersburg in 1966, when the Miami Dolphins began as an expansion team in the young and struggling AFL; it moved next to De Land in 1974, where the Jacksonville Sharks opened camp as the Florida entry in the WFL; and now it has come to Tampa. And everywhere it plays, the plot is the same: Men from all over the country, traveling wherever necessary to practice their trade, which happens to be football. Names, more names than anyone can remember. Men fresh out of college who would never have been in uniform if it were not for expansion, and others, veterans cut from other clubs, given one more chance because of the additional jobs. Many had quit, given up football and made a life for themselves in more conventional businesses, only to leave them and return to two-a-day drills and rubbing liniment for one more try. For some it was a lighthearted pass, a few painful days in camp trying to get into shape, sweating under the hot sun to replace fat with muscle, then out, back to the civilian world of gray suits, two-hour lunches, and anonymity. Others were more dedicated, more tenacious. One of these, John Stofa, a quarterback pretender at that first Dolphins camp, was cut, and then was either cut or traded by Pittsburgh, Cincinnati, twice more by Miami, and then finally by Denver before retiring to run a fast-food restaurant in Cincinnati. But when the Sharks opened up their camp, there he was. One more try.

Names. Endless names. Billy Joe and Ross O'Hanley, Frank Lasky and Tom Moore, Frank Cornish and Ernie Park, all men who came to one camp or the other with the thought that they could make it, all now long out of football. By the time we have finished with our story, that is what will have become of most of the names on the Tampa Bay roster. It has already begun. Two men failed their physicals and have left camp. Of the men here and dressed today, only twenty-five will make it to the season's final game.

These men know that, and it is one reason they are so quiet. They call it the numbers game.

It is now twenty minutes to three, and the first players are beginning to walk through the big, brown double door at the end of the corridor. All carry their shoes and helmets, and some of their pads and jerseys. One by one, hesitantly, they come out, squinting against the bright, strong sun. It is not only anxiety that kept them inside so long, but the heat outside. The official temperature is 89 degrees, but official measurements are taken in the shade. There is no shade out here. Just sun, intensified as it reflects off the building and the silver fence.

They sit on the green carpet just outside the one-story complex and finish dressing. Everywhere are rolls of white tape, and they are passed from one player to another as pads are secured to bodies and arms. Some running backs and receivers meticulously tape their shoes to their feet, running the rolls over the instep and around the rubber sole just at the arch, over and over, to prevent the shoes from slipping. This is no time to miss a pass or maneuver because of unsteady footing. With so many men in camp, cuts will come quickly, even with caprice.

As three o'clock approaches the players begin to spill out onto the field, and go through whatever exercises they use to prepare themselves mentally and physically. Some stand with their legs spread apart, and bend the top half of their bodies first toward one foot and then the other. Some sit on the ground, one leg stuck straight out to the front and the other to the rear, and they lean forward, stretching to touch the tips of their toes. Others run laps around the field or sprints back and forth between the line markers. Over on the sidelines, one large tackle, a free agent, slams his arms violently against the pads of one of the blocking sleds, over and over.

It is a strange sight. Men, with helmets on their heads and numbers on their backs, going through ceremonial routines. Names, more names.

A few remain against the wall of the building, and watch the men on the field, men, mostly strangers, against whom they are competing for a job. They watch the gathering of spectators on the other side of the chain-link fence, and the ten or twelve sportswriters standing along the sidelines, silent and judgmental. They watch as a glass door opens farther along the wall, and the coaches file out. It is one of those coaches who has promised that every player in camp has an equal opportunity to make the team, regardless of who he is or what kind of contract he has signed. That includes, he has said, Steve Spurrier, the high-priced quarterback acquired by trade from San Francisco, and John McKay, Jr., who happens to be the coach's son.

Now the last few players put on their helmets and make their way down the little grade in the lawn and onto the practice field. It is only moments before three. One man, the last, pauses at the base of the grade and looks up at the clear blue sky. Just how long will it be, he wonders, before that sky turns dark, before the earth begins to shake with thunder and the rains come to wash him away? How long?

1
IN PURSUIT OF THE GAME

It is the city of Baltimore during the third week of the 1976 baseball season, and Reggie Jackson has appeared in an Orioles uniform for the first time. Traded from Oakland during the closing days of spring training, he had refused to report to his new team until now.

Jackson did not play in tonight's game against his former teammates, the Athletics. He was dressed and on the bench as Oakland won, 11–1, but will not be eligible for a game until tomorrow or the next day because of some kind of technicality.

Now, however, back in the Baltimore clubhouse, having spent forty minutes in the batting cage after the game, it is Jackson who attracts the attention. A sometimes brooding and sometimes flamboyant man who is approaching his thirtieth birthday, he appears almost timid as he stands by his newly acquired locker and addresses the horde of media people around him.

In many ways Jackson is the essence of the successful modern professional athlete. Temperamental and articulate, he has always played well before the cameras. While he can be a disruptive force in and out of uniform and is at best an inconsistent fielder, he excels in the two categories most necessary to make a baseball player famous—hitting home runs and attracting press coverage. That combination has made him a superstar in a sport where more complete athletes go virtually ignored.

He stands there now, stripped to the waist and talking to the members of the radio, television, and newspaper press. Not an unusually tall man—he measures just six feet—he is obviously powerful, with thick, broad shoulders and strong, muscular arms. When he talks his voice has the even, well controlled tone of a man who has been through it all before. He has, and it's clear by the way he conducts himself that he takes pleasure in the attention.

Yes, he says, he is glad to be here in Baltimore. Why has it taken him a month to decide to report? Well, it is a complicated matter. Money is not all of it. Business interests in the Oakland area, and a desire to remain close to his friends on the west coast, all that and other, personal factors. It's very complicated.

His answers are courteous and full, for this is the cooperative Reggie. He speaks clearly, and with an air of erudition he occasionally has difficulty carrying off. Misused words here and there trip him.

Jackson steers the conversation away from his as yet unsigned 1976 contract, but the accepted information is that he is asking for a five-year contract approaching $3 million, and that the Orioles have offered around $1 million for the same period.

"I want to play ball—this is the thing I do best," he is saying, not in response to any particular question but as a general policy statement. "I appreciate that Baltimore's organization bent over backward to make me happy, and I want to bend over backward for them."

Some of the reporters are impressed and some just smile. The pace of questioning picks up. The Orioles are a team of quality players, but quiet quality. The press feeds on more sensational types like Jackson, and they in turn are nurtured in a kind of symbiotic partnership. The men with microphones and pads record every word, photographers take pictures of every change in expression; the entire drama is punctuated by the blinding of electronic flash.

The noise and the lights and the wave of commotion obliterate the fact that a baseball game was played here tonight, a game the Orioles lost. Many of the men involved in that effort have already left, and most of those remaining hardly seem aware that anything else has occurred.

Jim Palmer, who surrendered three runs and ten hits in six and a third painful innings, quietly combs his hair before leaving. Normally it would be he, the two-time Cy Young Award winner, who would be entertaining the press after such a game, but he seems pleased to relinquish the honor. Ken Singleton, the team's fine young right fielder who went hitless in three trips to the plate, pauses before the clubhouse's two boxes of Bazooka Sugarless Bubble Gum, one containing the regular red packages and one the spearmint-flavored green. The green, Singleton has learned, possesses special powers for him—"It gets me out of slumps"—but he decides it is not yet time for rash measures and scoops up three packets of the red.

There is a burst of temper from the interview. One of the reporters has asked Jackson about his feelings toward team responsibility in view of his long holdout, and the fielder snaps back in rage, "Don't start that shit with me. I'm a man with seven college degrees and I know exactly what you're trying to do."

The reporter, a young man from a suburban weekly newspaper, recoils in surprise. He has had no experience of this belligerent side of Reggie (who, incidentally, left Arizona State after his sophomore year). Jackson points his finger at him and continues his harangue. "You're trying to cause a split between me and my teammates," he says. "I'm on to you—I'm on to all you guys. Now cut it out."

As quickly as the tantrum erupted it subsides, and Jackson continues answering questions, talking about his affection for Hank Peters, the Orioles general manager, and about his desire to play out his career in Baltimore.

By now most of the players have showered and left the

clubhouse. One player remains. Since the little scene began he has been motionless, watching silently.

The player is Andres Mora, and he has been standing off to one side, out of the way. A twenty-year-old outfielder from the charming Mexican village of Saltillo, about half a day's drive from the U.S. border, Mora is on his first trip to the big leagues. In fact, until joining the Orioles last month, he had played in only eight regular season games in the United States, and those with the Montreal Expos' farm club in West Palm Beach. The rest of his professional career—all four years of it—has been spent with teams in the Mexican leagues.

But he knows about Reggie Jackson and he has been standing almost at attention in admiration, his spiked shoes held in his hands. He knows about Jackson's credentials, about his long home runs, and about his flair. He's heard about his life style off the field. And ever since Jackson was traded to the Orioles, he's heard about the huge contract he's been negotiating. While there are no beautiful women in attendance here, no Rolls-Royce car or armed guard to help carry his salary, the aura of making it big is clear and present. Mora cannot understand much of what is being said—he speaks little English—yet he remains entranced.

As the press conference disbands and Jackson strolls off toward the shower, Mora stands firm for a few seconds, looks around, then walks over to where they had all been gathered.

He does not touch anything in the open locker, nor does he even look inside. He just stands there, in the place where Jackson stood, and takes a deep breath.

He says nothing. He doesn't have to. It's all over his face. Andres Mora—future star. There is magic in the very thought.

The forces which bind a professional athlete to his sport are as many and varied as the forces keeping a husband and wife together. But the lure of that sport—the prime attraction—this is pure and simple, like the first time two lovers kiss.

It begins for most at an early age. On a dusty field in St. Louis or a sandy lot in Miami or a well manicured Little League diamond in Scarsdale, a boy stands at home plate and waits. Out on the mound the pitcher fidgets with the ball. He winds up, and suddenly a white blur comes sailing in at eye level. The hitter cocks his bat and swings, sending the ball whistling over the third baseman's head.

It's that simple. He's hooked.

The reaction is chemical; something inside clicks. A clean layup on an asphalt driveway in Indiana, a well thrown pass cutting across three lawns in California, a leaping catch made against a South Side Chicago storefront. They are all allied. For one brief piece of time, the trials and frustrations of being locked into a life situation are lost in the glory of a physical act well done. The satisfaction is complete, isolated from everything around it. It is an accomplished fact, capable of standing alone, much as a fine book or painting exists on its own merit. That people may be rushing to offer their congratulations only magnifies the satisfaction.

Millions of us have experienced such a moment sometime in our lives. We did it, enjoyed it, and catalogued it along with a thousand different moments, and went on to become doctors and writers and butchers and teachers. While these professions are not quite as exciting, they are not supposed to be. What they are is more realistic, more pragmatic. More safe. We would no more consider hitting line drives for a living than we would consider an occupation of making love or eating chocolate cake or flying kites.

For some people, however, that is exactly what they do. The magic they feel when bat strikes ball is so satisfying that they pursue it in a perpetual effort to make that moment happen over and over. They are known as professional athletes.

If this discussion were going on fifteen years ago the matter of money would never come up. It was the rare athlete in 1963 who was making $100,000; a few stars, men headed for the hall of fame in their respective sports, but no one else. That isn't so today. Many players are demanding and receiving six-figure salaries, and the impression among fans is that such contracts have become a major incentive for young men to enter professional sports.

In some cases it's true. Athletes today make an inordinate amount of money, especially in basketball, where the base salary is $30,000 a year for anyone who can stick with an NBA club, and the top is, well, very high and going up. The other sports are not quite so well paying, primarily because of the nature of the sports themselves. Only 242 men play major league basketball, and the necessary equipment consists of little more than eleven gym suits and eleven basketballs per team. Baseball, with 638 players at the major league level, has an entire minor league system to help support; football, an extremely expensive sport to operate, has over a thousand players. Starting salaries for these sports are $19,000 and $16,500, respectively. Still, considering the life, professional athletes are well paid. At an average of between $40,000 and $60,000 for six to eight months' work, it seems to most of us like fair pay. Even generous.

It is. But it is also immaterial. For all the strikes, the involved negotiations, and the fantastic contracts, money has little to do with why a man becomes a professional athlete. He is there because he is a player, and he became a player long before money was important. It is both what he does and who he is. How much he gets paid for doing it is a completely separate matter.

Just what it is that does make an athlete commit his youth to his sport, however, is complex. It is more than the simple joy of a boy hitting a ball or throwing a pass, though that is certainly part of it. It concerns the fact that sports in our society is something special, something around which a mystique has grown that encircles not only the games themselves but the players and everything they do. The star fullback rushing for the winning touchdown knows it, and the third man listed on the three-deep chart knows it. Not only do they know it while they are playing, do they remember it long after their last game, but it is a major force in their lives years before they put on a major league uniform.

In 1976 Donn Seidholz was a minor league third baseman in the Southern League. A tall, lean Chicagoan who had nearly completed work toward his degree at the University of Indiana, he was suffering through a mediocre month while playing for a team that was far out of the league race. On one particular night in Charlotte, in a game that was played in a light but steady rain, Seidholz went hitless in four turns at bat and, while usually a good fielder, misplayed a ground ball into a double.

"Sometimes there are nights like this," he said, toweling himself off in the dank and barren locker room after the game. "Sometimes you can't even remember why you're here."

He stopped short, as if catching a thought before it could be etched in stone, made permanent and irretrievable.

"But you do," he said, "you do remember. I remember. I remember the hours of playing catch with my father when I was just a kid. I remember playing on every rumdum team I could find. And when I wasn't playing I was listening to whatever game was on the radio. The Cubs during the day and the Sox at night. And when I'd fall asleep, I'd dream about being a baseball player."

A bright, introspective young man who starred on his high school team in Winnetka, outside Chicago, he was nonetheless ignored by the scouts who buzzed around this team in his senior year. Two teammates, pitchers, were signed, and Seidholz was left with his dreams.

"I guess I wasn't good enough," he recalled. "I know I wasn't very big. I was a peewee when I was seven, and 5 feet 1 my freshman year. But when they signed, all the attention, the hoopla really got to me. I put every spare minute into working on baseball."

He entered the University of Indiana that fall, outlining a course of study aimed toward medicine, though his mind was on baseball.

PHOTO BY ERNEST ROBERTSON, JR.

Donn Seidholz, from the depths of Class AA: "I just casually let it drop that I happen to be a professional baseball player. Lawyers, doctors, businessman. It gets 'em every time."

"I didn't want to be a doctor," he said, continuing to dress. "All I wanted to be was a baseball player. I worked so hard on baseball that I really wasn't studying, and had to change my major to stay in school. Even on weekends, when everybody else was playing football and in bars drinking, I'd be over working out by myself. But I never minded because I knew what I wanted. This. This is what I wanted."

Seidholz paused and looked around the dimly lit locker room, the floor wet from the leaky shower that was so dirty half the players refused to use it.

"I know," he said, "it doesn't look like much. But you have to realize what it means. It means they think I'm good enough to make it. It means they've signed me to a contract and invested money in me.

"Do you realize how many guys would give their left nut to be here, to have a chance to be a major league ballplayer?" he asked, very serious now. "Do you realize how many guys throughout America dream the dream, and end up selling it for a $10,000-a-year job at Procter and Gamble? They regret it for the rest of their lives. I know, this looks like a hole to you, but this is it. This is the ultimate."

In his third year then as a pro, he had improved steadily and received repeated words of encouragement from the coaches. ("You can always tell when you no longer figure in their plans," he said. "They stop talking to you.") And his size had improved. In that summer of 1976 he stood 6 feet 3 and weighed 190 pounds, and had the ungainly look of a boy still growing, his arms long and hanging from his broad shoulders as if they were occasionally removed for stretching.

"It hasn't been easy," said Seidholz, who had been drafted by his hometown White Sox after a junior year in which he led the Big Ten in hits. "My second game was in Columbus, Georgia, and I hit against James Rodney Richard. He'd been up and down with Houston. He was six-eight and he threw hard. He struck me out four times, and all of a sudden Procter and Gamble looked pretty good to me. I had the shakes for days. My hands and knees—I couldn't keep 'em still. But that passes. You learn."

Collecting his gear into his small, imitation-leather athletic bag, he walked outside to board the bus that would take the team to their game the following night. He stopped for a moment in the darkened stadium, signed his name for a kid who had no idea who he was, and smiled.

"You know it isn't just the playing," he said. "It's the being. Every time I walk into a room full of people I don't know and we start to make conversation, I wait for them to ask me what I do. I'm very cool. I just casually let it drop that I happen to be a professional baseball player. Lawyers, doctors, businessmen. It gets 'em every time."

Growing up in America today, it would be difficult not to be affected—one way or another—by the attention given to sports. It is all around us, and generates as much interest as a presidential impeachment or a man walking on the moon. Though that interest may be most visible when 56,000 people cram into Dodger Stadium to watch a World Series game or 62 million watch the Super Bowl on television, it is pervasive.

A few years ago when a baseball dispute closed the official training camps for the first three weeks of the spring schedule, players got together in little groups at playgrounds and college campuses throughout central and south Florida to play at spring training. They didn't do much: Just groups of ten and twenty men, wearing shorts and sweat suits, running laps and taking batting and fielding practice. But everywhere they showed up to work out, hundreds of fans waited for them, having traveled from across the state and often across the country to stand and watch big league ballplayers run and sweat and gasp for breath.

That's how fans got their name. "Fan"—from "fanatic." They are interested not only in what an athlete does during a game, but in everything about his involvement with that game. There is a longing on the part of the people in the stands to know what goes on in the locker room before the game, a desire to experience the feel of the rosin bag and even the sticky paste pass receivers spread on their hands. The game is why they are there, but their interest extends far beyond the actual contest. They arrive early at a baseball game to watch the players take batting practice, and at football games, come hours before the kickoff, then huddle in the stands under blankets as they wait for the players to come onto the field and go through their loosening-up exercises.

We go to the theater and enjoy a play, and we are enriched. We go to a concert and we are thrilled by the music, and we applaud our appreciation until our hands tingle. We go to a basketball game, one of 17,000 people in an enclosed gymnasium, and as our team grabs a rebound and races downcourt on a fast break we cheer. When a penetrating guard flips the ball behind his back to a forward streaking toward the basket the stands erupt, shouts and screams reverberating off the roof and walls. You can feel the vibrations of the stands up through your legs as the foundation of the building seems to shake. It happens all the time. It happens with the home team 15 points behind with minutes to go and no chance of victory.

Share with me one spring afternoon in New York City, a pleasant day that just happened to be the opening of the baseball season.

It was April 1976, and Yankee Stadium was opening after two and a half years of reconstruction. I had promised to take a friend's son to opening day. Both of them showed up at my West Side apartment two hours before game time. My friend, who was just dropping off his son, was bored by the entire idea. The mention of anything connected with sports sent him into an uncontrolled fit of yawning. Not so his son Ian. A Yankees cap on his head, a fielder's glove on his left hand, he was literally gyrating with excitement. But then he was a kid, thirteen at the time.

The two of us boarded the subway at Broadway and 72nd Street. It was about twelve-thirty on a Thursday afternoon, and, for that time of the day, the train was crowded. All the gray metal seats were taken and, with the center aisle full, it seemed almost like rush hour. People clung to the thick metal handles and leaned against the support poles, steeling themselves against the train's swaying and lurching as it jerked its way first to 96th Street and then to 110th.

I held on to one of the overhead handles, and Ian held on to me. "Are all these people going to the game?" he asked.

I shook my head paternally. "Calm yourself. They're just going uptown."

But when we got off to change trains at 149th Street and the Grand Concourse, there was a strange buzzing all up and down the platform. And when the Lexington Avenue express came it was jammed. There were lots of teenagers, but nearly as many businessmen. As the train raced north, I watched them in their conservative three-piece suits. First they loosened their collars, then stripped off their ties and stuffed them into their attaché cases. I leaned down to Ian and proclaimed, cleverly, that indeed most of these people were going to the game.

The buzz of conversation grew louder as the train sped through the darkness of the tunnel beneath the Bronx. I envisioned trains and buses from all over New York, from New Jersey and Connecticut, converging like some military exercise on Yankee Stadium. Then, as the subway emerged into the bright sunlight and the first sight of the Stadium flashed into view, cheering broke out all through the car, through the length of the train. It built to a crescendo as the train stopped at 161st Street, and we all poured out onto the platform and headed for the ball park.

It happens every spring, all over the country—opening day. And every time it happens it's special. Not special as in a week at Caneel Bay or a flight on the Concorde—things out of reach for most of us. Special, yet at the same time accessible. That's the key to the popularity of sports, its accessibility.

Whether it was in high school or college or in a sandlot game as a child, the vast majority of American males have experienced some part of the sports phenomenon. We may appreciate a fine musician or a great surgeon, but we don't identify with him. We know what he does is beyond our capability. But a baseball player! Hell, we've played baseball. Enough, certainly, to identify with the man on the field. We live out our lives—as perfectly happy plumbers or lawyers or teachers—but we remember the day we connected on eight straight passes in a pickup football game and we wonder, if things had been different, could we have made it in the pros? Sitting in our seat at Three Rivers Stadium as the announcer calls out the starting lineup and the Steelers run onto the field, it's so easy to see ourselves under one of those black helmets and hear our name being called. It's a common fantasy. Almost universal.

Rod Steiger and Marlon Brando sit in the back seat of a sedan in *On the Waterfront*. Brando is berating his brother for convincing him to throw that fight so long before. "I could have been a contender," says the young Brando in anguish, "I could have been somebody, instead of a bum, which is what I am." In the title scene from Philip Roth's novella, *Goodbye, Columbus*, Ron Patimkin stretches out on his bed in his parents' suburban home in Short Hills, New Jersey. A recent Ohio State graduate who is about to marry and enter his father's sink business, he is reveling in the sound of his senior class record. It is the Minnesota game, and the narrator is describing Ron, number 11, dribbling out before the cheering Buckeye fans for the last time. Christian Darling, in Irwin Shaw's brilliant short story, "The Eighty-Yard Run," is only a substitute on his college football team when he runs for a touchdown during practice. It is the greatest glory he'll ever know—all the world seems to be watching him that fall afternoon. The rest of his life is a failure by comparison. The money, position, and family, all that he accomplishes in later years, are little consolation.

But the best is Douglass Wallop's classic novel, *The Year the Yankees Lost the Pennant*, the basis for *Damn Yankees*. Best because it is the most fun, and is the most direct. We meet Joe Boyd, who, in the late 1950s, sells real estate in Washington, D.C., while gaining his emotional sustenance from love of the lowly Washington Senators. Joe had a chance to play baseball, but he got sidetracked. How often he thinks of that time in high school, that fateful day of tryouts when he permitted some girl to talk him into walking her home. That was his moment, and he missed it. When offered a second chance by the unearthly Mr. Applegate, Joe drags his middle-aged body before his mirror and thinks, *A baseball player*, and his chest swells beneath his pajamas. To be young and strong, to run and throw, and, above all, to hit—surely a worthwhile trade for one soul.

In one form or another, it is a fantasy more common than striking oil or running for President, because we have all had a piece of it. Scratch a Supreme Court justice or a congressman and you'll find a frustrated quarterback. Ask a famous surgeon about his operating successes and he'll tell you about the time he almost qualified for the Olympics. Even Gerald Ford, while he was still President, confessed to a secret desire to be a ballplayer. "I've had a lifelong ambition to be a professional baseball player," he said in a radio broadcast, "but nobody would sign me."

The fever is part of the American heritage. You can see it in schoolyards and on sandlots, and at tryout and rookie camps for every professional team in the country. Sportswriters, skilled at spotting the symptoms, have a name for it. They call it The Dream. Capital T. Capital D.

The Dream, of course, is the glory of sports. It is the aura of the game and all that surrounds it. Winning, and the incredible excitement it generates. The wonder of standing at home plate in the bottom of the ninth inning with the tying run on second base and 60,000 people shouting your name. It is immediate. One instant you swing, the next instant the ball carries over the left-field wall, and you are circling the bases to a standing ovation. No wait-and-see what the test results are, wait-and-see if the order goes through, wait-and-see what the jury decides. Instant gratification.

But for only a small percentage of athletes is it available with any regularity. We call those men superstars, and they are rare. Pete Rose and Kareem Abdul-Jabbar, Muhammad Ali, O. J. Simpson, and a few others—only they are good enough to perform brilliantly day after day. Only for them is the magic routine. They drive the Rolls-Royce cars and fly their own jets, endorse hair tonic and popcorn machines. They are exceptionally gifted athletes, and we learn about their eccentric behavior, their bizarre taste in clothes and living styles through newspapers, television, and magazines. We learn so much about them that we sometimes forget that they make up only a tiny percentage of professional athletes.

For the average athlete, the world of professional sports is nothing like what is in those articles. It is a world geared to his talent, which is painfully human in its limitations. His occasional sparks of superior play are blended into a broad pattern of quiet adequacy. He is a man of reasonable intelligence and competence, who, like most of us, functions in the middle range of his professional scale. And, like us, he has his good days and his bad days.

The fundamental demands on these men are the same, regardless of their sport. Each must be strong enough and skilled enough—and determined enough—to beat out the other men competing for his job. He must be willing to commit himself to his sport from the time he is a child (early high school is probably as late as one can begin to build toward a pro career) though, realistically, he can look forward to only six or seven years of playing time. He must be capable of accepting the fact that while he is playing he is property, to be bought and sold at will—someone else's will—to play when and how another wishes, and that so long as he plays he will be in constant jeopardy of losing his place to a prize rookie or a player from another team, who may be no better than he but a little younger. Lastly, he must be able to perform before people who feel the $6 they paid to get in entitles them to open expression. This often translates into the player's getting booed, spat on, and occasionally sprayed with Coke, beer, or anything else that's handy.

None of this is news to an athlete who has been a professional for more than a single season. Yet neither is it a deterrent. Athletes have a remarkable facility for pursuing their sport, even if they must spend a season or two playing in the boondocks at slave wages. They'll go wherever is necessary, do whatever they can to get the chance. When their efforts earn them a season with a championship team, that's a dream come true. When some phenom comes up from nowhere and they're traded to a losing club, well, that's just the dark side of the same dream. They can handle it so long as they are still in uniform, as long as they survive.

This is the story of those men and their world. Not a story about losers, but about men whose frequency of winning is low enough to make their continued devotion to sports enigmatic to most of us. The star athlete and his affection for daily glory is no mystery. The world of the marginal athlete and his fondness for it are not nearly so clear. Yet their commitment is identical. It is only that we, the spectators, are often confused by the glare and intensity of the spotlight trained on the superstar.

Just how many men are we talking about? Though the actual numbers vary from sport to sport and team to team, certain generalities hold firm. Nearly every team has at least one star, one man around whom the franchise is built. So long as he remains young and healthy, he can pretty much dictate his own future. If his salary demands remain within the range considered reasonable by his organization, he will remain part of that team. Around him are a small number of high-quality players, and they too are relatively safe. That small group makes up the nucleus of the team, those players who remain there year after year. In the 1972–73 NBA season the Baltimore Bullets were led by Elvin Hayes, Phil Chenier, and Wes Unseld. Eleven other men played for the Bullets at various times in the season, and many made solid contributions. But less solid than the big three. When the basketball season got under way in 1977, these three were still leading the Bullets (who by then had moved their home down the turnpike and were known as the Washington Bullets). None of the other seven players was with the team.

Our focus is on these others. On the average, nine men on the eleven-man basketball squad, thirty-three on a forty-five-man football squad, and eighteen men on a twenty-five-man baseball team. They are the midstrata players, the marginals and fringe players, men without any security in an already insecure profession. They remain on a team only so long as someone a little better doesn't come along, and new challengers appear at the gate daily.

These are our subjects, and our story is their story: life on the fringe of professional athletics. What that life is like, and what it is that makes men love it so desperately.

Answers come generally from two perspectives. First, from young players reaching for the glory that they hope and in most cases genuinely believe is within their reach. Such faith is so strong in young athletes—most of whom view themselves, at the start of their careers, as potential stars—because simply to reach the pros means they were the best among their teammates. While that faith may soften with exposure to superior talent, some semblance is necessary for players at every level, and is equally important for their sport. No sport can survive with only superstars, and not even a player at the lowest level can perform at his best without supreme confidence in himself.

A more realistic perspective comes from the older players, veterans who have put enough time in to know their place in their game, and exactly what staying in means to them. Some might even have had a piece of the glory at some point along the way, but now their battle is more limited. They no longer fight for the immortality of superstardom, only for a temporary extension of whatever they have. Their fight is for one more season.

It is five-thirty in the afternoon of a game day at Yankee Stadium. In the visiting locker room the California Angels are beginning to remove their street clothes and ready themselves for the night's game with the Yankees. Tall, straight young men with lean, hard bodies, they joke with one another as they carefully remove brightly printed shirts and flared trousers and hang them in their lockers. It is June 1976, and already New York has shown itself to be the class of the American League East, and the Angels have shown they are going nowhere. But for the twenty-five men gathered in this room, there is no sign of gloom. What was a lovely day is rapidly turning into a lovely evening, and at such times there is nothing they would rather do than play baseball.

One man seems apart from the main flow of banter. Not isolated—not left out—but not fully involved. He passes a few words with a teammate, and talks to a visitor, but generally goes on about his business. He had come in a few minutes earlier than the other players, and now, wearing only a pair of rubber shower shoes, walks down a hall toward a small room where a steel whirlpool tub stands in a dimly lit corner.

The man is Tommy Davis, once one of the finest hitters in baseball. He is still what people in the business call a pure hitter, the kind of man who could, the legend goes, be awakened in the middle of a February night and hit line drives in a darkened ball park. In truth, at thirty-seven years old, he requires more preparation.

He does not wait for instructions from the trainer or help from any of the clubhouse attendants. Tommy Davis is no rookie. He flicks on the light, and looks down into the greenish water in the high-walled tub. Even at his age—advanced for an athlete—he is an impressive looking man. His tan skin is stretched tight over his thick, powerful body. His shoulders are broad, his arms and legs well toned, his chest hard, and his stomach flat. He turns on the machine and watches it rattle and shake on the uncovered floor. As an unseen mechanism whips and churns the water into foam, he gently climbs over the edge and lowers himself into the surging froth.

"It takes a little longer now to get ready," he says, raising his voice over the grinding noise of the machine and pointing to his legs. There is a smile on his face, and a lilt to the words that he offers. They are the words of a man glad for the need to get ready, regardless of the extra effort that is required or the time it takes.

PHOTO BY SKIP ROZIN

Tommy Davis, standing with Yankee manager Billy Martin. "You'd think a man who collected more than 2,000 hits and drove in more than 1,000 runs would be treated better."

I had not seen Tommy Davis since the previous spring, when we spoke at the Yankees camp in Fort Lauderdale. New York had signed him as a free agent, and Davis was pushing himself back into shape. He had thought he had been brought to Florida with a job, but when he arrived he found that nothing had been decided, that he had to prove he could still hit, prove he could still run out a double. He talked one afternoon in the shade of an otherwise empty dugout, talked about being in camp, and about having to fight for a job. Then, as the conversation began to drift, he talked about happier times, about coming up through the ranks in the Dodgers organization, about places like Hornell and Kokomo and Spokane. He smiled when he came to Spokane, for it was there that he hit .345 in 1959, which got him into a Dodgers uniform for one game at the end of the season. One game, one at-bat, one strikeout. That was the beginning. He was back the next season, the first of seven fine seasons with Los Angeles.

There was no smile on his face when he spoke of the Dodgers' trading him in 1966—only hurt. He had been a star with Los Angeles, a talented outfielder who had played in three all-star games, leading the major leagues in hitting in 1962 and 1963. Then, a season later, he broke his ankle while sliding into second base. The prognosis was that it would take two years for him to recover fully. The Dodgers waited a year, then peddled him. The trade marked the beginning of a second career for Tommy Davis, that of a journeyman athlete who would make twelve moves in the following ten years. His wife and children began by moving with him, but when the pace quickened—he played with three teams in 1970, and two teams in 1969 and 1972—they took up permanent residence in Los Angeles. He missed his family badly, but he loved baseball, loved to hit, and he knew if he wanted to continue playing it was going to be that way, fitting in wherever he could for as long as his bat was needed. He understood and was willing to make this bargain, but he was not always happy with the terms that were forced upon him.

"You'd think a man who collected more than 2,000 hits and

drove in more than 1,000 runs would be treated better," he said, snapping off the words in anger.

Mostly, when Davis spoke, it was in a blend of accents from the many places where he'd lived and played, but when he got angry what came through was mostly Brooklyn, where he was born. When he talked about the way the different clubs had dealt with him during those last years he sounded like an old Dodger—mad. He accepted being sold and even traded as part of the game, but he had been released three times, and this was a blow to his pride. It had also shrunk his salary down to where most of the veterans on the field that afternoon were making more than he, even though he still carried a healthy lifetime batting average of .295. He had always done what they'd asked him—which was to hit the baseball—and he thought that should count for something. It proved to count for very little, and deep inside he knew that. As if to remind him, the Yankees released him a few days later.

"I was surprised when they released me," he said after it happened. "They called me—asked me to come to camp—and then they cut me. I was bitter and I was disappointed."

But that was March. Now, as he emerges from the whirlpool, there is no sign of anger. He is a man with a place. For however long it lasts, he is back in the game, and that is enough to make him happy. Last night he held a New York homecoming in his room at the Sheraton, with friends stopping by until late to wish him well. That was a fine thing, he says, and smiles. He turns off the machine and light as if he is walking out of his own bathroom, and heads back down the hall.

He sits now in front of his locker. It is still early, not yet time for the Angels to take batting practice, and as he slowly dresses he talks about those months after the Yankees had released him. He talks about the phone calls to different general managers, and how few called back. Those who did—Bing Devine of the Cardinals, Joe McDonald of the Mets, and a few others—had nothing to offer. Slowly, painfully, it began to sink in—it was all over.

"I wrote baseball off," he says. "I began to get acclimated, because I knew this was the way it was going to be. I took my boys fishing for the first time. And I started to think, hey, maybe this is where I should have been in the first place."

Two of Davis' friends own a record company, and they wanted him to be their national promotion man. It was a good job, one with a chance for advancement, and he took it. His wife was delighted and he was, well, pleased. Then, just as he was starting work, the California Angels called. They needed a right-handed hitter, and asked if he wanted to play baseball.

Davis interrupts himself. He has been dressing as he talks and he stops that, too. His arms fall to his sides.

"It was a tough decision," he says. "My wife didn't want me to go back. She asked me why I wanted to go through all that again. I really wasn't sure. But I figured I'd go out to the ball park, take a few swings, and see how it feels. I guess I should never have accepted the invitation to work out," he says in mock seriousness. "Once I put the uniform on I said, 'Ah, shucks.' I got that old feeling."

By now the smile covers his face, and he hurries to finish dressing as he fills in the rest of the story—catching the noon flight that Wednesday to Bloomington, where the Angels were playing the Minnesota Twins, coming to bat in the eighth inning as a pinch hitter, with two men on and the score tied. He waited until the count was two balls and two strikes, then hit a curve ball sharply into left field to drive in two runs and give California the lead. Like a movie script, heavy with drama—Tommy Davis was back.

"I thought I had some more base hits in my bat," he says as he puts on his cap and starts out to hitting practice, an exercise he hardly seems to need. In the week he's been back in uniform, he has been hitting for a .429 average.

As he reaches the clubhouse door he stops as if he'd been called, and turning around he says, "Baseball's my life, my life and my love. I had to come back if they wanted me."

The feelings of Tommy Davis are anything but uncommon.

Few athletes, knowing that their most productive years are over, pick a time to retire and stick to it. Most just don't want to quit. Stars like Brooks Robinson and George Blanda, or journeymen like Ron Swoboda and Norman Snead. They haven't considered what they'll do when they retire, and most push the date away as if it were their own death. They don't want to think about it. A sportswriter can call an athlete clumsy and even mediocre and get little static. But let him suggest that the man is getting old—too old to play—and he's made an enemy.

And why this desperate clinging to a life style designed to be temporary? It's really simple. For most athletes, being inside their sport—at any level—is better than being out. Winning is certainly better than losing, but even losing is better than not being in the game.

2
THE GARDEN OF DREAMS

The afternoon traffic, loud and busy the way it can be on summer weekends, isolates this little park, turning it into an island in a sea of cars. The sun, suspended above the dark gray buildings of Lenox Avenue, is tropical in intensity. And the vendors, doing a fine business in hot dogs and cold drinks, add a vacation tone.

But the people do not come for the sun or the refreshments. The attraction here on the edge of Harlem is basketball.

It is just after four o'clock, and the last of the high school division games is running late. The outcome's not been in doubt since the middle of the final period, when the Restoration Flyers got into foul trouble and lost their two big men. Only five Flyers showed up for today's game, and the three men left on the court had been unable to protect the lead carried throughout most of the game. Now, with less than a minute left, the Milbank Orphans have moved in front by a comfortable six points.

The game is one of six scheduled today in the semifinals of the Holcombe Rucker League, and through most of the morning and early afternoon the interest has been light. It usually is for

PHOTO BY SKIP ROZIN

Holcombe Rucker Park in Harlem. Straining for a view of the best schoolyard basketball in America.

the lower divisions, those made up of players between the ages of twelve and eighteen. Less than a hundred people were here at the beginning of this game, vying for the shade.

But for the last fifteen minutes a crowd has been gathering for the first of the unlimited classification games, the games showing off the pride of the Rucker tournament. In other years that has included such future professional stars as Kareem Abdul-Jabbar and Julius Erving and schoolyard legends like Herman (The Helicopter) Knowlings, and this island known as Buddy Young Park is now nearly full because of that tradition. The 360 or so spaces on the two sets of wooden stands boarding the court are jammed, and people are still coming in.

As the game between the Flyers and the Orphans ends and the fair on the loud-speakers switches from play-by-play to rock music, the teams for the next game enter through the opening at the south end of the court, a fence-enclosed rectangle on the corner of 145th Street and Lenox Avenue. They go directly to their benches. There is no fraternization before the game. A few players wave to friends in the stands on the way in, but there is little conversation. This is serious stuff. The championship of Harlem is at stake.

Sticks of Juicy Fruit are passed among the players of both teams, the Milbank Hammerheads and the 131st Street Rockets, and the blaring music is abruptly replaced by the starting lineups. By now the park is packed. A hundred or more people stand in the out-of-bounds area, and another thirty or forty cling to the outside of the fence, hanging there like No Parking signs. There is a charged quiet as the teams get their last-minute instructions and proceed to the center of the court.

The whistle blows, the ball is tossed into the air, and the crowd erupts as Willy (Dynomite) Young emerges out of a pack of black bodies, dribbles the length of the court, fakes the one man between him and the basket, and rams the ball through the metal rim. Joyful bedlam resounds, and the Hammerheads lead by two points.

Schoolyard basketball is what it is, the finest amateur one-on-one competition anywhere. Outside this wire fence is the world of the street, where drugs and crime breed early death. Inside, within the painted lines of the basketball court, is a place where fantasies are born and acted out, where young men of vision reach out beyond their natural barriers toward the magic of professional sports. Some make it; some do not. But this is where it starts. This black asphalt court is the garden of their dreams.

No one is born with fully formed fantasies of glory running around in his head. It is more gradual than that. First comes a sport, and then the discovery of proficiency. A kid in blue jeans and T-shirt pitches for his neighborhood team, and finds he can get batters out. A few years later he hurls his Little League team to the national finals. A boy plays halfback on a sandlot team, does well, and tries out for high school football. In his senior year he leads his school to the state championship. That first taste of victory is followed by a growing appreciation for the flavor, and a need for more. From there it is an easy step to thinking it can go on forever.

None of this happens without help. It doesn't have to. The young man gifted with the ability to hit a baseball or throw a football gets ample support as he envisions his glorious rise. The star system begins early on our playgrounds, is fostered in programs like Pony League in baseball and Pop Warner football, and blossoms in high school, the first fully rounded imitation of the adult world.

In that miniature society the athlete has an assured place of honor, and nowhere is it more visible than at an awards assembly. Most schools have them, usually toward the end of the academic year. Each of us has sat through at least one, if only as a spectator. All kinds of awards are given out—prizes for scholarship, recognition for the best student journalist and the best musician, for citizenship and service to the school. They are all important, and generate enthusiastic applause.

But the big moment of the assembly—almost always saved for the end—comes with the athletic awards, those given to the best basketball player and the best football player, the star pitcher and star hitter on the baseball team. And rarely are the recipients simply introduced. Their names are preceded by some capsule report of their heroics: the night our hero scored 45 points against the school's arch rival, or the afternoon he pitched the no-hitter in the city finals. The master of ceremonies works like a skilled conductor, manipulating the audience into a frenzy. They applaud and stamp their feet and cheer as the best young talent in the school walk down the aisle to pick up their awards.

That's heady stuff for a seventeen-year-old kid. In the audience are nearly all the people important to him: his teammates, his girl friend, his teachers. That is his world, and everyone in it is applauding him. What healthy American boy would not want to make such a moment happen again as often as possible?

He gets a lot of help there too. No high school star goes ignored in the establishment of athletics.

If his game is baseball he's probably been talking with professional scouts since his sophomore year. (And if he starred on a winning Little League team, they've been watching him for much longer.) Most baseball players sign directly out of high school. Baseball people prefer this because they feel the average college program is not well developed enough to warrant a four-year investment of time. They would rather have a player in their own farm system early so they can work on his skills.

But if our schoolboy star excels in football or basketball, the colleges and universities of America are the minor leagues. And, like the pros, they begin shopping early, sometimes when a boy is just entering high school, but more commonly during his third and fourth years.

In 1977 Bernard King was the most valuable basketball player in the Southeastern Conference, scoring 25.8 points a game as a junior for the Tennessee Volunteers. But his path to Knoxville began long before he first visited the campus.

As a student at Brooklyn's Fort Hamilton High School, the 6-feet-7-inch King was one of the top players in the city. A power forward who used his nearly 200 pounds as both a shooter and a rebounder, he was a consistent performer throughout his career, averaging 25 points and 25 rebounds per game each year.

And with his success came the hunger for more, spurred by dreams nurtured since he was a child.

"I used to go down to the playground in the summer and watch the stars from the NBA," said King, who has a quick, even glib way of speaking, but was nonetheless cautious with every word, as if listening for how it could be misinterpreted. "I'd stand there, pushed in by people, and know it could be me out there."

It is in those playgrounds, and in the youth centers and

parks, where the stars of New York are made. The high schools of the five boroughs may hold the official championships, but the real tests come on other courts.

"I played in every tournament and every league I could find," said King. "I played after school and on weekends, and during the summer I played till it got dark. Sometimes, when the basket was near a street light, I'd play till two and three in the morning."

From a family of five boys and one girl, all growing up in the rough Fort Greene section of Brooklyn, King began talking about some of the talented boys with whom he'd played, boys whose abilities, by his evaluation, rivaled his own.

But when asked what ever happened to them he stopped and shook his head, and the smile that had been a mask on his face slipped. Despite their ability, so few had managed to escape the old neighborhood. Most were still there, many still playing basketball in the same rundown parks.

"You've gotta be careful," said King. "You gotta play it right. I seen too many good players get caught in one fix or another and never get out. You gotta know what you're doing and where you're going."

That was all. Nothing sentimental; nothing maudlin. Just a moment's recognition of the talent that gets trapped in the city's streets.

But why do some get trapped and others pull free? King shrugged. "Breaks," he said. "Getting to know there's something else out there, and that it won't hurt you. For me it was going to Fort Hamilton [an attractive, middle-class section of Brooklyn, within sight of the Verrazano-Narrows]. That's a world away from Fort Greene."

The full range of Bernard King's talent did not become widely known until his senior year at Fort Hamilton, a fact which is a mystery to him. ("I was just as good a ballplayer my sophomore and junior years," he says.) But sometimes it takes a while in the city for reputations to spread from league to league, from one all-star game to another.

And King was not a finesse player. He accomplished his job

NETS PHOTO BY BARBARA ANN GIOVE

Bernard King, cutting short his collegiate career by signing a pro contract with New Jersey Nets coach Kevin Loughery (left) and president Roy Boe. "You gotta know what you're doing and where you're going."

on the court with power, and that is often less impressive to fans than more fancy moves. But, once the word was out, it spread.

"During my junior year I got a few letters from colleges," he said, "but by my senior year the coaches began contacting me personally. First I think it was Dayton, and then Oregon. A coach from New Mexico came to see me, and one from a school in Washington, D.C. And there were others—I can't even remember them all now."

King paused for a moment, then talked about the attention. "It gets to your head. You're an all-star and you're written up in the paper—you're sitting on top of the world. And all these people come knocking at your door, offering you—everything. It can really get to you."

And why didn't it get to him?

"I don't know," he said. "Being from New York helps. Not that everybody's poor there, but there's a lot to cut through just to get by. You live in that environment for so many years and you really start to think when somebody starts offering you this and that. You look for his angle. You know, 'cause reality's where you live. The city, the city keeps you alert."

He narrowed his choice to three schools—Arizona State, Dayton, and Tennessee. He visited all three—his first trip, to Arizona State, was his first flight in an airplane—and liked them all. But relying on the same street sense that had gotten him through the first seventeen years of his life, he took a skeptical look at what they were offering.

"You have to sit down and sort out all they're trying to hand you," he said. "They offered me cars, they offered me money. They offered to take care of my family. You have to get away from all of that and look at the school and what they're really offering. They want you to play basketball. They've got to offer me something I need—an education and a chance to make it to the pros."

King said that Tennessee offered him nothing but a chance to play ball and go to school, but that the people there treated him "like a person, not a piece of equipment," to be used and discarded. His instinct paid off. In the course of three years at Knoxville, through difficulties with the NCAA about his high school records and problems with the local police, the school never abandoned him. Many a ghetto star in similar difficulty has been dumped by his university, never to be heard from again.

The competition for top high school athletes is so intense that the King story is common. It is a story that was not only repeated three years later with Bernard's brother Albert, but magnified. As one of the top prospects in the country—maybe the top one—he had begun hearing from some universities when he entered high school, and by his senior year had received over a hundred scholarship offers. Finally he decided upon Maryland.

Once a player makes the jump to collegiate ball and establishes himself, he begins drawing the attention of professional scouts. Sports has gotten extremely sophisticated in the matter of seeking out and evaluating talent. Large scouting services function in football, baseball, and basketball, agencies whose representatives go from university to university—anyplace there is an athletic program—in search of athletes who could possibly make the pros. They analyze the players, then file reports on their physical qualifications and skills. This information serves the subscribing clubs as a survey of the talent in the country, and from there they send their own scouts and coaches for a more personal and in-depth report on any player in whom they are specifically interested. By the time the pro draft is held the participating teams know which players they want. In many cases they have already met and talked with them.

In the college basketball draft in June 1976 the New York Knickerbockers chose nine players, six of whom were interested in playing in the NBA and were subsequently invited to the Knicks rookie camp. (Of the remaining three, two decided to accept offers to play basketball with professional teams in Europe, and the third was suffering from a leg injury and decided not to play ball.) In addition to those six, eleven other players—either free agents, veteran players without teams, rookies not drafted, or men under contract to the Knicks but not on the team—were invited, along with one player picked up from the recently disbanded American Basketball Association.

The hottest prospect in camp that September was Lonnie Shelton. A 20-year-old Californian who played center for Oregon State University, he was the club's first pick in the draft. Not only was he a talented player with a fine college record, he fit the Knicks's need at the time, which was for a large man capable of scoring and rebounding. New York had been looking for a player of that type ever since their all-star center, Willis Reed, retired in 1974.

A man not as highly touted but given a chance of making the team was Rick Bullock, also a center, who had played at Texas Tech and was the team's third choice in the draft. He had many of the same qualities as Shelton—he, too, was big and strong, having set his school scoring record and become the first player in the Southwest Conference to accumulate more than 2,000 points and 1,000 rebounds—but was considered less of a prospect.

The presence of the two in the same rookie camp set up a classic situation in sports: one man standing in the glow of center stage, and another off in the shadows, straining for recognition.

Despite the edge that a player has, the first day of camp is an ordeal. Everything he has accomplished up until that point falls into one category—amateur—and this is a closed category. It has served to get him this far, and no longer has more than sentimental value. Everything starts fresh from the opening of camp.

Watching the Knicks hopefuls warm up at the Monmouth College gym in New Jersey that first afternoon, it was hard to recall that love of the game had brought them to this point. They all looked terrified. There was no laughter. There were no smiles. Players with blank expressions and wearing numberless practice jerseys did whatever was their custom to loosen up their bodies and minds: shooting foul shots, dribbling in for layups, fading away for hooks, or taking jump shots from a favorite spot on the court. Everything was done with concentration and great self-consciousness. So much was at stake. So much depended on being able to perform up to full potential in that short time.

The official mood of the day was definitely serious. The official emotion, anxiety. No one was immune.

That first day it was Shelton who felt the main weight of the pressure. He was the number one draft pick, the man designated to fill the Knicks's gap at center. Even before practice began, he was surrounded by the press, asking questions about what he thought his chances were and how he was responding to all the attention. To the rookie's credit, he evaded nothing, responding in a straightforward manner to what he called "being in the New York spotlight."

"There are a lot of eyes on me," he said. "People are expecting a lot of things from me. I think they expect me to fly."

Knicks coach William (Red) Holzman and his assistant Dick McGuire broke the squad into four teams, and each took charge of a separate scrimmage. Without exception, the play was sloppy. Players missed shots and passes, handled the ball badly, and played loose defense. All the things they had worked out of their game as amateurs were back.

Then, about midway through the session, Shelton began to slow down. He trailed the play down the court once, and a second time, then jogged over to Holzman. He told him that he didn't feel well, that he thought he was going to be sick, and the coach excused him.

The young center, who had looked no better or worse than anyone else in the early going, walked slowly through the door that led to the locker room. He paused at the water cooler, leaned down for a drink, turned, and crumpled to the floor.

For a few seconds no one knew anything had happened. Then a student screamed into the gym—"Your player's down," she called—and everybody rushed out to the corridor. An ambulance was called and Shelton, unconscious, his large body twitching convulsively, was carried out of the fieldhouse and rushed to the Monmouth Medical Center. The doctor diagnosed the problem as heat exhaustion (though the gym was not particularly hot), and Shelton was out for the remainder of the rookie camp.

"I don't remember a thing," he said later. "I just fell out, and when I woke up I was only half awake. I could see and hear people moving around me but it was like none of it was really happening. I thought I had died."

Another player, a free agent or a low draft pick, would have been in real trouble had he suffered through the same kind of debut. A new man's best chance to show his talent is always against nonregular players, a team of strangers. Once the veteran camp began, there would be a lot more experience on the floor. But Shelton, a first pick with a guaranteed contract—the club had to pay him even if he were cut—knew there was a place for him with the Knicks.

"I didn't worry," he said about his inauspicious beginning as a pro. "They'd told me what they thought of me and what they wanted me to do. And they were going to give me time to come along."

Even Red Holzman, in his statement to the press after the incident, talked about how much talent he saw in those few minutes of playing time before Shelton had collapsed.

So for the next four days, with star rookie Shelton in the hospital, the direct pressure intensified on the others.

Though the daily workouts were scheduled for eleven in the morning and five in the afternoon, nearly everyone was on the court an hour early, shooting foul shots, practicing hooks, and faking out phantom defensemen before starting their moves to the basket. One player, a free agent named Hershel Lewis, was always dressed and working out by nine-thirty in the morning, always waiting for the college students to free the court in the afternoon.

"I need all the floor time I can get," he said one afternoon while waiting for the court. "That's the only way I know to get into my game and stay there."

And when the appointed times arrived and practice began, it was an hour and a half to two hours of basketball—basketball conversation, basketball instruction, and more basketball. Holzman, a gentle man of somewhat less than average size, light red hair (hence the nickname), and an affection for large cigars, conducted the camp like a school, explaining what he wanted done and then backing off the court and letting the players execute.

With each day the progress was more evident, reflected not only in the play of the men but in their whole manner. Those who were doing well—Bullock and John McGill, the team's second draft choice, and two of the free agents, Charlie Criss, a star from the minor leagues of basketball in one of his efforts to gain some NBA recognition, and Dennis (Mo) Layton, who had played in the league before and had, from time to time, played well—showed the easing of tension. They looked loose. They even smiled. And they played better. They no longer missed easy shots, their passing was crisp, their defense was more tenacious.

Criss looked especially sharp. A 5-foot-7-inch guard from Yonkers, New York, he knew this was the best opportunity he'd ever had at the big time, and he was making the most of it. At twenty-seven, he had spent most of his adult life reaching for this. He won All-America honors at New Mexico State and was drafted by Pittsburgh of the ABA, but the team folded before he got a chance to play, and he shifted his efforts to the Eastern Basketball Association, a minor pro league operating mostly in Pennsylvania and New Jersey. He was a star there, scoring close to thirty points a game, but it was all to get him this far.

For Criss and the others who were doing well, what had happened after that first awkward day was that they had seen the quality of the players who comprised their competition, men whose abilities had been a mystery before camp. Once they figured they could handle the challenge, they relaxed. Even those not having a particularly good camp seemed more at ease. They didn't smile as much, but at least they settled down to the business of playing basketball.

During the camp the difficult hours were not on the court but off. Away from the gym, spending their off time lounging around the Harbor Island Spa there on the New Jersey shore, the players looked horribly out of place. A spot where the overweight and elderly from New York and New Jersey come for reconditioning, the Spa did not offer much to seventeen strong, young, and mostly black athletes. They sat in their rooms and watched television during their free time, or drank beer and played cards. Some, like John McGill, who was from Mississippi and not accustomed to the ocean, just sat and watched the waves striking at the shore. But wherever they were seen, in the lobby or the dining room, or walking through the halls, never were they mistaken for any of the Spa's usual guests.

Though the hotel had complete dining facilities, few of the players had any meals there except breakfast. They preferred the Either/Or Deli down the road, and during their time in camp it became a quasi-student union, as it had for so many before them. It was there one afternoon between practices that Rick Bullock talked about basketball and his chances.

As might be expected of a man 6 feet 9 inches tall, Bullock has difficulty squeezing into his side of the booth. He sits now with his back against the wall, his body draped across the bench, and his legs angled out into the aisle. The table is next to the kitchen, and he talks in between volleys of noise uncontained by the double door behind him.

"I was talking to a guy today and he was just shaking his head, saying how tough it was trying to make it," he says in a deep, slow Texas voice. "But that's his hope and that's his dream—the money and the glory."

There is a strange detachment to what he says, as if what he's describing were happening to someone far away. He pauses and shifts his weight in the booth. He wears a pair of jeans and sneakers, and a shirt that his mother must have bought him before he left San Antonio. It is one of those nondescript pullovers that only mothers buy, and the collar is all askew under his blue-cloth zipper jacket.

He turns and looks at some of the other men from camp who are also in the restaurant, then continues. "In the back of their minds they're thinking about the announcer calling them out at Madison Square Garden and 20,000 people yelling at them," he says, and his eyes begin to widen as he sketches in the scene. "All that noise and all those lights. I understand that. I thought about it a lot. It's been on my mind since the season was over last year."

No longer is Bullock engaged in an analytical description of somebody else's dream. Now his words are filled with feeling. From somewhere behind him a phone rings, and he waits the four, five rings until it is answered. He waits a little longer until the rattling of the dishes stops, then lowers his voice.

"I would like more than anything in the world to play professional basketball," he says. "That would be a dream come true, to play on the Knicks. Frazier, Monroe, people like that, people I know. Junior high school, high school, looking at TV, they were my favorite team. The Knicks, the Knicks, I'd just about fight somebody for talking about the Knickerbockers."

He stops and looks down at his large hands. "My mother, she wants to see me on TV saying 'Hi, mom,' " he says, smiling. "She knows what I want and she wants me to have that, but she's got her own thing. My dad, he says I'm better off at home, getting a regular job, something steady. He don't go for none of this stuff. Says it's like gambling."

He starts to talk about his family, about growing up on a nice street in San Antonio, in a nice, three-bedroom house. His father, employed by the federal government as a cataloguer of freight for the several Air Force bases in the area, his older brother, a teacher studying for his master's in educational systems, and his younger sister, a college student. A solid family.

PHOTO BY A. T. DRAKER

Rick Bullock, playing for his high school team in San Antonio. "They all got something that's their own. Basketball's always been it for me."

"They all got something that's their own," says Bullock. "Basketball's always been it for me, since I was eleven years old. It's been good to me. It helped me when I was little—it gave me something that was mine. It let me be somebody so I didn't feel so lost. I don't want to lose that."

A full minute passes before he continues. "It ain't the money," he says. "I've never had a lot of money but I never needed a lot more than I had, either. It's playing, and proving you can do it. That's it—letting everybody know you made it."

He stops again, and straightens up in his seat. "That's the way it is with most of these guys," he says, "regardless where they come from. Basketball's what makes them what they are. And being here, in the NBA, that's what they all want. That's what I want."

Rick Bullock was just one man and he had not polled his fellow players, but he might as well have. What he wanted was exactly what they wanted—to be a professional basketball player. Not everyone was as open about his emotions. Some hid them in bravado at first, while others described their time in camp as "worthwhile just to see what it's all about." But during the long September nights at the Spa, while passing the hours between workouts, shields came down and the importance of the week's proceedings was revealed. Wherever they lived and whatever other choices might have been open to them, basketball was their chance to remain on that marvelous merry-go-round they had been riding since high school.

"I don't want to ever be in the stands," said Hershel Lewis one night. "I know what it's like there—I've got friends out there. On the court is the only place to be."

But everyone knew that only a certain number of players were going to be asked to return with the veterans, and by the third or fourth day most had a good idea who they were. In a camp of rookies and free agents, it doesn't take long to separate the average athletes from the men who might be able to play in the NBA.

The camp was scheduled for five days. On the morning of the fifth day, before the final practice, the players exhibited a strange and totally out-of-place sense of well-being. At breakfast there were joking and humor liberally mixed with eggs, toast, and coffee. All appeared to be sunshine and light.

It was a charade, a ruse led by some of the older free agents, who had been through it before and knew the importance of tension breaking. The rookies readily fell into the mood.

"I've seen it before," said one of the free agents as he stood outside and waited for the bus that ran to the college. "Guys laughing 'cause they don't want to show they're scared."

As the bus pulled to the entrance and the seventeen players began filing out of the hotel lobby, Larry Fogle, another of the free agents, paused at the door. Fogle, a second-round draft pick by New York the season before, had survived the exhibition season his rookie year only to be cut after two games.

"Lotta rooms gonna be cleared out today," he said as he looked around the lobby. "Lotta us gonna be gone." And then, taking a firm hold on his equipment bag and turning to leave, "But I'm okay."

Whatever degree of jubilation had been generated at breakfast or on the ten-minute bus ride to the gymnasium disappeared as the men took the court for the last time in the rookie camp. The morning workout was carried out in near silence, as the candidates either tried to guess who would go home and who would stay, or prepared themselves for what they knew was coming.

They didn't have to spend much time guessing. The practice was brief, and by noon everyone was down in the basement where the lockers and showers were, waiting.

Of the seventeen men in camp, eight were to be asked to return for the veteran camp, beginning in two days. Eight, plus Shelton. Nine others would be thanked and dismissed.

One by one, Holzman spoke with the players being released. He was careful to get to each man alone and explain what had led to his decision. He brought one into the coach's dressing room, and talked to another at the far end of the long line of steel lockers. One player kept walking as the coach talked, and Holzman followed him into the entranceway of the shower, giving his explanation there. Most just stood there and listened, having already guessed what was coming. Others fought back the tears, biting at the sides of their mouths or digging their fingernails into their palms, because it's always worse than you expect.

A veteran of thirteen seasons as an NBA coach, nine with the Knicks, Holzman had never reached the point where cutting players came easily. He had been a player, and though that sometimes seemed like a forgotten part of his fifty-two years, he shared the agony of every man being released.

"It's never easy," said Holzman, one of the most respected coaches in the league, a man with a reputation as a teacher of athletes. "You're telling them their careers are over. You're telling them it's finished. I explain that they just don't fit our present needs, that they're fine athletes but there's no place on this team for them. But all they hear is 'No—it's over.' It's the worst part of my job. Worse than losing."

Walking through the locker room, one could see the hopes and dreams of the players who had been cut cluttering the cement floor like the limbs of men felled in war. Boyd Batts and Brent Wilson, Tim van Blommensteyn and Bernard Hardin, men who had compiled impressive records at Nevada–Las Vegas and Colorado State, at Princeton and New Mexico, said nothing as they showered and stuffed their gear into their bags. There was nothing to say. They had tried, and failed.

Sitting on a bench away from the other men and waiting for the time to go upstairs and catch the bus back to the hotel was Larry Fogle. His face was stony and his gaze fixed as he sat with his equipment bag between his legs.

"Lotta guys make this into a big thing, like it's the end of their lives, like it's everything," he said, looking down at the bag. "It ain't. I'm glad they did it now, 'stead of keeping me around all camp like last year. I gotta chance to catch on now. I'm gonna make some calls. I'm okay. I'll make it."

But it was not all gloom. Eight men were safe. And Charlie Criss, for one, was ecstatic. After four years in the Eastern league and six years of hustling every other semipro, industrial, and pickup basketball league he could find, he had his chance to play in the NBA. He had a $30,000 contract in his pocket, with a promise of a bonus, if he made the team. He had no guarantees—the $30,000 would be his salary if he made the squad—but at least he felt he had a chance.

Any training camp is a series of crisis-level tests, one after the other. Pass one test and you can go from the rookie camp to the veteran camp. Pass the next test and you survive the first cut. Every week or so there is another crisis, another test, as the team is pared down to the player limit. This was only the first.

Of the Knicks prospects who survived the rookie camp, only three were what would be considered traditional rookies, men who had played basketball in college during the previous season. They were Shelton, McGill, and Bullock, the club's top three draft choices. The rest were playing basketball someplace, under such banners as the ABA in Virginia, the U.S. Army in Heidelberg, the Eastern league in Scranton, and, in Mo Layton's case, the YMCA in Phoenix. And all of them, just waiting for their own season to end so they could get a crack at the NBA.

The veteran camp officially began on a Thursday morning, though the opening session was devoted to the press, to picture taking and interviewing. Not until that afternoon did the full squad of twenty-two men work out together. For the veterans it was just another opening of camp, but for the rookies it was more. First, it was their initial opportunity to wear Knicks game uniforms—with their names on the back and "New York" on the front. And, second, there was a lot of talent on that court.

John McGill, who ranked fourth among all-time scorers at Alcorn State and had participated in the Hapoel Games in Is-

PHOTO COURTESY NEW YORK KNICKS

Rick Bullock, a New York Knick for five weeks. "That's something. . . It's the dream."

rael, played much of that first practice with his mouth open. It was not only that the Knicks were so good—and they were good, he later confided—but at 6 feet 7 inches he was considered big in college, and had rarely played against anyone as tall as 6 feet 9. And right there on that court were three men who were 6 feet 10. John was impressed.

Bullock was impressed, too, but for a different reason. "I tell you," he said after the first workout, "that was a sight to see. I've seen these guys on television, and there I was within touching distance. I'm setting picks on Walt Frazier and Earl Monroe, and blocking Spencer Haywood and people like that off the boards. That's something.

"The dream," he added. "It's the dream."

Whatever awe Bullock, McGill, and Shelton, who was just returning to camp, may have felt that first day, eased during the next week of two-a-day workouts. While talent and experience separate athletes even in training camp, the painful process of working into shape and sharpening skills has the opposite effect. The daily suicide drills—running at full speed up and back to the foul line, then to the half-court line and finally the length of the court, over and over—the playing of one-on-one, the scrimmages, and the other drills designed to improve basketball proficiency, had the added effect of breaking down the barriers between players. What began as hero worship among the new men was quickly replaced by professional respect.

Easing that distance between the veterans and the new men in camp was assisted by the older players. They'd been through it before. Every year a new crop of rookies and free agents comes in, and, by the time the season starts, most of them are gone. It doesn't take much to help a newcomer get acclimated, to at least make him feel welcome and show him how to get a new athletic bag or where to get his stereo fixed. Most veterans are happy to make that effort.

Phil Jackson was beginning his ninth season with the Knicks that September. A good, steady player with well developed defensive skills, he was never a star or even a starter, and never had the security that went with those positions. But he knew his situation with New York, and he knew what he could give and what he couldn't.

"A lot of new guys these days don't want any help," according to Jackson. "They figure they know it all. But those who want a little help—and you have to wait for them to ask—you tell them what you can. What can it hurt?"

But he did not hesitate to say where he would draw the line. "I wouldn't help somebody too much. I wouldn't help him to take my job. He'll have to manage that by himself."

Jackson paused, thought for a moment, and added a note of candor. "This is a funny business, and ego is a big part of it.

Maybe a guy doesn't want to really help a rookie, but he won't admit that he's threatened, not even to himself. So he tries to look as helpful as he can, as if to say, 'Hey, I'm going to give you a hand but it isn't going to do you any good, because you can't take my job. I'm too good.''

And, pausing again, "It's just another way of coping with the pressure," he said. "Some guys get very helpful and some guys get all tight. Some just shrug and say it's in the hands of the gods."

And Phil Jackson, how was he dealing with the pressure of yet another camp?

"There's just so much that I can do," he said. "It's obvious what my talents are, and if someone doesn't want them they don't have to have them."

And, smiling, "There are always other places to play."

As long as a coach gets his team together and down to the player limit by the league-designated date, which is usually the opening game, he may set up his own schedule of cuts. In 1976, when the limit was twelve, the Knicks determined that they would cut their unwieldy squad of twenty-two players by at least four before the first exhibition game, scheduled for a Thursday night. So everyone knew that Wednesday was the day.

The effect of that on each man in camp depended on his position. The veterans were unconcerned—no veteran would go in the first cut. Any of them could be seen Wednesday morning eating breakfast in the Harbor Island Spa dining room as if it were just another day. But for the men from the rookie camp it was not just another day. They were painfully aware of its special significance, and few managed breakfast.

Most of them could be found in the lobby of the Spa, wandering around like waifs as they waited for transportation to the gym. John McGill stood in the hallway just off the main entrance, staring out toward the road. He smiled, and confided that he wasn't worried because he had done all he could.

"I played my game," he said. The words were strong, but there was little enthusiasm behind them.

"Lots of difference between these guys and the rookies," he added. "Bigger. Faster. And they know the plays." His voice began to trail off. "So much to learn."

Some of the players had managed to get over to the gym early, and by nine-thirty were already shooting baskets. Hershel Lewis had gotten there first, as always, and Charlie Criss, Shelton, and Bullock joined him. They shot layups and fouls, jogged in small circles, and did pressing exercises against the walls, all in an effort to loosen up and get warm in what was a cool and otherwise empty gym.

Lewis, a quiet young man with a pleasant smile, was uncharacteristically talkative. He talked while he shot at the basket, then stopped shooting but continued to bounce the ball on the hardwood floor.

"It's been tough," he said in response to no question, "but I think I've played well." And then, "Did you know they're making cuts?" he started to ask, then smiled, embarrassed, and withdrew his question. Everybody knew.

"You ask me and I'll tell you I been playing good enough to make this team," he said. "Lot of other people told me the same thing. But they don't make the decisions, and neither do I." With that he went back to the baskets, shooting one, following it up, and shooting another.

Practice began promptly at eleven o'clock. No one needed a schedule to know it was cut day. It was etched in the face of every rookie and free agent in camp. Even those safe from any threat could feel the tension. The coaches, Holzman and McGuire, in an effort to ease the strain, ran a few plays with Butch Beard, a veteran guard. With Beard handling the ball, the two coaches double-teamed him, trying to keep him from scoring. They roughed him up playfully, one holding him while the other tried to slap the ball away. It was a funny routine, and effective. After a few minutes of this the practice went on as usual, with the only noticeable difference being an occasional burst of showmanship by one of the rookies. There was no way of knowing if it was a last-chance attempt to impress or a release of pent-up anxiety.

It is now twelve-thirty, and practice has just ended. The players run for a few minutes, then break into groups to practice their foul shooting. It is the way every practice ends.

Holzman walks over to the members of the press and requests that they give him five minutes in the locker room with the players before they come down, and he signals for the squad to head for the showers.

That is it. By the time the reporters reach the lower level, three of the four men who've been cut have already cleared out their lockers. Charlie Criss and Hershel Lewis are gone, and Benny Clyde, the free agent who once played with the Celtics, is in the shower.

John McGill is walking slowly up the stairs. "I knew it," he says as he reaches the door. "I felt it all along. I needed to tighten my defense. I needed to work on it and I just didn't."

He speaks slowly, in short, choppy sentences. On the drive back to the hotel he reaches into his pocket and pulls out a cigarette.

"I knew something bad was going to happen so I brought this," he says. "I usually don't smoke." He lights the cigarette awkwardly. "Donovan [Knick General Manager Eddie Donovan] talked to me about playing in Europe. He told me to call him Monday. I will."

Now he is speaking more easily. He leans back in the car seat and puffs on the cigarette that he does not inhale. "I want to play," he says. "If it's Europe, I'll play there. I'm married, but that won't matter. I won't quit now."

At the Spa, McGill pauses before getting out of the car. "The hard part's coming up. The next few days. Going home, facing my mom and Connie [his wife]. And all those people who had faith in me."

As McGill enters the Spa, Hershel Lewis, bags in hands, is coming out. First again. He stands there by the door for a few seconds, then puts the bags down.

"It looks like I'm handling this okay, but I'm hurting inside," he says. "People think this is easy, basketball, but it's work out there. It's hopes and dreams, and when it's over it hurts deep."

He bounces up and down on the balls of his feet as he speaks. His head bops and his hands jiggle, and his words come out in rapid spurts. "Yeah, I'll be okay in a few days. But it'll take that long. I worked hard out there. I wanted to make it bad."

He stops talking, obviously trying to compose himself. Within a few seconds his body ceases its frenetic motion. "I don't know what I'm going to do," he says, and fights again for control. "It's pain . . . deep pain."

Still in his room packing is Charlie Criss, agonizingly putting off his departure. For no one else has the experience of the veteran camp been such a blow.

His first camp had been a triumph. In basketball parlance, he ate bigger and better publicized guards alive. Mo Layton, who'd played for Phoenix and Portland, and Ticky Burden, the sharp shooter from the Virginia Squires in the ABA who'd been signed to a fat contract—Criss had played them all tough. He'd played his game against them; no one had been able to stop him. With Shelton out of the picture, surely he was the best-looking basketball player on the court.

But that was the rookie camp. And though Holzman carried him over to the veteran camp "because he'd played so well and so hard," he was never given serious consideration thereafter. While he worked out with the veterans in the scrimmages and hustled as hard as ever, no one paid any attention. The camp was overrun with guards, most of them on long-term contracts. And, after all, he was 5 feet 7, and how can anyone 5 feet 7 play in the NBA? Everybody knows it's impossible.

So now here Charlie Criss sits, on the corner of his bed—a Lilliputian castout from the world of Gullivers—his small, hard body wound spring-tight from the day's happenings, his face, broad and round, strained from the effort he is mounting to call his girl in New York and break the news.

"I've had it," he says. "I'm not going through this again. I've had it with the industrial leagues and the Eastern league. What's left to prove?"

He excuses himself to call the woman in his life and explain that "it just didn't go." They speak for a few minutes in low tones, and then he hangs up.

"Do you know what it's like?" he asks. "To have to tell everyone that you failed. All the people who waved goodbye and sent you out to win, to tell 'em that you lost."

He packs his new pair of basketball shoes, given to him by one of the sporting goods representatives, and talks some more about going back to Yonkers to face his mother and father and all the people who will be disappointed. He tries to force a smile, but it will not come.

"You know I lost my job," he says, "Yeah, I had two weeks of vacation, but it was up yesterday. I talked with them and they said sorry, I'm fired."

He looks around the room and stuffs a few hotel towels and an ashtray into his bag. "Well," he says, "I guess that's it. There's nothing keeping me here."

Back on the porch, the players appear one by one with their bags, standing around the car which will take them back to Manhattan, the first step toward home. The men from the rookie camp who survived the first cut are there, too, and there's a brief exchange of goodbyes. Nothing sentimental. Just a touching of fists, or pat on the back, and a wave. And then they are gone.

The real business of blending a basketball team is done during the exhibition season. Eight games over a three-week period, and two-a-day workouts on most days when there is no game. The method is to select which of the new players can improve the team, and then to try to work them and the veterans into a cohesive unit. Those who work the best together, theoretically, become the men who form the team.

Though Bullock started off slowly, he began to loosen up during the exhibition games. He didn't play much during the first night, a game against the Nets out on Long Island, but was gradually worked more into the lineup as the preseason wore on. And the more playing time he got, the better he played, learning what was expected of a center in professional basketball. He was bright and learned quickly. And by the third or fourth game he was playing more, even more than some of the veterans on the team.

With confidence on the court came the trappings of a new life style. Gone was his blue windbreaker, replaced by a leather jacket similar to those worn by veterans Earl Monroe and Spencer Haywood. And he began to grow a beard. (Seven other Knicks had beards.) He was relaxing, getting more comfortable, and began joking with the other players in the locker room before and after games. His play improved, and he received more attention from the coaches during practice. And as each day passed and he was still there, he began to feel there was a tenuous permanence to his position with the team.

"It's been going okay," he said after one game. "I'm learning. There is a lot to learn, but I feel it all coming, and that's good."

But the odds against him were great. Many factors beyond just how well a man does dictate the decision on his future in professional sports. There were five centers in camp—two from the previous season, Shelton and himself, and Spencer Haywood, an all-star forward who had been working out at center during the exhibitions. "That," as Bullock observed, "was the wrong direction."

But his biggest problem was Lonnie Shelton, a quiet and complex young man from Bakersfield, California. Because of the financial pressure on himself and his family, Shelton decided to leave Oregon State after his sophomore year and join Memphis in the ABA. His father had died when he was eleven, the youngest of his four brothers is mentally retarded, and the family house was in a condition of steady and advanced decay. Money, clearly, was a problem.

But before playing in a single professional game he reconsidered his decision, based on some sound logic. The ABA looked to be in rocky shape in 1975, and since he was betting his professional future on it, he opted to return to school. A year later he left Oregon for good (after becoming the highest scorer in the university's history) and was the first pick of the Knicks in the draft.

"Financially," said Shelton, "it was just too much of a burden. My family back in California needed help—I had two younger brothers and a younger sister living at home. And I had just gotten married."

A strong, bulky man with a large nose and a slow, soft way of talking, he paused and smiled shyly. "Anyhow, I was getting tired of being broke."

Though only 6 feet 8 and twenty years old, on the small side for a center and young for the league, Shelton was an unusual athlete. He combined great natural ability with intelligence and the kind of basketball hunger that coaches and general managers love. He handled the ball well, shooting from close to the basket and the outside, was an exceptional rebounder, and had, as one veteran said, "the quickest hands I've ever seen."

The product of all these qualities was a young but strangely cool and experienced athlete. He could rebound off the opponent's basket and fire an outlet pass to a teammate racing down the court, block a shot and recover the ball, steal the ball from smaller, supposedly quicker players, and still be an effective scorer and passer when the Knicks went on offense.

To the Knicks fans he was the most exciting big man since Willis Reed had been a rookie, and everything he did seemed to turn them on. They screamed when he was introduced, and cheered when he stole the ball or charged after a rebound. At one exhibition game, after he had blocked an opponent's shot, a well-dressed, middle-aged woman at courtside stood up and yelled, "We love you, Lonnie, we love you. Do it again."

And as if his athletic abilities were not enough, Shelton by nature was quiet and serious, a man who worked hard at what he did and enjoyed the rewards.

"I feel good about this game," he once said during an interview. "Everything I do I want to do well. I want respect."

That attitude was perfect for the media and the fans. Serious young athlete, striving for perfection on the court, while off the court he quietly tended to his own business. With the money from the lucrative contract he bought his family a new house in a better neighborhood of Bakersfield, and moved himself and his young wife, Paula, into a comfortable apartment in the pleasant Floral Park section of Queens.

About the only outward manifestation of ego-tripping on his fame was a fondness for reading his own press, and Paula's keeping a scrapbook.

"I like to please the people," he said. "I like to hear 'em cheer. And I like to read when the papers print nice things about me, especially when there's a picture."

That's a tough act to follow. And Rick Bullock, a good basketball player but quite human, had trouble keeping up. As the exhibition season wore on, the difference between him and Shelton became more clear. There was little chance the team would keep them both, and Bullock could tell by the signs when they had made up their mind. He received less attention during practice, and less playing time in the games. Then, in the last game before the season began, he did not play at all.

Two days later, during a workout at Monmouth College, Bullock was sitting in the dressing room. He looked particularly quiet, even downcast.

"How's it going?" I asked.

"Why?" he responded.

" 'Cause I care!"

"Then you the only one besides my mother and my little sister."

The following morning, one day before the season opened, the Knicks were down to fifteen players. Two were not available to play because of injuries, and therefore did not count.

NEW YORK
11

This meant there were thirteen—Rick Bullock and twelve others. Bullock knew what was going to happen, and after practice it did. First Holzman talked with him, explaining the situation, and then Eddie Donovan.

Donovan told Bullock that he was pleased with the way he had played, and that they had kept him so long because there had been "deals in the works," though they had fallen through. The choice, however, ended up between the two rookie centers—him and Shelton—and the Knicks felt Shelton could help them more.

What Donovan did not explain was that he also felt it was more than just talent, that a player's background often had a lot to do with what kind of basketball he played.

"You take a kid like Bullock," said Donovan, "from a comfortable home, and he doesn't have the hunger. A kid from the ghetto is used to fighting for every inch of life. Shelton's got that hunger, and he shows it on the court."

The general manager, who looks more like a middle-aged businessman from upstate than the front office wizard who engineered trades that brought New York two NBA championships, suggested that Bullock stick around for a few days. He mentioned the possibility of working something out with the Eastern league, or with one of the European professional teams. Both had expressed interest in him.

Bullock thought for a long, silent moment. He didn't know about the Eastern league, but he had played in Italy during the previous summer and didn't like it. Donovan told him there was a room for him at the City Squire in midtown Manhattan. He could wait in comfort. Bullock thought about it, then offered his thanks and said, "I wanna go home."

And he meant it. The team arrived back in New York at five-thirty that afternoon, and Bullock headed straight to the

PHOTO COURTESY NEW YORK KNICKS

Lonnie Shelton as a confident rookie. "Everything I do I want to do well. I want respect."

airport and waited there for the first available flight to San Antonio. It was well after midnight by the time he arrived home.

"It was a long night," he said from his home in Texas. "I knew it was coming. I saw the writing on the wall. But it's still hard, especially when you think you're doing the job. I thought I was. I think I shoulda got a better shot."

He asked how the team had been doing, about several of the players, and if any progress had been made toward the trade that had been rumored during the latter half of the training camp. Then he went back to the flight home.

"I worried about going home," he said. "I worried about what to say to my mother. She always had high hopes for me, and I knew she would be disappointed."

He paused for a second, and when he began again his voice was harder. "I just wanted to know what clown would come up to me and start asking 'bout me getting cut. They'd read it in the paper like everybody else, and still they'd want to come and ask. I didn't want to hear all that lip from people."

Another pause.

"Well, it happened," he said, "and I knew I had to live with it. But I took it. It's funny how many people you think are your friends."

It is a hard thing for a young man who has always been a winner, who has been a star in high school and a star in college, who has always been on top, to go back home as a loser for the first time in his life. And not a loser in private, but right out there in the newspaper.

"I didn't want to go out," said Bullock, going back over that first month after his return to San Antonio. "I didn't want to see anybody. I just stayed in my house. I didn't go anywhere because I didn't want to hear anything about it. Nobody really gives me any shit, but you get a lot of kidding from little kids. You just can't go around beating on no ten-year-old kid."

Years from now, when Rick Bullock has rechanneled his life away from basketball, he will look back with pride and talk about the pursuit of his dream. He will take satisfaction from knowing he did everything he could to make it happen, while others around him—his classmates at Texas Tech and his friends in San Antonio—traded their dreams off on jobs and Chevrolets.

It will bring him pleasure then. But in that fall of 1976 he had only the pain.

3

ONE LONG STEP FROM THE BEST

Someplace east of Asheville, North Carolina. The bus once belonged to the Trailways Bus Company, but that was some time ago. The name is only barely visible on the outside, faded by the sun and washed by rain and wind. The inside, too, has seen better days. The seats have long since been recovered in institutional plastic, and the padding—bonded original—is depressed and hard. Some of the seat backs tilt and some don't. Some of the foot rests work; some don't.

But it runs, and if it were only being used to go around town, or out to the country now and then for a picnic, it would be a wonderful bus. Unfortunately, more is expected of it. As the official means of transportation for the Knoxville Sox in baseball's Southern League, much more is expected. Monday night it drove from Savannah to Charlotte, about 250 miles, and tonight it is making the trek from Charlotte across the mountains to Knoxville, which is shorter in distance but takes close to seven hours because of the road. Of course the killer trip is the overnight ride from Orlando back to Knoxville—645 miles. For the twenty-one minor league ballplayers sprawled inside this rocking dormitory, that represents the world series of endurance. Games played the night following an Orlando trip are special.

Most of the players are sleeping now, and contentedly. Pitchers of beer consumed at dinner before leaving the outskirts of Charlotte contribute to the mild euphoria. They ate in little groups, each according to his palate (pizza, fried chicken, or double-deck hamburgers) with the bus strategically parked at a point equidistant from three franchise restaurants.

It also helps that they managed a 5–3 victory over the Charlotte Orioles, their first win in the last five nights. Though Double A hangs in the minor league structure midway between the majors and the playground, winning is still important. These young men have enough time in to know they are professionals, but they are paid so little and are so far from "The Show" that an occasional good game is necessary for their egos. The problem for the Knox Sox, as they are known, is that there has been all too little winning during this second half of the season. A team that played well in May but stumbled in mid-June and lost the first-half pennant on the last day, they are now hopelessly out of the second-half race. With five weeks of the season remaining, the players dread the remaining time.

Winning in the minors is not always a matter of assembling the better team. Teams are part of organizations, and often suffer in favor of them. That is what happened with the Sox. Knoxville's bullpen was crippled at midseason when an organizational decision was made that Kurt Best, their top relief pitcher, was needed more in Triple A. It was a loss from which the team never recovered.

But at least for tonight, all that is forgotten. Like children who have been rewarded for a good day in school, the Sox sleep soundly as the bus rocks on its soft springs, dipping first to one side and then to the other. Most are curled up in their seats, one man to a two-seat unit. A few planners have brought foam-rubber pads and stretch out in the aisle, while one lone man has climbed up into the overhead luggage compartment and sleeps, a gently snoring duffel bag.

The memory of past errors and wild pitches and their

second-half collapse is lost in the beating of hard rain against the metal skin of the bus, and they can dream of the glories of playing for the Iowa team in Triple A, or even for the parent Chicago White Sox. That is what keeps them sane, along with the knowledge that they are still young and that all this is traditional apprenticeship. As one player said before falling asleep, "If Hank Aaron could handle this, I can."

A young professional football player who had also starred in baseball in college explained his choice of one sport over the other by saying that he didn't want to get stuck in the minors for two or three years.

"In football you go out and do it," he said during the opening week of his rookie camp. "Then bang, you're right in there where the main action is."

There is no question about it. Decisions are made with relative quickness in football, as they are in basketball. An athlete is drafted—or comes to camp as a free agent. He gets from a few days to a few weeks to display his talent, and is either kept or let go. Instant acceptance or the man is gone, and there aren't many places to go but home. That can hamper a career.

In baseball final decisions are much slower in coming. A young athlete signs a contract out of high school or college and is assigned to one of the classifications of the minor leagues. But once he signs, he will be given time—at least two years, often longer—to show some of the promise that led to his signing. He is brought along, from level to level, at whatever rate the organization feels is suitable. This presence of a structured minor league system, in which athletes prepare for play in the majors, is one of the main differences between baseball and the other American team sports.

Even to mention the minor leagues is to tempt images of the vast network that existed during the 1940s and 1950s. At their healthiest, in 1949, the minors consisted of fifty-nine leagues divided into eight classifications, with teams located in over

450 cities and towns. The Brooklyn Dodgers alone had over 600 minor league players under contract at their Vero Beach camp. But that was before television and expansion. There were only sixteen teams in the majors, and none farther west than St. Louis. Now there are twenty-six teams, six of which are on the west coast and two in Canada. Every week during the heart of the season at least two games are televised nationally. With big league baseball so available, interest in anything less has depressed the condition of the minor leagues from its postwar wealth to its current poverty. Sixteen leagues remain, with most organizations operating either four or five teams.

Most players signing out of high school go directly to the Rookie League, which is the lowest of the current four classifications. Players with college experience usually begin at a higher level, either at Class A or Class AA, depending on the organization's opinion of the man's ability. In some rare instances a highly touted player will start off in Class AAA, which is the closest division to the majors.

What life is like there for the young baseball player depends on the individual and what his standing is with his organization. Players designated as future stars—the Johnny Benches and the Vida Blues, the Rod Carews and the Tom Seavers—move quickly and smoothly through the various classifications, spending two or maybe three seasons "honing" their talent before they are presented to the big league club.

But for the average player the journey from his first pro camp to a spot on a major league roster is a quest not unlike that of Don Quixote. It is a journey filled with detours and dead ends, marred by poor visibility and inadequate road signs. Many lose their way. For every hundred players who enter the minor leagues, less than five will ever see anything approaching regular service on a major league club.

In 1976 Larry Foster was in his fourth year in the Chicago White Sox farm system. An outfielder who had a reputation for good hitting and questionable fielding, he had repeatedly proven the former—he led the Gulf Coast League his rookie season with a .383 average, and was on his way to leading the

Southern League that year—and was working hard on the latter.

But try as he did, he could not seem to get above Class AA, not a comfortable place for an aspiring baseball player to be stuck.

"I just can't figure it out," said Foster, who at twenty-five was older than most of his teammates. "It seems that I can't get out of this league. No matter how good I play, I always end up here."

There was a strained tone of frustration in his words, spoken in a southern accent that placed him in his home state of Alabama. Frustration and disappointment.

Baseball had been the center of Larry Foster's life since he was eight. He was a star in grade school, and a star at Etowah County High School in his hometown of Attalla. People in the county got used to seeing pictures of Larry and his twin brother, Harry, in the paper. They were local heroes.

"We all played baseball," said Foster. "We were nine brothers, and every one of us was on a team. My dad was our coach, and he was proud as he could be of all of us. He didn't push us or anything like that—we just all loved the game."

Of Foster's brothers, only one, his older brother Max, ever played pro ball, for just one season with a minor league club in the Cincinnati organization.

"We all wanted it," said Foster, "but I guess I wanted it more than any of them. I used to watch major leaguers Saturday afternoon on television. I couldn't see much difference between what they could do and what I could do. I knew I could make it."

He wasn't drafted out of high school by any major league team, which was disappointing but not crushing. Alabama was not a big baseball state, he reasoned, and he did want to attend college.

He played baseball at Jacksonville State University in Alabama for four years, and never hit less than .400. In 1972 and 1973, his last two seasons, he won All-America honors. But still he wasn't drafted.

"It was terrible," said Foster. "After the senior year I had—I batted .440 and hit 17 home runs—I knew there was no way they couldn't draft me. But they didn't. I didn't know where to look, so I talked to my coach and he started calling some scouts. Finally the guy from Chicago gave me a chance. He signed me as a free agent."

Why should a healthy athlete with an excellent career in college ball be ignored by all professional teams in their annual selection of amateur talent, so completely ignored that he is forced to call and beg for attention?

"I don't know," said Foster. "I know I can hit—they know I can hit. It's always come down to, Can he play defense? Can he play the outfield? They decide you can't, and you're stuck with that. I may not be a great outfielder, but I've worked hard on my fielding, and I do a lot in the field to get the job done. I've improved, but that doesn't seem to matter. That's my reputation, and I'm stuck with it."

He stopped for a moment and shook his head. "It almost seems like there's a plot," he said.

This reasoning is not something totally constructed in Foster's head, a paranoia devised by a frustrated athlete to soothe his ego. In all professional sports, decisions are made on athletes early in their careers, decisions which usually shape the future of those careers. That can be helpful for a player designated as a future star, but deadly for a man tabbed early on as a loser.

Pat Gillick is a baseball man who knows both sides of the game. He was once a minor leaguer in the Baltimore system, but, having recognized his limitations early in his career, he moved over to the administrative side. For the last eighteen years he has been involved with evaluating young athletes, first with Houston, then with the Yankees, and, most recently, as vice president in charge of player personnel for the Toronto Blue Jays.

"Basically, players fall into two categories," says Gillick, a tall, sun-tanned, nice-looking man in his early forties, "those who are prospects and those who are not."

Pat Gillick, a talent shopper: "Players fall into two categories: those who are prospects and those who are not."

PHOTO COURTESY TORONTO BLUE JAYS

A prospect is a player who, in Gillick's words, "has all the tools." This means that he can run, hit, throw, and has power—that "he's an athlete." If all of these qualities are present, the theory is that with time and instruction—and assuming that none of these skills diminishes along the way—the man will make it to the majors. And he will be helped. He will receive special attention—much the way a first-round draft pick would in football and basketball—and be given every opportunity to fulfill the prophecy that was made when he signed (usually for a respectable bonus).

"He's a prospect until he proves he's not," says Gillick. "And he will be moved up through the various levels steadily, often before he appears ready. We know that he can do the job, and feel at some point he will catch up with his potential."

The other side of the story is the player who is deficient in one of those vital areas. Maybe he can hit but is a poor fielder;

maybe he's fast and can field but cannot hit; or maybe he's considered too small. He possesses some important intangibles, such as desire and confidence, which have helped him perform well and succeed at lower levels, but scouts and executives remain skeptical because of his lack of some essential ability. Such a player will receive minimal attention and assistance, because no one truly believes he can be as good as he appears.

"A player without all the tools has got to prove himself at every level, in every classification," says Gillick. "He must hit .300 in Rookie League, and then do it again in Class A, Double A, and Triple A. Then, maybe, the parent club will give him a crack at the big leagues."

And though Gillick did not put it into so many words, his implication was that once given that "crack" at the major league level, such a player had better perform very well and very soon after his arrival.

"The feeling about those players is that, despite their good statistics, they will not succeed in the majors," he says. "No one believes they're for real. So the minute they begin to play poorly, the tendency is to let them go."

Gillick admits that a lot of evaluating talent is guesswork and taking calculated risks. "We gamble," he says. "We gamble that a player who's got a man's body at eighteen doesn't have the potential for improvement, so we look for a player who is physically immature and then try to project him into maturity. It's a risk, but we can't concentrate on every kid in our system."

For those young ballplayers considered not worthy of special attention, the long shots who are guilty until proven innocent, the minors are an endless night in which they are doomed to stumble throughout their youth. For Larry Foster, a large portion of that night was spent in Knoxville, Tennessee, home of the Knoxville Sox, Double A farm team of the Chicago White Sox.

Knoxville is an acceptable enough city of nearly 200,000 people, a large percentage of whom work in the metals and chemicals plants that support the economy there. It lacks the electricity and character of Nashville's music interests or the

Bill Meyer Stadium, home of the Knoxville Sox, midway between the playground and the majors.

beauty of Memphis, fertile and scenic by the Mississippi. It's just a medium-sized, rather grubby city.

Little of this affects the members of the Knox Sox. They bus in and bus out so quickly, and are so occupied with baseball and sleeping when they are there, that any local charm not wearing a skirt or tight pants would probably escape them.

But tourism is not what has brought them to Tennessee. Baseball is, and in this respect Knoxville is nothing more than a stopping place. For kids just up from Appleton in Class A, it's a pleasure to be there. They've been promoted. They all know about the Southern League, about the long bus rides, poor fields, and old stadia. They're willing to put in their time. But for the men who've already done that, who have spent a year or two with the team—or, worse, who have been up to Iowa and then been sent back down—there is great frustration. For men like Larry Foster, it's hard.

It is nearly eleven o'clock at night. Larry Foster sits in the general admission seats of Bill Meyer Stadium. All of the fans and the maintenance crew have left, and the last light has been turned out. The stadium is dark, and the outfield wall is but a shadow against the blue-black sky. On the wall in left and center fields, signs for Reeder Chevrolet and Pabst Blue Ribbon, Knox Federal Savings and Flagstaff Beer, are mute, their messages locked in the umbra of night. Over the right-field wall

Larry Foster (front row, center), with a grin, ten-year-old member of the Attalla All Stars. "Nine innings of baseball—I'd rather do that than go home and eat."

the towered lights of a softball field are visible in the distance, and from behind the stands comes the lonesome sound of a Southern Railroad freight train, its whistle cutting through the heavy air.

The Sox have just beaten the Savannah Braves, 3–0, before 572 happy but not too vocal Knoxville fans. Foster, the team's leading hitter with a .321 average, suffers the burden of being a Knox Sox as if it were an albatross around his neck. Of his four seasons as a pro, this is the third in which he has spent some time in Knoxville.

"It gets ya down," he says, staring from midway up in the stands out at the blackness that is the infield. "I been four years in baseball—three of them hitting over .320—and I'm still here in Double A."

There is a pleading in his voice as he talks about his struggling career. He is not a very tall man, just 5 feet 11, but even in his loose-fitting street clothes it is clear how strong and well developed his body is. For one so trim, 190 pounds is a lot of weight.

"This game turns me on," he says. "I like the challenge of me being in the batter's box and saying that guy [the pitcher] can't get me out. I love to play ball, but not here. I'm no kid, and this is a kid's league."

He stops and stretches his legs out over the wooden seat top ahead of him. It is a close night, about what one would expect from Knoxville in July, and a warm breeze blows in from the outfield, circulating hot and heavy air under the overhang of the single-deck ball park. Peanut bags and hot dog wrappers swirl through the empty seats, up and down the aisles, and one lone cup bounces noisily down the steps nearby. Foster ignores the competition and talks about having completed work for his bachelor's degree, and having spent some time teaching. He could teach now, he says—full time—but he doesn't want to be a teacher. He wants to be a ballplayer.

"It tears me up to be on a team, to be doing well and get nowhere," he says. "And all the time, guys keep going up to Triple A around me."

PHOTO BY ERNEST ROBERTSON, JR.

Larry Foster, fifteen years after the Attalla All Stars, as the leading hitter and MVP in the Southern League. "It tears me up to be on a team, to be doing well and get nowhere."

He talks about hitting .383 in Rookie League, then .328 in his second season, split between Appleton and Knoxville, and .310 during the first half of 1975 with the Knox Sox. Then, in the second half of that season, he was called up to Chicago's Class AAA team, then located in Denver.

"When I got there all I did was sit," he says. "I got into 32 of the 80 games, and hit .250. A man just can't get into the groove doing that. He's gotta play."

Throughout spring training of 1976 Foster played with the Triple A squad, which by then was the Iowa Oaks, and he was scheduled to be their left fielder. But as the last day of training approached, the White Sox sent down three outfielders from the major league camp, and Foster was moved back down to Knoxville.

"Things happen," he says. "I can understand that. But as the season goes on and I'm hitting .330 and those guys in Iowa are hitting .230, why are they there and me down here?"

Without leaving time for a response, he begins talking about his fielding and how hard he's worked on it, getting his throws off faster and covering more ground. Two errors in all of 1975, he says, and just two this season. But it does no good—the label is there, and it sticks.

He stops and shakes his head. "It's not just me," he says. "I got a wife and a little girl. They've looked out for me these four years. All this time it's been my career that's been everybody's main concern. Soon I'm going to have to start looking out for them."

He talks about the moving—"I won't leave my family"—back and forth across the country. From their home in Attalla, near both of their families, to Appleton, then back to Attalla. Then to Knoxville, and back to Attalla; to Knoxville, to Denver, then back to Attalla. And so on.

"It can drive you crazy," he says. "You never know where you're going to be, and just when you think it's going to be one place they send you someplace else."

He stops again, and slumps down in the seat. "Jolene," he says, referring to his wife, "she's really something. She knows how important this is to me, how much I love it. Whatever happens, she goes along. The last time they sent me down to Knoxville, I told her I wanted to quit and asked what she thought. She said I'd have to live the rest of my life with that decision. She was right."

A smile comes to his face as he talks about the girl he'd married when they were both juniors at Jacksonville State. His love of baseball was not something to which she had to adjust—she always knew it came with him. Though they met in high school, she had heard about him since she was twelve years old. In the small towns of that section of Alabama, in the Appalachians northeast of Birmingham, reputations are everybody's business, and Larry Foster has been a local hero for a long time.

"She used to live a block from where I played ball," he recalls. "She'd come to the park and watch me play and I didn't even know it."

Still talking about his young family, he works the conversation around to the way they live, tiny apartments in Knoxville, then going back to find a place for the winter in Attalla, "a settled area" where people expect you to sign a lease and stay, where finding work is hard when everybody knows you'll be leaving in the spring.

"Money's tight," he says. "I make $1,000 a month in Double A. With rent, car payments, insurance, that's about $100 a month under my expenses. And that's only for the months I'm playing. Winter's another story."

He resumes talking about Knoxville, about having to come back each season and prove all over again that he can hit Double A pitching, but then he stops himself.

"Hey," he says, "don't get me wrong. I love to play. Nine innings of baseball—I'd rather do that than go home and eat. But if something don't happen after this year, I'm probably gonna hang it up. No matter how hard I try and no matter what I do, it seems I don't get ahead."

Larry Foster's plight is not exceptional. Though young ballplayers rarely consider the possibility when they sign that first contract, getting stuck in the quagmire of the minors is the pattern for most men climbing toward the majors. The projected apprenticeship for the average player is five to six years, but that often turns into seven and eight and even nine years, especially for those considered by their organizations "not quite ready" for the majors.

Sometimes success requires a little more than getting out of an organization where, for one reason or another, a player's abilities are not being fully appreciated. Nolan Ryan spent seven frustrating seasons as the property of the Mets before he was traded to California, and has been setting pitching records ever since. Claude Osteen bounced around in the Cincinnati system for five years before the Washington Senators rescued him from the Indianapolis roster and brought him to the majors in 1961, the first of fifteen years as a big league pitcher.

But the outcome is not always so pleasant. With a player limit at each of the four levels, with each organization signing as many as twenty to thirty new players a year and only a few spots opening up at the major league level, somewhere along the way a lot of baseball players get lost in the shuffle. The procedure is called an "unconditional release," which is a euphemism for being fired. Few things are more sad in sports than an athlete who has been playing since he was a child, who has been a professional since his late teens, and suddenly, at twenty-five or twenty-six, has been released.

On the same Knoxville team with Larry Foster in 1976 was an outfielder named Fred Norton. Norton's skills profile was just the opposite of Foster's. He was a fine fielder and a weak hitter. A tall, lean center fielder from Pennsylvania, Norton signed with the White Sox right out of high school in 1969.

In seven years with the Chicago organization he played for every farm team in every classification. And after three fine seasons—he was a leading fielder in each and twice made league all-star teams—he began to level off. His fielding became less impressive, and his hitting tapered off from mediocre. With the Knox Sox in 1976 he could manage only a .223 average.

"My defense has always been good," he said that summer, "but my hitting just hasn't come along. The Sox don't have a minor league hitting instructor anymore, and I've done what I could on my own. But when I make the show, it's going to be with my glove."

He rattled off the names of some outfielders who had made respectable careers in baseball on the strength of their defensive abilities, men like Jim Rivera and Bill Virdon, Jim Landis, Tommie Agee, and enough others to show that he had done his homework.

The following February Norton was at his parents' home in

the mountainous southwest section of Pennsylvania. He was waiting for his air ticket to arrive from the White Sox for spring training—his eighth—when the phone call came.

"It was C. V. [Carol V. Davis, Chicago's farm director]," said the twenty-five-year-old outfielder. "He told me I couldn't play with them anymore."

His voice dropped as he mouthed the words, a child cast out. "He told me no one in the organization wanted me on their team, and that he'd checked around with other teams and that they weren't interested either. He said I was through, and that he was sorry."

He started talking in run-on sentences about having trouble hitting at Knoxville, that he'd done better in Triple A but that the White Sox seemed to feel his performance in Double A was important, and then he stopped short.

"I don't know what I'm going to do," he said. It was a statement suspended, followed by nothing.

A minute later he continued. "After that call I went down to Florida anyway. I didn't go near camp. I went fishing in the Keys. It was the strangest feeling, to be in Florida in March and not to be playing baseball."

Norton took a minute to think. "You see guys get cut all the time," he said. "You're sorry to see them go 'cause they're friends, but you're glad it isn't you. And at the same time you can't imagine it happening. It's just not real."

He drew in an obviously tense breath and went on. "Baseball's all I ever wanted to do. I never even thought of anything else. During the off-season I'd work on construction jobs, things to stay in shape, 'cause the season was coming. Now there's no more season. All those summers, back to back, playing baseball. Till now."

By the time he returned from the Florida Keys the letter from the White Sox was waiting. Simple confirmation, so there could be no confusion. The message was brief. Thank you, but we feel you have not shown sufficient progress. We've tried to make a deal for you, but no one has shown interest. Goodbye, and good luck.

And that was it. Before it ever began, the career was over. The Dream ended.

But it is unfair to concentrate on the negative side of life in the minor leagues. The frustrated ambition, the players getting released—other players watching, sad but relieved—they represent only a small part of the overall experience. And while that dark side of the game remains hidden in the corner of every player's mind, his active hours are spent with baseball, if not the actual playing and practicing, then endless talk about it. And while analyzing a pitcher's motion or chasing down a line drive or practicing a drag bunt, there is little thought of promotion or release. Even when things are not going well, when his team is fifteen games out of first place in the last month of the season and it may be tough to block out the despair, that condition is transitory. The season ends, and everybody starts again fresh in the spring.

Spring training, the annual rebirth of the baseball season, is a unique occurrence in sports. Unlike the training camps of basketball and football (where there are normally twice as many players on hand as jobs available) almost every player in uniform has already signed a contract. Certainly all the minor leaguers have signed. Those not coming back—like Fred Norton—have been released during the winter. So with the exception of a few free agents, invited to camp on the chance of finding a spot, and here and there a veteran being challenged by one of the top rookies, everyone is assured of working someplace for the upcoming season.

Overall, it is a happy experience for the minor leaguers, one to which they look forward. It represents for them the best conditions of their entire season. Whatever disappointments were suffered in August and September have been softened by the off-season. Even the memories of the jarring bus rides, the damp and fungus-ridden locker rooms, and the overcooked meals eaten on the run fade in the warm, gentle sunshine of Florida and Arizona, lost in the pure and graceful act of drifting back under a fly ball on an even, well-groomed field.

It is what every kid envisioned as baseball when he signed his contract, and what now comes to pass but once a year.

One of the fine training facilities of the spring is Allyn Fields in Sarasota, used by the Chicago White Sox. It was there that Fred Norton was heading when the Sox released him in 1977, there that Larry Foster thought he had won his Triple A job in 1976. The Sox's major league camp begins at Allyn Fields at the end of each February, then moves into town to Payne Park in the second week of March. The farm teams then take over the huge complex for the four weeks of their spring training.

It is a mammoth operation, and beautifully maintained. Four baseball fields on one tract of land. The four home plates are neatly clustered at the center, forming a large octagon of space from which all fields are clearly observable. Each diamond has a small set of stands positioned directly behind its batting cage, so that spectators may watch the game on any field they like. At the center of the octagon is an observation tower, which has complete command of the fields surrounding it. From the canopy-topped second-story landing, club executives and coaches have a clear view of the entire facility, from the batter's boxes less than one hundred feet away to the fielders' positions all around.

There is also a complete clubhouse with showers, lockers, and a training room, and nearby are two batting cages with automatic pitching machines.

The players arrive early in the morning, go through some calisthenics and loosening-up exercises, then break up into groups and head for the four fields for instruction and intersquad games. By one or two in the afternoon they have finished (except for those days when games are scheduled with other minor league teams) and the rest of the afternoon is free, to go to the beach or sleep or do whatever they choose.

During the five or six hours of working time the facility is alive with baseball. Intersquad games or batting practice occupy all of the diamonds simultaneously, players run in the outfield, and coaches bat a random assortment of balls to infielders. Baseballs—bouncing grounders and great, arcing flies—are everywhere at once. And from the batting cages off to the side comes the endless sound of players hitting the flawless strikes of the two mechanical pitching machines.

It is a glorious time, especially during that first week, when nothing seems to be beyond a player's reach. The hard decisions come later—who will play where; who will be traded and who will stay. Now it is fantasy time. Anything seems possible. Who is to say what fruits a great spring could harvest?

It is also a time of renewing old acquaintances. Baseball players are mostly gregarious by nature, and friends made during their early years often remain close, despite the fact that so many are in direct competition for advancement. A lot of White Sox expense money is spent during the season calling from one farm team to another, from Knoxville to Des Moines to Appleton, just to keep in touch. Spring training is the one time they are all together, and can sit and share the horrors and joys of the season past.

But primarily the business of the day is still baseball, and to that end spring training is a most productive time. There are pitching coaches and batting coaches, coaches to help players with their base running and stealing, with all facets of the game. If a pitcher wants to develop a screwball or work on his pickoff move, if a batter wants to turn himself into a switch hitter or change his stance, this is the time and the place to do it.

"It's the only time during the year when a guy can depend on getting help," says Bob Palmer, a young catcher in the White Sox organization.

"Managers mean well, but how much can one man do with twenty-five guys who need help?" he says, referring to the absence of coaches at the lower levels during the season. "Like last season. Gordy [Gordon Lund, Palmer's 1975 manager in Class A] did his best, but he was a shortstop. What can a shortstop tell me about catching? I have to save all my questions for spring training."

This is one of the amazing flaws in the workings of the minor leagues: with so much money invested in their operation, and so much reliance placed on their success, that so little is done to provide qualified instruction during the season. Organizations bring all their coaching talent to the Triple A and major league levels—where it is least needed—and let the young players struggle along except for those few weeks of spring training.

While coaches and minor league managers are working with young players during the spring, they are also evaluating them. Not only the tangible things, a man's ability to hit and run and catch a baseball, but things that do not show up directly in the box score—hustle and concentration, along with more subtle aspects of playing the game, the judgment to tag up on a long fly ball and take a base after the catch, the ability to hold a runner on second base while handling a ground ball. The process goes on throughout the minor league camp, but rarely do any of the players concern themselves with it until the results become known.

Toward the end of every spring camp, the days start to get tense. This is when players are assigned to the levels and clubs for the upcoming season. It is rarely a life-and-death situation. Players know they are going to play; the only question is where. A good spring can push them ahead an entire classification; a poor spring can cost them a year's labors. But the tension builds each day.

"Those last ten days can drive you crazy," said Larry Foster, reflecting back on his annual ordeal in the White Sox camp. "The guys who've had a good camp talk like they're going north with the big club. The ones who've been flat are worried about falling back. It's just like getting your report card when you were a kid and looking to see if you were promoted."

It was a problem that Foster knew well, not only from the side of an athlete dealing with his own future in his sport, but of a man trying to make immediate plans for his family. How does he make arrangements for a season when he doesn't know where it will be spent?

"When it's just you it's one thing," he said, "but what do you do with your family? All you can do is try and guess. If you guess wrong, you end up calling pay booths on the turnpike and leaving messages for your wife halfway across the country."

There was a smile on his face, but it faded when he talked about his own adjustment to having guessed wrong.

"It's hard going back," he said, referring to Knoxville. "You've been there and you've done it. You keep asking yourself, How many more times?"

No one sits down with a player and explains where he's going to spend the season and why. Most organizations have the same ritual: an assignment sheet is posted at some prominent place inside the clubhouse, and each day more names are listed under the team where they will play.

The assignment sheet at Allyn Fields in 1976 was posted just inside the front door, tacked to a bulletin board that hung from one of the front lockers. About a week before the end of camp the teams began to take shape. Each morning the players would start trooping in for the day's practice, and the first thing each man checked was that list, just to see what was happening to his life.

While some organizations fill their top-level teams first, that spring Chicago started from the bottom. First to be filled was the Rookie League team, which would play right there in Sarasota. Then the Class A team in Appleton, and the Class AA team in Knoxville.

Every day more and more players were classified, and from then on they worked out with the players who would be their teammates for the coming season. And as decisions continued to be made (players being dropped down to the level where they would spend the season) those remaining on the top formed the Iowa club, Chicago's Triple A team in the American Association.

One of the players left was Kevin Bell, a fair, farmboy type from California. He was twenty, though he looked younger—what appeared to be baby fat was in fact muscle—and was in only his third year as a professional, having signed in 1974 after his first year at Mount San Antonia Junior College.

Calling Bell's year at San Antonia his first is misleading. It implies a second, and one was never intended. For Kevin Bell never planned to be anything but a baseball player, and all decisions were carefully directed toward that goal.

He was an aggressive player, even at eight when he started in Little League, pursuing that kind of play through Pony League, Colt League, Connie Mack and American Legion ball, and right into high school, where he earned all-league and all-valley honors. It was while he was a junior at Northview High School in Covina, south of Los Angeles, that he began seriously planning for his pro career.

He talked with scouts from the Minnesota Twins and the Boston Red Sox while still in high school, but the bonus money they offered—ranging from $2,500 to $8,000—was not what Bell had in mind.

"A lot of my friends were playing in the minors," says Bell, "and they all said the same thing. You sign for a couple of thousand and nobody gives you a good look. You sign for $15,000 and they give you a lot more attention."

To let the market better appreciate his talents, Bell needed time. Not a lot—about a year or so.

"I didn't want to start at a four-year university," he recalls, "because then the pros can't take you till your junior year or you're twenty-one. Then the coach from the junior college where I live suggested a year with him might be just what I needed. It made sense."

That one season with San Antonia, where he batted .366, hitting five home runs and six doubles, increased his value to the point where Chicago gave him $20,000 to sign. And once the White Sox had him under contract, they treated him like quality merchandise—patiently and with affection. Though he set no records in his first two seasons in the minor leagues, Bell progressed smoothly from Appleton to Knoxville.

Then during the winter of 1975 he played ball in the Dominican Republic, which was arranged for him by the White

Sox. Baseball is popular in several Latin countries, and many men play twelve months a year by catching the seasons on both sides of the border. It is especially good for young players who want to add to their experience quickly.

Bell, however, had a poor winter in the Dominican sun. He was young and so far from home for the first time, in a foreign country where he neither spoke the language nor liked the food. He missed California and his friends, got sick and lost weight.

"I was really miserable," he said later. "We stayed in a poor little town, worse even than Tijuana. I had mosquitoes biting me all the time. Try to eat and there'd be fifteen, twenty flies around your food. I even got sick from the water."

Worst of all, he couldn't hit. His batting average—a healthy .304 in Knoxville the previous summer—dropped to .132. After five weeks he was sent home.

"I felt like I was never gonna hit again," recalled Bell. "But the White Sox were really nice. They talked to me and told me not to worry about it. They said they knew I could hit. They said that kind of thing sometimes happens to people down there, and that I shouldn't worry about it."

And, smiling, "They also said I didn't have to go back there again."

It was obvious what the White Sox thought of Kevin Bell that spring. First, they invited him to attend the veteran camp, along with some other prospects from the Chicago organization and two free agents (established major leaguers) looking for jobs. And when he got there, they looked hard.

The Chicago camp was the only one to open on time in 1976, because of the dispute between the players' association and the owners. All other teams had locked their training sites tight while negotiations were in progress. But Bill Veeck, the Sox's maverick president, back in baseball after several years of being locked out himself, decreed that his camp would open on time with whatever minor leaguers and free agents he could find. He managed twenty-five of them, one of whom was Kevin Bell.

PHOTO BY ERNEST ROBERTSON, JR.

Kevin Bell, a certified prospect. "I felt like I was never gonna hit again . . . but they told me not to worry about it."

It is fascinating to watch baseball men look over a young athlete whom they consider a real prospect. One could almost describe their interest as lecherous, not so different from an old man staring at a beautiful young woman as she cavorts in a bathing suit.

That is how Veeck and his manager, Paul Richards, whom he had brought out of exile with him, looked at Kevin. And with good reason. He was a powerfully built kid, 6 feet tall and 185 pounds, with blond hair and fair skin that reddened after the first day's workout. He played a respectable third base, though he probably would still be in school if defense were what he was selling.

It wasn't. Hitting was. And as he stood in the batting cage and savagely attacked the pitches offered by the other minor leaguers, you could see the lust on the faces of Richards and Veeck. They would sit in the president's golf cart and watch him, swing after swing after swing. *Whack! Whack! Whack!* Even the coaches and other players would stop and watch. *Whack! Whack!* The ball literally leaped off the bat, carrying deep into center field and left center, each shot a straight line that seemed to pick up speed as it passed over the infielders. Bell stood there with a serious look on his face as if he were dispensing divine justice with that long, light-colored bat. *Whack! Whack! Whack!*

Finally Richards, a leathery man of sixty-eight who spoke very little to anyone in camp, would lean over the side of the cart to spit some accumulated tobacco juice, and then turn to Veeck. "That kid can hit a baseball," he'd say. Both men would nod seriously and turn their attention back to the field. You could see it happen, day after day.

When the veterans finally reported in mid-March and the major league camp got started, the attention quickly shifted from even the most promising minor leaguers as management rushed to cram five weeks of spring training into the remaining eighteen days. Bell spent the rest of the time with the same players who had been his teammates for two years.

"I was planning on going back to Knoxville," he said later.

"I'd finished up there pretty well, and they told me I needed to polish up on some things. I figured another year, fine."

But as the training season drew to a close, the lower classifications began to fill. Without Kevin Bell.

"There was about five days left," said Bell. "They had filled out the rosters for every team but Knoxville, and suddenly the last cut from Iowa was made and I was still there. I couldn't believe it. I had set my mind to go back to Knoxville—that's what they told me was going to happen—and there I was in Triple A. Really, at first I couldn't believe it. But then I figured, why not? They must know. Right?"

A broad smile flashed across his face as he said it, and he explained that he had done well during the nonroster camp, but had not hit at all when he moved over with the rest of the minor leaguers. But by then the decision was made, and Bell was on his way. When camp broke he proceeded to Des Moines to play on the American Association club there, and on June 16, when his teammates were flying from Evansville to Denver, Bell was boarding a Delta flight for Chicago, having been called up to join the White Sox.

The dynamics of such decisions appear to be one of the great mysteries of sports. Athletes use the expression "being in the right place at the right time" (usually while shaking their heads) as a vital factor in the progression of a career. And they are correct, as far as they go. But more of a factor is the attention and support given to the player considered a prospect in contrast to the player whose potential is viewed as limited.

In that respect, baseball is the same as all other team sports. Men like Larry Foster are destined to be given little attention because they do not fit whatever formula has been devised for what comprises the successful athlete. Not coming from a prestigious sports school, being drafted in a late round—or worse, not being drafted at all—all these are stigmas. Free agents are the most suspect, and they must overcome this handicap throughout their career. If he wasn't good enough for someone to draft, coaches and executives reason, how good can he be?

This is the kind of attitude that can discourage an athlete. It also tends to create its own reality. An acknowledged prospect is given time and attention, made to feel comfortable and secure in his future. If he has any real talent, it will develop. The same player, stripped of all this support and put on the spot with the knowledge that one poor season will get him dumped, will be home selling shoes before you can say Bobo Holloman.

The unique quality about baseball is that a man of average talent who is truly committed to the game and that talent can test the system while remaining part of it. So long as he is willing to put up with the low pay and often intolerable conditions in the minors, he can hang around until that perfect combination of circumstances—being in the right place at the right time, and then being able to produce—offers him his chance. If he doesn't run out of seasons, he just might wait out a pretty decent career.

Football and basketball do not afford even the most tenacious of athletes that privilege. Once cut by a big league team, there are not many options which will permit a player to stay in his sport. A few, but not many. And the number is fewer than it once was.

Throughout the years a variety of minor football leagues have sprung up across the country, held on for a few seasons, then died. Some of them had working arrangements with National Football League teams, so that when a man of particular promise was cut a team could place him where his progress could be monitored. Others functioned without any affiliation, official or otherwise, filling their teams with men unwanted by the pros or who just loved the game and wanted to play. Some paid their players, but many did not. Minor league football is mostly for love, not money.

When they were the only alternative to the NFL—and to the corresponding Canadian Football League—the quality of play was often quite high. But with the increased popularity of pro football came expansion, both within the NFL and with the birth of the American Football League in 1960. It meant more teams and more jobs, and reduced the flow of better players to the minor leagues. Then the World Football League began in

1974, and, while it lasted only two years, it placed an added strain on the minors, further depriving them of players and also draining off much of their fan support. It was not unlike the effect that expansion in major league baseball had on its minor league system.

Today, aside from the NFL, there are few professional leagues that have survived, and almost none that still pay their players. Gone are the Seaboard Football League and the Continental League, and many others. Those which remain—the Interstate League and the Central States League, the Florida League, and about a dozen more—manage to hang on through the dedication of their backers and coaches, and the men who come out each weekend to play.

The Jersey Oaks, a team in the Gotham Division of the New York Conference, have been playing football for the past twenty seasons. Based in Plainfield, New Jersey, the team plays its home games at Seidler Field, a local park whose adjacent swimming pool to the south requires that all field goals and extra points be kicked toward the north goal post.

It's a casual kind of operation, the kind that draws fifty or sixty men out for a practice session in the summertime when the nights are light and warm and that old high school spirit spreads infectiously over the field and into the locker room. But come October and November, and they're lucky to get twenty-five men to an evening practice.

One particular Thursday night late in October 1976 was unusually cold, somewhere in the mid-thirties, and the conditions took their toll on participation. Only about a third of the fifty-two-man squad showed up for practice, some coming from neighboring towns but others driving from as far away as Allentown, over an hour away in Pennsylvania. Arriving at the little park and seeing the pickup trucks, the vans, and the odd assortment of vintage Fords and Chevrolets that lined the street, it was easy to think of the parking lot adjacent to the New York Jets camp in Hempstead, Long Island, replete with Continentals and Cadillacs and the occasional Jaguar.

They ran through some plays quickly that night, mostly

trying to get warm. A few pass patterns, a running play or two, and ten or fifteen minutes on kickoffs and punts. Then they decided that prudence dictated an early evening. After practice, Carl Giosa, the Oaks's wide receiver, sat in the locker room, trying to get the circulation back into his fingers, talking about his professional football career.

"I lasted two months at the Cowboys' spring camp when I first got out of college," said the 1975 graduate of Kutztown State in Pennsylvania, "and then had weekend tryouts with the Colts, the Jets, and the Philadelphia Bell in the WFL. Every time I got cut."

Giosa, who is slightly built and did not seem as tall as the 5 feet 11 inches listed for him on the Oaks's roster, had driven in from Easton, Pennsylvania, as he did three times a week—twice for practice and Sundays for games. It was his second season with the Oaks, which he called his "ticket to the big time."

"I'm not like some of these guys," he said. "It hasn't been part of my life since I was six, and I don't see myself driving around in a Caddy. It's just the game."

As he talked he was taking off his football shoes and pulling on a pair of sneakers, and he stopped to slip his arms into an unlined windbreaker, for it was cold in the long, narrow room and all he wore was a sweatsuit.

"I guess it's been going on since high school," he said, "that feeling I get in a game."

Though he had been talking in a slow, easy voice, the words suddenly began coming faster and with an excited thrust.

"It's such a great thing when you catch a ball when your team needs a touchdown," he said, and his eyes widened with the thought of it. "You score and you come back and everybody grabs you and hugs you. It's that thirty seconds of glory. It makes you weak."

He let a moment pass, as if to let that rush of emotion pass with it, and started talking about his weekly schedule to keep in shape, the running and lifting of weights, the handball, and more running, then he shifted abruptly into the tryout camps he had attended.

"You know what they're like," he said. "Five hundred guys in a day. They run ya through the forty, then watch ya catch a couple of passes, and that's the name of that tune. Guys get cut if their pants aren't on straight."

Trying out for the NFL is a favorite topic among the Plainfield players, he said, and it seemed that there were two philosophies. Some men go to the better clubs, figuring if cut they'd have a good chance of getting picked up by the lesser teams, who are always interested in the cut list of the teams ahead of them. Others figure they would get more attention trying out for a team which is less rich in talent, and go directly to the second-division clubs.

"I've tried the good clubs," he said, "and next season I'll try the others."

He got up to leave. It was after nine o'clock, and early the next morning he had to be at the Easton YMCA, where he worked as a physical education instructor with kids.

"Next year I'm gonna play it a little smarter than in the past," he said, "I'm gonna try to go to the camps where I know they need receivers."

He zipped up his jacket. "I'm not willing to bend my life out of shape chasing this," he said, "but I figure I've got about two years of trying left. After that age will be catching up with me."

And, heading for the door, "Twenty-six in this game and you're an old man," he said, and started back for Easton.

That Sunday the Oaks played the Boonton Bears before barely two hundred people on a cool but bright and sunny afternoon. There was a lot of socializing, and nearly as much attention was paid to some children playing touch football on the sidelines as to the main attraction on the field. There was only a slight stirring when, early in the game, Giosa shook loose from his defender, headed straight down the sidelines and waved frantically to his quarterback, drifted easily under a strongly thrown pass, tucked it under his arm, and carried it into the end zone for the Oaks's first score. But, then, minor league football has always been less for the benefit of the fans, and more for the players.

That same maxim applies to minor league basketball. In pro leagues in Pennsylvania and Indiana, around Detroit, Chicago, and San Francisco, the people most benefited by the night's game are the players. A man cut from the NBA can still play good, competitive ball in one of those leagues, and can earn $50 to $60 or even $75 a game. Many NBA teams, when cutting a prospect, will try to interest him in the closest minor league team—unofficially, of course—just to help him keep in shape and help them keep him in their view.

The atmosphere at a basketball game in Indianapolis or Syracuse is not so different from a football game in Plainfield, New Jersey. The men in the game are supplementing their dreams with a little live competition, just, as the song goes, until the real thing comes along.

This is not to imply that every man playing minor league sports is waiting for his shot at the "bigs." Most of them are there because they love their sport, because scoring with a jump shot—or hitting a home run or sacking a quarterback—does something for them emotionally and physically that they can find in no other way. But that is why most major leaguers are in their game. Aside from the trappings, there isn't that much difference. It's what they like to do most.

But most athletes would rather do it at the top. Some players deny that they have any more grandiose ambitions than the game in which they are playing, but many are willing to talk with more candor. And one of the most candid, and most persistent, is Charlie Criss, the 5-feet-7-inch guard cut by the Knicks after one week of their veteran camp in 1976.

On that afternoon in September, Criss swore he'd had enough, that he was finally giving up. "That's it," he had said. "No more tryouts, no more basketball. I've had it."

But that's not so easy, not for a man as committed as Criss. Ever since he was in the eighth grade and the coach at school told him he wasn't good enough for the team, basketball had become the central goal in his life. He returned the following year to make that team, went on to win a basketball scholarship at New Mexico State, then played AAU ball near there at Las Cruces. After returning to New York in 1972 he worked at a variety of jobs, for the parks department, an insurance company, and a tape manufacturer. But they were all avocations. For whenever the opportunity arose he would step into the nearest telephone booth, change into his shorts and sneakers, and emerge as Super Criss—basketball player nonpareil.

"I just wanted someone in the NBA to notice me, and that's why getting cut was so tough," said Criss, reflecting back on the New York camp. "Six years I had worked for that chance, and when it happened it was nothing. They ignored me. I really thought I'd had enough."

It was almost seven months later when Criss was talking, sitting in a high school gymnasium in Allentown, Pennsylvania, site of the first game of the playoffs in the Eastern Basketball Association, the minor league whose letterhead reads: "One Step from the Best."

"When I got home and started talking to my family," said Criss, "they kept reminding me how hard I'd worked. Six brothers and four sisters—that's a lot of support."

Criss's family had shared his dream of making the NBA, and would frequently appear en masse—including cousins and eighty-seven-year-old grandmother—at a game in which he was playing. But his biggest fan was his father. He had always urged Charlie on, and was involved in every stage of his career. But in that fall of 1976 he was involved in his own battle against leukemia.

"He just told me not to quit," recalled Criss. "He said I'd come too far and fought too long to give up. I knew he was right. I knew that no matter what happened, the world was going to keep on revolving, and as long as it was I wanted to be playing basketball."

So Criss returned to his perennial role in the Eastern league. Five years he'd played there, for teams in Hartford, Connecti-

POLLOS
14
32
22

cut, Cherry Hill, New Jersey, and Scranton, Pennsylvania. His first season, 1972, he had been on reserve, playing on the taxi squad. By 1973 he was not only a starter for the same Hartford team but its star.

"It's not bad," he said of the thirty-year-old league. "It has the feeling of being organized, as if there's something there. Games don't get canceled because nobody shows up, or because nobody can find the key to the gym. You get that a lot in some of these leagues."

He paused, and looked around the sparsely filled gymnasium of William Allen High School.

"What it isn't is big league," he said. "You never forget that. You're playing in places like Trenton and Hazleton for $50 and $60 a game, and that pays for everything—equipment, gas, everything. Teams fold and move in the middle of the season, guys get fed up and quit. And there isn't much chance to practice. So when you play, it's mostly run and shoot."

Because the yelling of a woman seated just behind him was so loud, Charlie had to stop talking. It wasn't even the regular game—he would play in that, for Scranton against Allentown—just a preliminary between a local team of doctors and hospital workers and a group from the city hall.

"That's another thing," he said. "They can be unpleasant. I've had 'em call me midget and freak, and yell to get me off the court. Mostly that stuff just gets me going better."

This was a typical EBA crowd that night in the clean, modern Allen High. Most of those who were going to attend the game were there, about 700 of the 2,700 capacity, and whatever noise they were making was but a warmup for the playoff game, scheduled for eight-thirty-five p.m. At that point nicely dressed, middle-aged, working-class fans would go berserk, screaming their hostility at the members of both teams, but

PHOTO COURTESY SCRANTON TIMES

Charlie Criss, attempting a shot for the Scranton Apollos in the Eastern league. "What it isn't is big league."

saving their choicest suggestions for the officials: "Blow yourself, ref" and "Stick 'em in the basket" are favorite comments from EBA crowds, along with an occasional "Screw the blind bastard to the backboard."

For anyone not accustomed to attending minor league sports events, it can be shocking. But it does not take long to understand that neither personality nor basketball has much to do with it. At $3 a ticket, it's just a good way to release hostility in a small town on a Saturday night.

"The toughest thing about the Eastern league is the traveling," said Criss, trying to ignore the commotion in the stands. "Two hours and a half to Scranton, nearly four to Lancaster. Sometimes I'd arrange to meet the team bus on the way, but often I'd have to drive it by myself."

All games were on weekends, Saturday and Sunday nights, which left Criss free during the week to play in the AAU leagues in New York. Four games a week in the city, then on the road for the Eastern league.

"I remember one game in Syracuse," he said. "It took me eight hours to drive through the snow. I just about made it by halftime."

After that first season, when he played in just four games, Criss averaged 20.5, 30.6, 38.5, and 34.4 points a game, and in his last two years an amazing 43.6 in playoff games. Twice he was named most valuable player in the league, and he still holds the single-game scoring record for his 72 points against Hazleton in 1976.

All that effort, and nobody from the NBA ever thought to give him a serious look. All the phone calls and the letters—ignored. Until the Knicks responded by inviting him to camp, and then they ignored him in person. And why not? After all, everybody knows the NBA is a league of giants. Putting a 5-foot-7-inch guard in with them could only be a joke.

"That drove me crazy," said Criss. "I knew I could play against those guys. Every summer, in the Rucker, I'd play against all of them, and I beat 'em. I beat 'em on offense, and I beat 'em on defense."

The Rucker to which Criss referred is actually the Harlem Professional League, which is the professional extension of the Holcombe Rucker Community League. It is the league which draws much of the best talent in the NBA to the playgrounds and gymnasiums of New York during the summer, and even within that select company Charlie Criss was a star. He would bring the ball across the midcourt line, teasing some of the best guards in the NBA with his casual way of dribbling. Then he would fake to one side, move to the other, and take a jump shot from the top of the large circle they call the "key," sending the ball through the center of the basket without its touching the rim. The announcer who did the play-by-play called Charlie "The Mosquito" and when he would connect on his jump shot the man would lean into the microphone and yell "Stinggg" over the sound system, drawing out the "ng" that way. When Criss wasn't playing there he was playing in the Bob Douglas League in Queens, or in one of the leagues in Yonkers or Brooklyn. It was a schedule which frequently kept him playing basketball seven nights a week during the summer.

It was nearly time for him to get changed, and he took hold of his athletic bag as he reflected back over all the years of great basketball he'd played with nobody but friends and family paying attention.

"But none of it was wasted," he said, "and getting discouraged really wasn't such a problem."

He smiled. "You've got to remember that all that time I was playing basketball, and there's nothing I love more than playing basketball. It does something special for me."

And, as he stood up to leave, "A lot of guys look at me and say I'm too small. But once we're out there"—and he motioned to the court—"I'm as big as anybody else. Basketball's the equalizer. I may be only five-seven standing here, but out there I'm big."

That was April 1977, and Criss went out and scored 54 points that night, and 42 points the following night up in Scranton. Soon after he left for a tour of Europe, playing for the Washington Generals as they provided the opposition for the

Harlem Globetrotters. (Exciting and lucrative as it was, the job bothered Charlie because it wasn't "serious basketball.") But when he returned, the man everybody said was too small to play in the NBA received a call from Hubie Brown, coach of the Atlanta Hawks.

"They called me," said Criss sometime later. "Nobody ever called *me* before. He [Brown] said he'd heard what I could do and he was going to give me a full shot. The whole exhibition season—eight games—to see if I could fit in."

According to Brown, formerly a coach in the ABA who was in his second season with the Hawks, "We were looking for quickness and scoring. The best man outside the league for that was Charlie Criss. We sent some of our people to watch him play, and they said he was better than any guard we had, so we invited him to camp."

Brown made a gesture as if to say that would be the only natural thing to do. "He'd been a free-lance basketball player for seven years," he said. "I told him if he could adjust to our game he had a job."

Criss went through the exhibition season with Atlanta playing good, steady basketball. He did everything Brown wanted of him. He brought the ball down the court and set up plays. He passed off effectively. He played tight defense. And only when the circumstances were right did he shoot.

And then, at the end of September, after Atlanta's last exhibition game and before the season started, he got permission to take a few days off. His father had grown weaker and was in the hospital, and Charlie was flying home to see him.

"Coach Brown and I shared a limousine to the airport," recalled Criss. "He asked me if I'd found a place to stay in Atlanta, 'cause I was going to need one."

Criss grinned. "I didn't say a word, but inside I was screaming."

Later that day, when he walked into his father's hospital room, the first topic of conversation was the Hawks.

"He asked me what was happening," said Criss. "He asked if I'd made the team. I said I made it. He said 'You made it!' and

HAWKS PHOTO BY C.W. SKINNER

Charlie Criss at a Hawks practice with 7-feet-1 Wayne Rollins. "I didn't say a word, but inside I was screaming."

I said yeah. He said 'I don't believe it.' I said that I did, I really did. He just smiled."

Charlie's father never saw his son play in the NBA. By the time the Hawks arrived in the New York area to play the New Jersey Nets, on October 26, he was too weak to leave his hospital bed, though he listened to the game on radio. By the time Atlanta returned to the area to play the Knicks at the end of December, he had died.

When Criss went home to Yonkers for his father's funeral, his mother told him of his dying wish.

"She told me what my father said before he died," he recalled. "He wanted me to stay in the NBA and keep on playing, to prove to all the people who said I couldn't do it. He wanted me to play for him, to just keep on going."

There is a bond between Charlie Criss and Carl Giosa, a bond shared with men who, in other places and at other times, have played in the minor leagues of every sport. They are men who love their game, men possibly not quite good enough to make it to the big leagues, or, possibly, men just never in the right place at the right time.

They are also men who share the belief that luck can change, can be waited out, that if they want it bad enough and work hard enough, they will earn their chance. And once given that chance—a real chance, when someone is watching—they're going to make it.

The crazy thing about sports is that guys keep making it, coming out of nowhere to make it. Not many, admittedly, but enough to keep the myth alive. Mike Riordan made it out of the Eastern league and settled with the Baltimore Bullets in the NBA, and George Johnson made it from the Western Basketball Association to the Golden State Warriors and the NBA championship. The NFL is full of established players who have come out of podunk little leagues from Connecticut to Texas.

In baseball it's only easier. Players like Mike Cuellar and Maury Wills spending eight and nine years in the minors before getting to the majors, and then making a name for themselves.

But it happens. And every time a Charlie Criss makes it, every player on every minor league and semipro team shakes his fist defiantly at fate and says, "Yeah, see what I mean? He did it. And if he did it, so can I."

And who's to say that he can't?

4

STANDING ROOM ONLY AT THE SHOW

The final session of the Philadelphia 76ers rookie camp is nearly over. The decisions on who will be invited to the veteran camp and who will be sent home have already been made, and, while none of the dozen or so men here today will admit it, they all have a strong sense of who those will be. In a short camp—four sessions of basketball crammed into two days—every man knows exactly what he has done, if he has played poorly or if he has played well. That is why it is so strange to watch them, driving relentlessly for a basket, twisting in midair as they force the ball up, diving to block shots and steal passes—hustling, hustling. Because it's too late for that. It's over. No minds will be changed in the twenty minutes which remain. They know that. Yet still they press and push and strain, as if one more move—one really good move—could make everything right.

There is a surreal quality to the entire scene, being played out in the near-empty fieldhouse here at Ursinus College outside Philadelphia. Though a few season ticket holders and members of the press are scattered through the stands, and a group of students is clustered around the basket at the far door, most of the seats are unoccupied. What during the season is a hall alive with fans, screaming their team on, is now a great, ghostly cave, the sounds of the basketball hitting the hardwood floor and the grunts and shouts of the players reverberating off the walls and the ceiling and the floor itself.

Though this is officially a camp of rookies and free agents, a few Philly regulars are here for an early start. The senior player is Steve Mix, sometimes sixth man and sometimes starter when the 76ers' aging star Billy Cunningham is injured. He is an attractive young man, with short black hair, a smooth, handsome face, and a body proportioned so evenly that at 6 feet 7 inches he appears unusually tall only when standing next to more conventional-sized people. Despite his position on the team, he has been here since the beginning of camp. Yesterday he ran during the afternoon session, and today he worked out during the scrimmage. Now he sits in the stands near midcourt, a towel draped around his neck and perspiration dripping from his forehead and the sides of his face. He sits quietly, watching the drama on the court. And it is clear, even before he speaks, that he identifies with the desperation of some of the men playing.

"I know what's going through their minds," he offers in confirmation. "I've been there."

There is a silence, as if he is going to continue, but he says nothing more. No one would have expected more. Mix's history in the league is common knowledge, especially in Philadelphia. Though he is officially credited with six seasons—three with Detroit and three with Philadelphia—that is only a fraction of his story.

He had been drafted by Detroit, struggled through two seasons there, and was cut soon after the end of training camp in 1971, his third season. That signaled the beginning of his basketball odyssey. He tried out with Boston and was cut, then tried out with the New York Nets in the ABA and was cut. He played with Denver for a while and was cut there, too. He fell back to regroup for the rest of the 1971–72 season, but returned the next year to try out again with the 76ers, and was again cut.

That last one was painful. The 76er team that he failed to make in 1972 went on to win 9 games and lose 73.

When he wasn't playing in the NBA or the ABA, or traveling from one camp to another, he was playing basketball wherever he could find a game, whether it was on neighborhood courts in his hometown of Toledo or in more organized circumstances. Among other tours that do not show up in the record book was his season in the Continental League, where he was the most valuable player, scoring 30 points a game for the Grand Rapids Tackers.

Then, before the beginning of the 1973–74 season, Mix and his wife, Maryalice, sat down for some serious conversation.

"We had a long talk," recalls Mix. "She knew how important basketball was to me. She'd been through it all, the frustration, the time on the bench, dragging myself around the league. But she pointed out it was different then, and she was right. I was nearly twenty-six, not a kid anymore. Our son had been born the year Detroit cut me, and was a year and a half. It was time to make some decisions. I had responsibilities."

Pausing to wipe away the sweat, he continues. "If I'd been single I would have gone on and on, but I wasn't. And we decided that I'd give it one more try—one more full try—and if I didn't make it I would quit."

Even while he talks, his attention is on the court.

"I never thought I wasn't good enough to play," he says, "but time was a problem. And I also knew that psychologically I couldn't continue to be cut without it having some effect on me."

For the first time he stops staring at practice. He looks straight ahead, his eyes narrow, then goes on. "I could see what was happening. The signs were there—the questions. I knew I could play, but to be cut by five teams, it's got to work on your head. And if you accept that they're right—that maybe you can't play—you're lost. You can no longer be effective on the court. They'll eat you alive."

He went to camp that fall with the New York Nets, and, though he played well, he was cut. But by then Gene Shue was coaching in Philadelphia, rebuilding from the disastrous season before. He heard Mix was available and invited him to camp. The rest, as they say, is history.

Out on the court, Lee Dixon, the 76ers' eighth draft choice, fights for a rebound. At Hardin-Simmons he had established the all-time scoring record by averaging 26.2 points his last season, but he is a forward at only 6 feet 5 inches tall and 180 pounds, and no one is watching him here. No one but Steve Mix, who shakes his head.

"Eighth-round picks don't get much attention, especially in two-day camps," says Mix, himself a fifth-round selection. "I've seen my share of two-day camps, too. With the Nets I had a weekend tryout and did nothing but play full court, three-on-three with the second string. In Boston I was there for a weekend, and the best thing I saw was the New England Patriots play the Miami Dolphins. I don't call those tryouts."

The focus of attention of most of the sixty or seventy students seated on the floor near the door is Darryl Dawkins, whom Philadelphia drafted directly out of an Orlando, Florida, high school in 1975. Dawkins, at 6 feet 11 and 251 pounds, is beginning his second year as a professional, and he is impressive to watch. He is obviously young and inexperienced—he is just nineteen—but his potential for development is awesome, even to the casual observer. He is a huge person, with great, broad shoulders and massive arms and legs.

Mix watches the action closely as it moves from one end of the court to the other. He watches the plays as they develop, spots those men who have learned their fundamentals and those who have not. And he spots the men having a poor camp, and empathizes with them. Three players from the ABA, all top prospects when they left college, all stars, are in trouble. Through the four sessions of basketball they have not found their game. One is Fly Williams, who was the fifth best scorer in the nation when he played at Austin Peay a few years before. Now he looks sloppy and disorganized. He, like most of the men on the floor, knows his opportunity for this season has slipped away.

"You have to get a chance to play," says Mix, never taking his eyes from the court. "You have to be given the time and the minutes. Then you can prove you can score in this league. But it takes time."

There is a tone of earnestness in his voice. He had come within days of quitting, of never playing professional basketball again, until Gene Shue gave him a chance. One full chance, one opportunity when a decision had not been made in advance. That changed his life.

At twenty-nine years of age, Steve Mix is unusually realistic for an athlete. Most are forced by the overwhelming odds against success to be compensatingly optimistic and positive. Mix knows himself as a player, knows his strengths and weaknesses, and seems comfortable discussing them. And the fact that he has made an appearance in an all-star game has not blurred his vision, though he readily admits it was the biggest thrill he's ever experienced.

"A thrill," he says, "but a shock, too. I don't consider myself NBA all-star quality. The Elvin Hayeses and the Abdul-Jabbars, they come down the court and score almost at will. Bang, bang, bang, they put it up in your face. I get my points on fast breaks and offensive rebounds, bumping people around. There's a difference."

He looks to the court as Darryl Dawkins leaps up above the rim of the basket to pull down a rebound, clearing a path for himself as he lands, then fires the outlet pass downcourt. One could almost see the improvement in him with each session. He was a boy, and they were teaching him how to play basketball. But Mix, a six-year veteran who had as much security on the team as most starters, what was he doing in a camp of rookies and free agents?

"I didn't have a good season last year," says Mix, measuring his response. "Oh, I scored my 14 points a game and averaged

PHOTO COURTESY PHILADELPHIA 76ERS

Steve Mix: "Nothing's guaranteed in this game. I'm no all-star."

seven or eight rebounds, but mentally I wasn't prepared to play every game like I should be. That's not going to be the case this year."

He stops himself in the middle of his thought to watch Terry Furlow lead a fast break down the court and slow up until he sees Lee Dixon enter his sight from the side, then hit him with a hard pass as the forward cuts in front of a defender.

And again the question: Why should an established player, a man who played more total minutes during the 1975–76 season than anyone else on the team, be here in an early camp, running and sweating with men who are already halfway to the Philadelphia International Airport?

"Nothing's guaranteed in this game," says Mix. "After last year I looked at myself and decided I had to dig down and come up with a little more."

And turning his attention back to the court, as if needing one more sight of the winning and the losing going on there, "I told you. I'm no all-star. I've got to work to make it in this game. And whatever it takes, that's what I'm going to do."

The glories of the world of professional athletics splash across the sports pages of our daily newspapers with an impact that belies the word "game." Only wars, presidential elections, and, when it was news, the conquering of outer space are so boldly trumpeted.

MARINERS SINK YANKS WITH LATE BARRAGE

MIAMI WINS 'EM ALL—MAKES NFL HISTORY

PORTLAND HUMBLES MILLIONAIRE SIXERS

REDS DO IT AGAIN—DECLARE DYNASTY

Big words over big stories. Pictures and articles which proclaim and examine the glory of sports. It's all very exciting.

Who won and who lost and by how much, heralded in big black-type headlines and embellished by active verbs and heart-pounding adjectives.

But those are only the results—who did what on a particular day in a particular event. We have become obsessed with that or, more accurately, the daily press is obsessed with it. Certainly results take up the vast majority of their coverage. Yet all the while a thousand tiny, life-and-death dramas take place every day in the world of sports. Real dramas that, if filmed and put on television between noon and five o'clock, could utilize the combined advertising budgets of Procter and Gamble, Colgate-Palmolive, and Lever Brothers.

But they are not on our daily television schedules, and rarely in our newspapers. For the human drama in sports to rate any attention beyond an occasional feature on a slow newsday, it must be of dire emotional importance: the tragic death of a young athlete, or a fallen star hitting skid row. Yet while less spectacular stories are not actively covered, their passage is chronicled.

Many sports sections devote a portion of a page—or sometimes an entire page—to data. Frequently collected under a set headline or logotype such as SCOREBOARD or just RESULTS, the daily potpourri of information includes league standings and box scores, bowling and boxing results, tennis summaries, golf scores, and a variety of other miscellany. It is a gray-looking page, rarely illustrated, and would seem more at home as part of the financial section or the classified ads.

But it is on these pages where the careful reader will usually find a little feature labeled PRO TRANSACTIONS. Though they are insignificant looking, printed in small type called agate, the items listed here are more vital than 90 percent of the headlines in the section. These little notes tell of the comings and goings of everyone in American professional team sports for the preceding day. They are, quite literally, the chronicle of men's professional lives. Take a minute to look back over the entries appearing in *The New York Times* on June 17, 1976:

PRO TRANSACTIONS

Baseball

CHICAGO (AL)—Sold Pete Varney, catcher, to Atlanta, and purchased John (Blue Moon) Odom from Richmond of International League for Iowa Oaks of American Association.

ST. LOUIS(NL)—Traded Reggie Smith, outfielder, to Los Angeles, for Joe Ferguson, catcher-outfielder, plus Bobby Detherage and Fred Tisdale of minor leagues.

TEXAS (AL)—Acquired Joe Lahoud, outfielder, from California for slightly more than waiver price.

Basketball

BUFFALO (NBA)—Acquired Tom Van Arsdale, forward, from Atlanta, in trade for Ken Charles, guard, and Dick Gibbs, forward-guard.

Football

NEW ORLEANS (NFL)—Traded Johnny Fuller, safety, to Tampa Bay, for Jim Kearney, safety.

Nothing more. The bare essentials, with no sketching in of further details. Just a listing of the names and the briefest of facts, printed in the smallest available type. Each listing, however, is a signpost indicating the progress of a career. The code—"traded" or "sold," "acquired for," and "sent to"—is easy enough to follow, and a handful of record books will translate each entry into a reflective fragment of a man's life.

The two men involved in the lone football transaction of the day were proven veterans, hoping that a change of teams would prolong their careers. Jim Kearney had spent nine of his eleven pro seasons with the Kansas City Chiefs, and with the Chiefs in 1972 had tied NFL records for most touchdowns on interceptions in a season with four, and in a game with two. But in 1976 he was considered expendable in the expansion draft, was selected by Tampa, and quickly traded to New Orleans. Johnny Fuller played for San Francisco and New Orleans in his eight seasons. The Saints traded him to Tampa Bay on June 16, and two months later he was traded to St. Louis.

The Tom Van Arsdale mentioned in the basketball trade was one of the Van Arsdale twins who starred at Indiana University during the mid-1960s. He had played for four different teams since beginning his NBA career with Detroit, and never did play with the Buffalo team which dealt for him on that June 16. He was traded on to Phoenix during the off-season, where he joined his brother Dick, for the first time on the same team since they were in college.

The Joe Lahoud purchased by Texas from California was a typical marginal ballplayer. An outfielder who came up through the Boston organization, he had played for three different teams during his six years in the major leagues before being sold to the Rangers. The California Angels had placed him on waivers the day before, and on Wednesday he was claimed by Texas, with whom he would perform adequately as a pinch hitter and part-time outfielder.

Careers, every one moving up or moving down, or just moving, not in any particular direction but on to some other place. Every agate line is another man's story. Read them quickly and you might think inanimate objects are being bought and sold, commodities dealt in some kind of barter. The trading of two pitchers for a shortstop; a place kicker for an interior lineman; a catcher and a dozen balls for one slightly used team bus. It all sounds alike, but it isn't. Men are fighting for their professional survival. It's all there. One name, one story. Look more closely now at one of the entries in that same published list of transactions:

CHICAGO (AL)—Sold Pete Varney, catcher, to Atlanta . . .

Richard F. (Pete) Varney is an oddity. An Ivy Leaguer in professional baseball. He graduated from Harvard, majoring in American history and psychology. The fact that he went to

Harvard, however, should not be misleading. Baseball was his main love, not academics. He was a bright and articulate kid who, since he happened to live in the Boston area, had a chance to attend Harvard. He took it, but the temptation to sign a baseball contract out of high school was strong.

When he did sign, it was with the Chicago White Sox, and he was assigned to their Double A Asheville team in 1971. In 1972 he played with Tucson and led the Pacific Coast League catchers in fielding, then led the Triple A catchers in 1973 and 1974 at Iowa. He spent the last part of the 1973 season with the White Sox, and also the last part of 1974. Then, in 1975, he played the entire season with Chicago, hitting a respectable .271 while playing behind Brian Downing, the first-string catcher.

He had progressed nicely through the ranks, improving at each stage, and in 1976, while not a starter, had every right to assume he was developing satisfactorily as an established major league catcher.

Then came the waning hours of June 15, two months into the 1976 season. For those not intimately involved with baseball, this may mean nothing, but it is one of those special dates which occurs regularly in sports—a trading deadline. There are different kinds, some affecting trades between teams in the same league and others affecting interleague trading, with all kinds of different conditions concerning how those trades may be made. June 15 is a big deadline in baseball, the kind that marginal ballplayers and even regulars who are not too secure sweat out each year. After the fifteenth at midnight, local time, players may not be traded unless "waived," or passed over by rival teams. Trading players is not impossible at other times later in the season, but it is not as easy.

One of the hundreds of players watching the clock that particular June 15 was Pete Varney.

"My wife and I had kidded each other that we hadn't gotten a phone call yet," he would recall later. "We were thinking about the deadline. You always do. As soon as the phone rang we both sorta looked at each other and gasped for air. We knew what it was."

At the time he was talking, Pete Varney was the catcher for the Richmond Braves of the International League. It was early on a warm July evening in the stadium at Lucas County's Recreation Center in Toledo, Ohio, about two hours before game time. He was sitting on a folding chair alongside the bullpen area, discussing the events which led to his wearing a minor league uniform there in a minor league city. That the uniform was Richmond's and the city was Toledo made little difference. What they were *not* was important. Neither was major league, and therein lay the source of Varney's hurt.

"It was about twelve-thirty at night," he said. "I picked up the phone and it was Roland Hemond [White Sox vice president]. He told me I'd been sold to Atlanta. At the same time he said I was optioned to Richmond, which was topping on the cake."

Varney stopped for a moment, shaking his head, and then went on. "My wife cried. She couldn't believe it. She had been through the minors with me, but we had made it. We were in the big leagues. We had an apartment in Chicago, and our friends there. Our son was just over two, and my wife was friendly with other mothers. Our life was in order. And then that phone call came."

He was a broad, powerfully built man, 6 feet 2 inches tall and 215 pounds, yet, sitting there, he resembled a little boy who had been scolded. He sat hunched over in the metal folding chair, his shoulders pulled tight around him and his large hands clasped. His eyes squinted and his brow was wrinkled as he worked laboriously over each word.

"It was traumatic," he said. "You think you're going to be with an organization for the rest of your life. I was very loyal to the people in Chicago, management as well as players, plus the fact that I had strong allegiance with the players who were there. I had grown up with them. I had seen them mature and I had matured with them as a ballplayer."

Pete Varney, on his demotion to the minors: "Being a baseball player is the utopian thing to do. But not here."

PHOTO COURTESY RICHMOND BRAVES

He squeezed his bear-like arms close to his sides. "I tried to be the kind of ballplayer they wanted to have around," he said. "I don't think I ever caused any problems or was a trouble maker. I tried to do what they asked of me. I worked extra. I tried to stay ready, even though I didn't play every day."

He pulled in a breath, slowly, taking as much time as he could. "When you're traded, your only reaction is that they don't want you anymore. The other side of that is someone else wants you, but at the time you feel only the rejection."

Even then, six weeks after it had happened, Varney said he had not recovered. Atlanta sent him directly to Richmond, where he played for a week at the end of June. He was recalled for two weeks with the Braves, but then sent back down to Richmond, where he would finish out the 1976 season.

"I'm disappointed in my mental approach," he said. "I can't seem to get out there and do the job. I feel like I'm physically ready to bust out, but mentally I'm still lagging behind and that really bothers me."

As he talked, the Richmond team was working out—pitchers throwing behind him in the bullpen, batters hitting, and fielders taking infield practice. But Varney seemed aware of none of that. His chair was in a closed room, without windows or doors. Nothing distracted him from analyzing his plight.

"It bothers me to be here," he said. "I had been in the big leagues and I had done the job asked of me, decently, and I thought I should be there. You come down here and you start questioning yourself. And I'm struggling. I don't know why. I'm just not with it yet, and when I don't do well I feel terrible."

Two players chasing a foul ball collided right in front of where he sat, but there was no interrupting Varney's conversation.

"I love baseball," he said. "It's what I always wanted to do. I remember being in Fenway Park in 1967 when the Red Sox won the pennant. I was thrilled. Being a baseball player is the utopian thing to do. But not here. Nobody wants to be here. The place to be is the big leagues, and everybody is shooting for that."

He paused for a moment, as if running his own words over in his mind, then, softening his tone, he forced a smile. "I don't want to give the impression that this is so gloomy. I'm still playing baseball. I still have the opportunity to be in the big leagues and I'm grateful for that. And damn it, if I'm good enough and a man, I will be there."

With that declaration he picked up his glove and walked to the far end of the bullpen to begin warming up one of the young Richmond pitchers.

Pete Varney's shock and humiliation were a product of his youth. Since he had put in his time in the minors and had moved up to the big leagues, he felt he was a major leaguer and would remain so. He felt his career had been launched, and that his only responsibility was to continue to improve, to work on his catching and hitting skills, and in return the Chicago organization would take care of him.

Varney's naïve feeling of security is common among young athletes. It comes from those years of school and the minors when the same athletes play together, year after year. Professional athletics is like that for only a small group of men. What true security there is belongs only to the stars, men who are good enough to become so identified with a team and a city that they live out their entire careers there. Al Kaline with the Tigers and Sandy Koufax with the Dodgers; Jim Brown with the Cleveland Browns and Dick Butkus with the Chicago Bears; Jerry West with the Lakers and Bill Russell with the Celtics. And even some of the greatest stars have been traded for one reason or another, personality conflicts with management and owners, or salary disputes. Wilt Chamberlain, the greatest scorer in the history of pro basketball, played for four teams during his career. Floating stars are even more common today, with athletes playing out their options and moving to whichever team will pay their price.

But stars initiate their own travel, which represents a tiny percentage of the transactions in sports. Most player movement occurs at a lower level, and is almost always involuntary. Average athletes, journeymen and marginal players—men whose usefulness to one organization has ended and who are being peddled for whatever they are worth, and young players, men who have not yet established themselves in their sport. Men like Pete Varney, considered not quite ready for the big leagues, being sent down. While there is a continual flow of athletes from team to team (an average week in the Pro Transaction column of *The New York Times* can list two hundred men from various sports), at those times of the season when squads must be pared down to meet league deadlines, the lists swell. Then the names of two hundred to three hundred men can appear in a single day. And most of those men are not being traded—they're being cut.

A baseball player's not making the squad is not so tragic. Being sent down to the minors may be a blow to his ego, but that is hardly fatal (painful, but not fatal). He has a place to go, and a channel through which to work his way back. But if his sport is basketball or football, the rejection is more serious. Some late cuts—high draft choices who have signed for a bonus but who just haven't worked out, or players who have shown exceptional promise but need further development—are helped to relocate with conveniently placed minor league teams.

But most of the players cut (usually close to half of those attending the opening day of camp) are shown nothing more than the open door.

What does an athlete do then? Twenty-one years old, and for the first time in his athletic life he's on his own. Before there was always a team ready and waiting for him, but no longer. Suddenly, after all the preparation, he is told he is not good enough to play in the big leagues. That's it. The climb up the ladder stops here.

In 1973 Jim Foote was one of hundreds of young football players cut from a National Football League camp during the exhibition season. A quarterback at Delaware Valley College in Pennsylvania, he had been the eighteenth and last man selected by the New York Jets in the draft. And though final-round picks have notoriously little staying power, Foote had high hopes. Unrealistic, but high.

"Football had been my dream since I was a little kid," said Foote. "I grew up with it all around me. My father played semi-pro ball for thirteen years, and coached our local team in Boiling Springs for nine years. My uncle coached college ball. Our whole town was football crazy. I was, too."

But Boiling Springs, a small town in the mountains of central Pennsylvania, is not exactly a magnet for big league college football interests. Out of his high school graduating class of 120 students, no athlete was courted by the grid factories at UCLA or Notre Dame, or even Penn State, the local power. So when Foote was offered a full scholarship to play at Delaware Valley, he grabbed it, figuring he'd make enough of a name for himself there to impress the pros.

And he did pretty well, throwing for 2,300 yards and 38 touchdowns, and, as a punter, averaging 40.2 yards a kick. Just about well enough to get noticed—and drafted on the last round. Still, he was optimistic.

"You come to camp with all the confidence in the world that you're gonna get a fair shot," he would recall later. "Just because you're a late pick doesn't mean that you're any worse a football player than anyone else. Look at Nottingham. Last man picked in the last round, and he's made it."

Don Nottingham, now a running back with the Miami Dolphins, is one of the patron saints of men on the outside of the NFL looking in. Nicknamed "the Bowling Ball" (he is 5 feet 9 inches tall and 210 pounds), he was the four hundred forty-first player drafted in 1971, chosen by Baltimore. In his seven seasons to date, with the Colts and then Miami, he has played in every game.

Jim Foote, however, proved not to be a very good disciple. "You feel in your mind you're going to get a fair chance and you feel that you can do the job," he said. "But once you get to camp it doesn't take long to find out there's no way they're gonna give you a chance."

The Jets camp to which he reported in 1971 already had three veteran quarterbacks. Joe Namath was one, and then there were Al Woodall and Bob Davis. They drafted Foote as a punter, but once he got there—"A kid from the mountains, there in an NFL camp with Joe Namath," he recalls—he wanted to play quarterback. They let him try for two weeks, then cut him.

He immediately tried to interest some of the Canadian teams in his services, but found no takers. A minor league team in New York State had been after him for months. Since that seemed to be the best offer he had—indeed, the only offer—he joined the Westchester Crusaders, serving as their quarterback for two games before the franchise ran out of money and folded. Then, out of options, he went back home to Boiling Springs.

"There was no other place to go," he said. "But going back was tough. I had told a lot of people I was going to play pro football—the only one ever from my town—and here I was, crawling back."

The one thing Foote was certain of when he went home was that he would not play for his father's team, the Cumberland Colts. He may not have made it in the big time—or even the not-so-big time—but he would not return to play for the local group of weekend athletes. He made that clear before he left.

"I will never come back and play for the Colts," he had said, and you can't get much more clear than that.

And had the Colts coach not been his father, it would never have happened. But the relationship between the two was very close. James Foote adored his son, the only boy after two daughters. And when his wife died, when Jim was just a child, football and his son became the focus of his life. He coached him from the time he was old enough to hold a football, hoping son would succeed where father had failed, to make the NFL. He taught him to be a quarterback because it was the premier position on the field, and how to punt because a man can always get a job if he can kick a football well.

So once Jim was back, settled in a new apartment with a decent job, and his father asked if he'd play, it became a family matter.

"He desperately needed a quarterback," said young Foote. "He didn't have any at all. So I said, oh, hell, I'll play."

His opening game before the hometown fans was a disaster. There had been a lot of publicity about his return home ("ex-pro football player" was the title that two weeks in the Jets camp earned him) and a big crowd turned out to see what he could do. He threw five interceptions as the Colts were routed. But by the second week he had his confidence back, and he went on to lead Cumberland to its first of eleven straight victories en route to the league championship.

"I was pretty happy about things," said Foote. "I liked being a hero, even if it wasn't in New York. I was the hometown hero, playing for beer money but leading the team to the championship. I enjoyed it. I might still be there, but not Suzie."

Suzie is Suzie Foote, Jim's college sweetheart and wife. And, to a great measure, the spur to his ambition.

"I was having a good time," said Foote, "but she couldn't stand it. She hates to be second. I thought that season was fantastic, but she was not happy. She wasn't happy for me; she wasn't happy for us. She wasn't happy, period. She could see me weighing 280 pounds, playing out my life as a football hero in a nowhere town."

During that winter he worked for a construction company ("a little selling, a little house painting—whatever"). Then one Sunday he and Suzie were watching the Superstars, a television program featuring stars from different sports in competition against one another.

"She just couldn't take it anymore," recalled Foote, "and we started talking about pro football again. Me, I wasn't too eager to try it again. As a semipro player I was fantastic, but to stick my nose back into a pro camp after what'd happened to me in New York, well . . . "

Suzie Foote, however, was feeling the full intoxication of an 11–1 season, and, watching the stars on television, she suggested that her husband write letters to some of the pro teams in the NFL, just to see what kind of response he got.

"Frankly, I was a little gun-shy," said Foote, "but not Suzie. She sat down and wrote a letter, then had it mimeographed, and sent out twenty-five copies—one to every team but the Jets."

Within ten days back came a special-delivery contract from the Houston Oilers. Before long, contracts came from St. Louis and New England.

"I was shocked," said Foote. "And I started to get excited. They were just free agent contracts—just to have me committed to them—but they wanted me to come to camp. They were really interested. Whatever enthusiasm I had lost was back."

He carefully examined all the rosters, and selected Houston, reporting to their camp in July 1974. It was two years later that I met him in Tampa.

Jim Foote leans against one of the heavy metal blocking sleds and waits for practice to start. He is one of four quarterbacks attending the first camp of the expansion Buccaneers. He is young looking, younger even than his twenty-five years. His face is tanned and his hair is brown and recently made curly, and he sits with his legs outstretched, shoulder pads in his lap and helmet on the ground beside him. As usual, he is the first player outside the air-conditioned building, which gives him time to talk about Houston.

"Maybe you remember," he begins. "That was the year of the strike. It was a camp of rookies and free agents, and I'd have to place myself fourth among the four quarterbacks there."

He pauses for a moment's reflection, then continues. "I can honestly say I went to camp thinking that I was gonna be able to make enough money to pay off some bills, and I'd be home again. After you get released once, you start to think that way."

Suzie Foote had strongly suggested that her husband stress his punting ability with the Oilers, and forget about the more heroic role of quarterback. (After all, she had written the letter, and that was what she had stressed.) But when Foote reached camp, a special four-day camp for free agents, and he received what he calls his first real instruction as a pro quarterback, he forgot the punting.

"They had this quarterback coach," he says, referring to King Hill, a veteran of twelve years in the NFL who was then working with Houston, "and he was fantastic. I knew he could help me play quarterback."

And, sure enough, he returned for the regular camp and by the time of the first exhibition game Jim Foote was the top-ranked quarterback in camp, and so he started against the Giants. The game was televised, and before the national audience that included his wife and father he threw for one touchdown and ran for another, leading the Oilers to a 16–8 win.

"Right away I became an instant hero in Houston," he recalls, smiling. "They had had two back-to-back 1–13 seasons and hadn't won a first preseason game in about eight years, so the people were fantastic as far as the rookies were concerned."

Jim Foote, while a Houston Oiler, conducting a quarterback class. "I became an instant hero in Houston . . . . Outside of Boiling Springs, I never had any of that."

The smile remains, but it is now buttressed by a smug glow. "There were stories in the paper with my picture. People began to recognize me on the street. Every day there was another pile of mail waiting in my locker. Outside of Boiling Springs, I never had any of that."

He methodically runs his hand over the painted surface of the block sled. "A funny thing happened that week. I began to feel like they couldn't stop me. I knew it was preseason, but I felt like that was it—I was there. I felt . . . bigger. You know, stronger. I talked to my father about his moving to Houston. I was that sure I was going to be there, playing for the Oilers."

The following game the Oilers traveled to Washington to play a team similar to themselves, rookies and free agents, and a few veterans defying the strike. Foote played the entire game, throwing three touchdown passes and leading Houston to a 48–3 romp.

"It was unreal," he says, the tone of his voice rising with excitement. "My wife came to the game; my father came to the game. Probably fifteen or twenty people from my hometown came to the game. It was the most exhilarating experience I'd ever had."

Then quietly, almost shyly, "There is nothing I like more than doing things like that for my father."

That following week the NFL players' strike was settled and the regulars returned to the Houston camp. While many coaches moved their veterans directly to the business of getting ready for the season, Houston's Sid Gillman promised to use only those players already in camp for that weekend's game with Dallas. He said, in fact, that he might use them all season. The Dallas coach, Tom Landry, took the more conventional choice and replaced the rookies with his returning veterans.

"It was one of the most awesome feelings in the world," Foote recalls, "being a rookie quarterback behind a rookie offensive line, looking across and seeing Bob Lilly and Lee Roy Jordan, Larry Cole, Cliff Harris."

By now the other Tampa Bay hopefuls are beginning to come out of the building, milling around in the morning sunshine, putting on their pads and shoes. But Foote is lost in the game two years before against the Cowboys. He clicks off the players on the Dallas line, one by one, end to end, as if it were a high school test of famous Americans. He talks about the feeling that the game would surely be a rout, and that people he knew were giving away 40 points. But at intermission the score was tied at zero.

"I went around talking with our guys at halftime and we figured they were just beat—they were tired!" says Foote. "It was 109 degrees on that field, and they were out of shape. Bob Lilly was sucking wind at the end of the half."

At the beginning of the second half the Oilers took the ball and marched 85 yards to score a touchdown. Back came Dallas, only to have a field goal attempt blocked.

"We were flying after that," says Foote, his eyes flashing. "On the next series we took the ball right down the field. I threw for a touchdown and we had a 13–0 lead."

But in the fourth period it all began to come apart. The Cowboys scored, cutting the lead to 13–6. Then, in the final minute, with victory seemingly assured, Houston got hit with a delay-of-game penalty on third down and, when they attempted to punt, the ball was snapped over the punter's head. Dallas recovered on the Oilers 28, scored, converted the extra point to tie the game, and quickly won in overtime, 19–13.

Sid Gillman's thoughts about playing his rookies all season lasted until the next exhibition game. It was against Atlanta in the Astrodome, and his veteran lineup started the game. But the welcome voiced by the 49,000 fans was for their rookies, who had performed so well in the previous three games. And by the middle of the second period the stadium rocked with the chant, "We want the rookies! We want the rookies!" It wasn't until the middle of the third period that Gillman sent Foote and a few of the other rookies into the game.

"The place went wild," says Foote. "It was fantastic. We didn't do all that much, and we ended up losing to Atlanta by 13–6 or something, but it was fantastic. It was also over."

Foote played three or four downs during the remaining exhibition schedule, and was never in a game once the regular season began. His father did move to Houston, to be near his son and watch him play, but Jim spent all fourteen weeks with a clipboard, charting plays. The following summer—1975—he was used sparingly in three exhibition games, and, four days before the season opened, he was cut. He and Suzie remained in Houston, Foote driving a beer truck for a living, and, after conversations with the Oilers and two other clubs, he arrived in Tampa, ready to try it all over again.

The area outside the door of the Buccaneers complex is crowded with football players, dressed and waiting to troop out to the field. Foote stands off to one side, holding his helmet in his hands and reflecting back on the experience at Houston.

"That's the way I always imagined it would be," he says. "That was my fantasy. It was super. It was magic. Forty-nine thousand people in the Astrodome—'We want Foote! We want Foote!' I dream about that."

Now it is almost time for practice to begin. Foote puts on his helmet and, before jogging across the field, turns.

"That's why I'm here," he says. "To make it happen again."

It did not happen in Tampa for Jim Foote. The Bucs staff had already decided by the opening of camp that their quarterback was going to be Steve Spurrier, a veteran backup player who had won the Heisman Trophy while playing at the University of Florida. They backed him up with a hard-throwing rookie named Parnell Dickinson.

It was a Tuesday afternoon, about a week and a half before the season opened, when Foote was released. He called Suzie to come pick him up early, not explaining why, then waited outside the Bucs offices for her to arrive in their little blue MG Midget. When she drove up he walked over, knelt down beside the car, and spoke to her. Suzie Foote put her head down on the steering wheel and didn't move for a long time.

"I know the realities of this game," said Foote from Houston, where he and Suzie returned to make their home and remain close to the Oilers. "But you've got to be there before anything can happen. And I still think I can make things happen. So here I am, waiting."

And midway through that season, with Oilers quarterback Dan Pastorini injured, Foote was signed on, given one more chance to, as he said, "make things happen."

The commitment and hunger of Jim Foote are echoed by thousands of athletes in professional sports who have not moved quickly and smoothly from being an amateur to stardom—or even acceptance—in their sport. Deep in the ego of every athlete beats the heart of a superstar.

In reality, he walks the thinnest of lines. That line represents the state of his security, and it is deceptive. Though he may be making $50,000 or even $75,000—a firm sign of stable success in any other business—a torn muscle, a fight with a coach, or a prolonged slump can make him expendable. "Expendable" can mean a trade, a trip to the minors, or being released.

The average athlete lives his entire career with the knowledge that he can be easily replaced. While the rosters for all-star games go virtually unchanged, season after season, marginal players are constantly in motion, their places being taken by men just a little faster or a little younger, or sometimes, a little better behaved. It is an endless shuffling of names and bodies. The farther down a player stands in his sport, the more threatened his position. Superstars may be clearly better than the average player and are therefore tough to replace. But once you get down into the pack, levels of talent are similar. The average starter on a mediocre team isn't that much better than his backup sitting on the bench. And the man on the bench isn't that much better than a hundred—even a thousand—men waiting in the bushes to take his place. The fringe player may dispute the evaluation of his ability, but he is not likely to deny the precariousness of his situation. He knows that he remains in his game only so long as he does his job adequately, remains healthy, keeps what is commonly called a "low profile," and is not challenged by a younger player carrying a smaller contract.

Through the mid-1970s the premier punter in the NFL was Ray Guy, first-round draft pick of the Oakland Raiders in 1973. Guy was able to kick the ball quickly, far, and high, the three necessary factors for successful punting. That talent earned him a secure place on the Oakland team, while he averaged 43.2 yards a kick.

About the same period there was another punter named Duane Carrell, who also kicked quickly, far, and high—though none of these quite as well as Ray Guy. His average kick traveled 39.6 yards, which is a little better than the league average. That difference—less than four yards a kick—spelled the difference in their careers.

The role of kickers is a unique one, for kicking is different from all other jobs in sports. Punters and place kickers—each team has one of each, and no more. Sometimes one man does both, but rarely. They are the ultimate specialists. A wide receiver will sometimes play on special teams (returning kicks) and a center in basketball will occasionally play forward. Center fielders play left field; shortstops play second and third. But kickers just kick, which makes their tenure in sports more precarious than most. They have no flexibility. They do their work, but if someone a little better comes along there is no place for them to go but to another team. Or home.

Duane Carrell was one of those. A kicker. He had been doing it since he was a little boy. He was born with a heart murmur, and was warned against strenuous involvement in sports. But shortly after he started school, an instructor came around to his Washington, D.C., elementary school and showed everybody how to kick a football, and Carrell found that he enjoyed it.

"I remember being out at recess, setting up the ball on a tee and trying to kick it over a fence," recalls Carrell, who was a short, pudgy child. "At home I'd go out in the street and try to punt over the telephone wires. It was always something I could go off and do by myself when there wasn't anybody around."

There was a lot of time when no one else was around. Carrell grew up without any brothers to play catch with, and lived so far from his school that there was little time spent hanging around the schoolyard. And while he wasn't forbidden most activities, his doctor had ruled out playing football as a precaution (an overprecaution, Carrell thinks).

"I was all involved in my studies through three years of high school," says Carrell, who stands only 5 feet 9 inches tall. "Then in my junior year my father died, and I felt I wanted to get involved in something. So the next year I got an okay from my doctor, went to the football coach, and asked if I could kick for the team."

Kicking was not a big part of the football program at Woodrow Wilson High School in 1966. There was no kicking coach, and not many kids were looking for the job of kicker. The team took what it could get, and that year it took Carrell.

"I was pretty bad," he admits. "But I guess I didn't know how bad, so I kept kicking. And I did like it. It didn't take long for it to get into my blood."

He kicked field goals and punted when he went to Florida State, and, after he graduated and was ignored in the draft, he contacted all twenty-six teams in the NFL at that time and asked if they might like to reconsider. The Washington Redskins invited him to a tryout camp, though they had an established punter in Mike Bragg. (That was the kind of kicking Carrell liked best, punting.) The Redskins promoted him first to their rookie camp and then to their veteran camp, where he lasted two weeks before being cut. The rest of the 1972 season he spent with the Hagerstown (Maryland) Bears of the Seaboard Football League, punting and kicking field goals for between \$25 and \$35 a game, and holding an office job in Washington. In 1973 he lasted three weeks with St. Louis, kicking field goals against Jim Bakken and punting against Donny Anderson, both established pros, and after being cut, returned to his office job and the Hagerstown Bears.

"Hagerstown was up in the mountains, about seventy miles from Washington," said Carrell, a dark, solidly built man with black hair and a full, black mustache. "I always enjoyed the drive. But we lost a lot, and the crowds were pitifully small, one and two hundred people. Still, I was having a good time."

Then in 1974 he and the World Football League discovered one another. He played with the Jacksonville Sharks for the fourteen games of their existence. When the team folded that fall, he returned to his pursuit of the NFL.

Carrell's timing was poor. The NFL season had already begun, and most of the teams were set. He had a five-day tryout with the Green Bay Packers in October, but they opted to stay with Randy Walker. He talked again with Washington, but they confirmed their satisfaction with Bragg.

"Toward the end of the month the Dallas Cowboys called and wanted me in for a tryout," said Carrell. "They'd become unhappy with Marv Bateman, and were looking for a replacement, so I flew down for a tryout."

He passed his tryout, Bateman was released, and Duane Carrell had a job in the NFL. Everybody seemed happy. He had such a good first game that the team voted him most valuable player and gave him the game ball. For forty punts during the season he averaged 39.8 yards, fourth best in the conference.

"I really thought I was set," he said. "I liked the city—I decided to make my home there. The organization was tops. I even met my wife in Dallas, and got married that next year."

Then draft day came, and on the eighth round the Cowboys selected Mitch Hoopes, a punter out of Arizona. During the following year's training camp Carrell was cut.

"It was a terrible shock," he said. "I loved it there. I was really looking forward to living and playing in Dallas."

He signed that season with Los Angeles, and had trouble from the beginning. He was unhappy with the organization, did not like kicking in the Coliseum, and his wife hated the city. And, most important to his game, he had begun hearing footsteps. The experience at Dallas had spooked him, and, to support his paranoia, each week in practice another punter was brought in for a tryout.

"I like football and I like punting," he said. "But the insecurity can drive you crazy. The tension is killing, always hav-

Duane Carrell, on his own insecurity: "You just can't live knowing the coach has a dozen guys and is waiting for you to make one mistake."

PHOTO COURTESY NEW YORK JETS

ing to prove yourself. You can never relax. You have to feel you belong someplace before you can really do a good job."

There was a nervous edge to his voice, as if he were expecting someone to tap him on the shoulder. He played out that uneasy season, and, determined to make things work with Los Angeles, spent all of his off-season in preparation—running and getting into shape. He came to camp that next July in his best condition since he was in college, but the Rams cut him anyhow.

"You do your best and you think you're doing the job, and the next week you come out and there's some other kicker working out," he said after he had signed on with the New York Jets for the 1976 season. "You just can't live knowing the coach has a dozen guys and is waiting for you to make one mistake."

There is an important element of truth to Duane Carrell's

words, and it is not limited to the world of sports. With the exception of those relatively few individuals who thrive in a crisis, everyone needs a sense of security to do his best. He has got to be given the opportunity to work into his job, to be given the confidence that one bad day will not signal his dismissal. Clearly, that luxury is denied the marginal athlete. The very nature of sports, with the pressure on winning, precludes it. An athlete must produce with consistency or he is vulnerable to being cut. In the case of the fringe player, knowing this only contributes to his inconsistency.

While the reasons why a player does not perform to his full potential may be one of the great mysteries in sports, the fact that he isn't performing well is no mystery at all. Anybody sitting in his living room with a morning paper has a pretty good idea who did what. A quick look at a box score from the previous night's baseball game may show "EVltn, rf," and the numbers "5, 2, 2, 5," which tells the fan that Ellis Valentine, the right fielder for Montreal, collected two hits in his five times at bat, while scoring two runs and driving in five. Though the codes are different, similar information is available from the published summaries for basketball and football. Certain conclusions are even possible. It does not take a genius to know that on the night that Pete Maravich scored 68 points for New Orleans in the NBA, the man guarding him, Walt Frazier of the Knicks, had a poor night defensively.

The less obvious aspects of an athlete's performance, available only to professional observers, are nonetheless recorded as assiduously as are statistics. Basketball teams keep shot charts, so that at the end of a game the coach knows not only how many points his players scored but from where they shot. Football games are filmed by each club. Two cameras record each play, one taking a broad view and the other focusing on just a few players at a time. The films are reviewed and each player is graded on his performance. How well an end runs a pass pattern and how well he blocks, how many tackles a defensive player makes and how many he misses—how well each player carries out his assignment on each play. It's all converted to a percentage, which is his grade for the game. A grade of 95 or 98 and a player's had a good game. A grade of 75 or 78 and, well, as a coach might say, improvement is indicated.

Such evidence is hard to refute, and even harder to ignore. Even if a player doesn't study his grading sheet, he knows where he stands. He knows by his salary and by how often he plays, by how often he gets traded and what his standing is on the team. If one day he's starting and the next day he's on the bench, he can assume someone isn't happy with his play.

Different athletes respond to that differently. Some who feel their talent being wasted openly rebel, complaining about the unfair treatment. When Lenny Randle, a twenty-eight-year-old second baseman with the Texas Rangers, was benched early in 1977 in favor of Bump Wills, rookie son of Maury Wills, he was furious. The ensuing "discussion" with Ranger manager Frank Lucchesi erupted into a fistfight, for which Randle was first fined, then suspended, charged with aggravated battery.

The other extreme is not nearly so sensational, but it is often more final. Few people notice when a demoted athlete sulks for a while, then quietly decides to leave the game.

Dave Gallagher was a star on the undefeated Michigan team of 1973, and a first-round draft pick of the Chicago Bears when he graduated. He signed a lucrative contract (most first-round picks do, even before they come to camp) and was happy, living in Chicago with his wife Carol and starting for the Bears. But at the end of his first season, a disastrous 4-and-10 one for Chicago, there was a major shakeup. The coach was fired, and many of the players with whom Gallagher had entered pro football were traded. It took until just before the opening of the 1975 season for the Bears to get around to him, and then they traded him to the New York Giants.

"It was crushing," said Gallagher, looking back. "I thought I'd found a home in Chicago. We had just moved into a new apartment in Skokie, and my wife had just been accepted at Northwestern to work on her master's. We had roots."

He never felt safe or happy in football after that. Though he started and played well for New York through the 1975 season, the weight of rejection and disillusionment hung with him. And when in 1976 he lost his starting job to a younger player, the newest top draft choice, Gallagher was inconsolable.

"There's no reason for them to bench me," he said the afternoon he lost his job. "This is a team having a lousy year and I'm being used as a scapegoat. I've played well and I know it. They never said a word to me, never told me I was being benched. I deserve more than that."

An average sized defensive lineman—6 feet 4 inches tall and 256 pounds—who relied on quickness to be effective, he spoke slowly and emphatically.

"I am bitter," he said later that season, still the Giants' second-string tackle, "very bitter. I've given up. I've lost weight; I'm going through the motions of playing. I've just been playing to get my paycheck, and I've always said that if it ever came to that I'd quit."

Gallagher, the son of a doctor, had considered medical school before, but through high school and college, football was his first love. And it was his first choice as a profession until that third season. Then, as the final game approached, he decided it was time to try medicine.

"I have my pride," he said, "and sitting on the bench for a 3-and-10 football team is not what I want to do."

But these are extreme reactions. The average fringe player adjusts to demotion and criticism, anything to go on playing. And that can be difficult. In a business where confidence is easily 50 percent of a man's game, how does a player who's been bounced around the league keep his ego healthy so that he can continue to perform? There is no simple answer, but those who succeed, those who survive, manage. Most create a little world of support within themselves. Call it selective reality—the art of taking the facts of the real world and magnifying selected items to get the most beneficial effect.

One of the best at this was Bob Miller, who, before a damaged shoulder drove him from pitching, was one of the two most traveled players in the history of baseball. (Dick Littlefield was the other.) In his seventeen-year major league career,

Bob Miller, one of the most traveled players in baseball history: "I wouldn't have wanted to stay in one place. That's boring."

PHOTO COURTESY TORONTO BLUE JAYS

Miller pitched for ten different clubs, two of them on two different occasions. In those years he was part of every conceivable kind of transaction: he was drafted in one expansion, traded five times, sold twice, and released three times. He epitomized the term "journeyman" pitcher.

In February 1977 Miller helped open the first camp of the expansion Toronto Blue Jays in Dunedin on Florida's west coast. He was their pitching coach, and in that first spring of the Blue Jays, with the lawn around the clubhouse still in unrooted sections of sod and their players not yet introduced to one another, he had time to talk about his career.

He had been a good, reliable workman, frequently winning more games than he lost, and often giving up less than three runs for nine innings of work, the generally accepted standard for good pitching. He had a couple of fine seasons, especially 1962, when he was 10–8 with a 2.89 earned run average with

Los Angeles, and 1971, when he gave up only 1.64 runs a game and was 8–5 while pitching for Chicago, San Diego,and Pittsburgh. Then there were other seasons, like the year with the Mets when he lost twelve in a row and was a winner only once. All in all, a pretty decent itinerant pitcher, winner of 69 games and loser of 81. But Bob Miller was unparalleled in his ability to adjust to the reality of his career.

"Living in one place may be easier for some," he said, sitting in the Blue Jays locker room, "but I like traveling. I can hardly walk into a ball park now and not say 'Hi, roomie' to somebody. I've played in all the ball parks and played for all the managers, and that's nice."

A tall, right-handed pitcher who had good control in his prime, Miller has put on several pounds since his best years. Now his face was round, and his stomach eased over the belt of his light blue uniform. He tugged at the tight-fitting double-knits, and admitted that getting relocated every time "was a pain," but he insisted it was well worth it.

"There are a lot of nice people in this game," he said, "and I've met most of them. I wouldn't have wanted to stay in one place. That's boring."

He talked about the different teams he played with, and had something nice to say about every one, adding that he was happy pitching wherever he was. But didn't he ever get traded because he wasn't doing a good job? He shook his head.

"It was always a matter of other considerations," he said. "You'll notice I was traded a lot to contending teams, clubs like the Cubs and Mets and Detroit, clubs fighting for a pennant. They needed an experienced relief pitcher. Sometimes it was a matter of my club losing and needing to change faces. And sometimes, even if you're very valuable to the club you're on, they can get something they need more."

It was all very neat. Bob Miller's view of baseball was predicated on his own experience during seventeen highly mobile seasons. That is a healthy attitude for a marginal ballplayer, since there is little he can do to control it.

Miller began in baseball as a starting pitcher, but soon

found his place as a reliever. If he didn't like that assignment—most pitchers consider it a demotion—he was not about to change it, so it was better to adjust. Miller wasn't always happy about being traded. He hated to leave Los Angeles. But complaining wouldn't have helped, so he didn't. That was a good decision. By accepting and adjusting to whatever situation confronted him, he managed to build a satisfying career, first as a player and now as a coach.

When Bob Miller finally did give up pitching, it wasn't being cut, traded, or released that did it. Those were all things he could cope with in his mind. But arm trouble, the curse of most pitchers effective enough to last more than a half-dozen years, was another matter. In Miller's case it was bone chips pressing on the nerves of his shoulder that finally forced him to quit.

"The pain never went away," he said. "It just got worse. And then in the last few years the shoulder would come out of the socket while I was on the mound. Finally, I just couldn't stand it anymore and I had to stop pitching."

Of all the things which conspire to limit an athlete's success, injury is the most dramatic. In a world of inches, subtleties, and delicate balance, injury severs a man's future like the surgeon's knife. The most promising of careers can end in an agonizing instant that sees nothing more spectacular than an arm or a knee bending the wrong way.

No one outside the game can understand the dominating presence of pain and injury in sports. It exists far beyond the view of millions of spectators. Fans are properly shocked by the visible explosion of pain: an outfielder, chasing a fly ball at top speed, crashes into a wall; a quarterback, rolling out of his protective pocket, is hit first by one linebacker who cuts him off at the knees, then by another flying in from the opposite direction. But after the fallen player is carried from the field and the game goes on, the fan's memory of the incident is short. He does not lie on the hospital bed the night before surgery and wonder if he'll ever play again—if he'll ever walk again. He does not go through the hours of surgery that may be necessary, or sweat out the weeks and months of exercise needed to return to playing shape. All that is out of vision, as if it did not exist. We see strong, young bodies on the field of play and we are impressed. This is the image we hold of a professional athlete. But walk through any major league locker room and the scene would shock the most sophisticated fan. Joe Namath, strapping on his knee braces before a game; Johnny Bench, his muscular body cut and scarred like a patchwork quilt; Curtis Perry, wired for the electric shock that numbs the pain of the damaged nerve in his back.

No one escapes. Pain is as much a part of sports as sweat and beer. To all athletes it presents a serious risk; to the marginal player it poses a special threat. A star who is injured will be tenderly watched and mothered. No one wants to chance ruining a fine and valuable athlete. But when a man fighting for a job is injured and does not respond satisfactorily to treatment, it is often "more practical" to replace him.

Wayne Mulligan was a football player who had, as the coaches like to say, learned to play with pain. A hefty, strong center who spent most of his seven professional seasons with the St. Louis Cardinals, he once played with a broken arm, and another time with a broken rib. When he came to the New York Jets for the 1974 season he started 26 out of 28 games, though he suffered two concussions, and played most of the 1975 season with an ankle so badly damaged that it required surgery that winter.

Then, early in 1976, in a preseason scrimmage against the Philadelphia Eagles, he sustained a serious injury to his left knee, and spent all of that season on the sidelines.

"It's like you're no longer part of what's going on out there," Mulligan said one morning, midway through the season. "You come every day, just like everybody else, but you attend none of the meetings and take part in none of the practices."

He was sitting on the bench outside the Jets training facility in Hempstead, Long Island, dressed in a pair of gray shorts and a T-shirt. Out before him, on the two practice fields, members

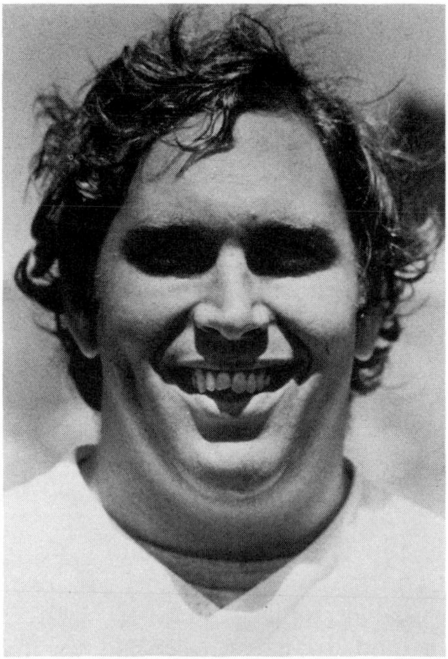

PHOTO COURTESY NEW YORK JETS

Wayne Mulligan, who spent the 1976 season as an injured New York Jet: "I'm sure people don't ignore you purposely, but they do it just the same."

of the forty-three-man squad were preparing for that Sunday's game.

"I'm sure people don't ignore you purposely," he said, "but they do it just the same. It's like they're afraid they're going to catch what you've got. They stay away. You have no contact with players or coaches. The only people who talk to you are the trainers, and even they are more interested in the guys getting ready for the next game."

Mulligan stopped for a moment and looked up at two players who were jogging along the perimeter of the field. They, too, were dressed in gray shorts and shirts. He gave them a half wave, adding, "And the other guys who are injured, they become your real teammates. You run together. You work out in the weight room together. You talk about football and cars, women and television, but not about your injuries. Nobody wants to talk about that."

An expression came over his face which appeared to be a smile, but which in fact was only a recognition of the irony.

"All you're thinking about is your damn knee and how bad you wish it was okay," he said, "about your job and the fact that you've lost it. And all you talk about is cars and television."

A strong, stocky man with light, thinning hair, he appeared to carry few effects of the injuries he had sustained. Then it became clear that he was taking gentle care with the injured left knee. As he talked, he stretched the leg out straight to ease the pressure.

"You want to go back and you know you're not ready," he said. "And all the while you're watching somebody else playing your position. You can't keep from wondering if you'll ever get the chance to win it back."

The longer he talked, the more uncomfortable he appeared. When he had to move his leg he used his hands for support. And, periodically, he would touch the inside of his left forearm, an eight-inch scar there marking where a metal plate had been inserted to reinforce the bone broken in two places. They fastened metal to bone with six screws, and Mulligan described the pain that he still felt as "deep and constant—often numbing."

"I've put out a lot for this team,"he said, "and I would like to think they remember, but they don't seem to. I guess I understand. You're only as good as your last game."

He started talking again about the feeling of being isolated and ignored, stopping to look out to the action on the practice field.

"Football's a special thing—like your own little group," he said. "It's like nothing else I can imagine being part of. It's a great feeling. And it's hell being isolated from all that."

The situation which confronted Wayne Mulligan, and hundreds of athletes like him each season, is a precarious one. Professional sports have rules prohibiting a team from releasing a player while he's injured, but nothing prevents that team from replacing him in the lineup, forgetting he exists, and then releasing him once he's well. That is a common pattern, and the marginal player's greatest fear when injured. A Joe Morgan or an O. J. Simpson is a player about whom everyone is concerned, who, when hurt, remains the center of attention. But men like Wayne Mulligan exist only so long as they are visible and out there playing. Out of the lineup for too long, they vanish. That was something Mulligan feared, and with reason. The Jets kept him only until the knee was declared sound, and then placed him on waivers, that great void where athletes go to be offered to other teams before they officially become unemployed.

That same dual set of standards—one set for the star and one for the survivor—permeates all of sports, affecting everything from a player's behavior to his play on the field. A star can miss an occasional practice or blast off about management in the press. The fringe player had better learn his place, be on time for all scheduled events, and wash behind the ears. And if last year's batting champion can't buy a hit the first month of the season, everyone is patient, knowing he is a proven performer and will return to form. If it's the second-string shortstop who's having trouble, he'd better shake the slump fast or start packing.

But this is all part of the same truth, the unyielding reality that the midstrata player has no security whatsoever. And every time he thinks of buying a house or putting his kids into school or joining a swimming club, somewhere in the back of his mind he must wonder how long it's going to last this time.

That question, however, rarely reaches the front of his mind. Whatever are the negative aspects of life on the fringe, for most players they are lost, overshadowed by what is positive.

For however long a man can stay in any of the major leagues, he knows he is going to travel comfortably, though often, and on the road the accommodations will be excellent. He will eat well, compliments of the team, and receive excellent medical attention. Being Duane Carrell or Bob Miller will earn a player none of the star's side benefits—no cover stories in national magazines, no lucrative television commercials, no long list of endorsements—but he can always pick up a little pocket money by making occasional appearances for the team's speakers' bureau. His salary is certainly generous enough, and as his time in the league increases, so do his pension benefits. And, so long as he stays in his game, he knows that he is likely to be recognized as a celebrity in his own neighborhood, as well as in a reasonable percentage of bars throughout America. He also knows that this earns him attention not only from hard-core fans, but from a number of women who collect evenings with athletes like some people collect baseball cards. "Groupies" exist for ball players the way they exist for anyone in the public eye, and some athletes (like some musicians and some politicians) are eager to exchange attention for attention.

But these are the externals. What holds a man's devotion to his sport is the sport itself, and his love for playing. Regardless of the trauma of training camp and the frustration of constantly being tested—and frequently being judged wanting—once he finds a place on a team and gets into a game, he's home.

Finding this home, however, can be an arduous task. Sometimes it requires difficult compromises on a personal level, adjustments in what a man wants for himself and his family. Often it means compromises for his ego, and that can be the most difficult adjustment of all.

But the real survivors manage. When it means settling for part-time play, they manage. When it means moving to a new city every season or two, they manage. And most are happy for the chance.

One of the all-time great survivors in professional sports is a man named John Stofa, who played football off and on for nearly ten years in a variety of different leagues, not only in the National and American Football Leagues, and in the World Football League, but even farther from the bright lights, in the North American League, and in the Southern Professional Football League.

And while no one can serve as the archetypical fringe player, there is a secret to Stofa's precious if limited success that is shared by every marginal athlete in professional sports: incredible tenacity, and a dogged refusal to accept that he is not good enough.

John Stofa heard a lot of people tell him that. If you were to look him up in any of the professional football record books, you would think that he materialized faintly onto the scene in 1966, was vaguely visible for a few years, and then quietly faded away in 1970. Not true. John Stofa, remember, was a marathon survivor.

He was a quarterback. Usually second string, but sometimes third. He had good size, 6 feet 3 inches tall and between 205 and 210 pounds, and he was a good, sturdy runner. In high school he had been a halfback. But what he liked to do most was throw the football, and when he entered the University of Buffalo in 1960 he was converted to quarterback. After three respectable years, he felt he was ready to burst into the pros.

Unfortunately, the pros failed to notice. Among the 280 players drafted out of college in 1964, the name of John Stofa was not mentioned.

"I knew it was a mistake," said Stofa recently, reminiscing about his erratic football career, "so I called a few teams and tried to work a deal."

He talked with San Diego and Buffalo in the AFL. Neither seemed interested enough to make him a firm offer, but he did manage to get some show of interest from the Chargers, and ended up playing that season for the Daytona Beach Thunderbirds, a team in the Southern Professional Football League with whom San Diego had a working relationship.

"They paid me $100 a game," said Stofa, "and I figured I'd try it for a year. It was riding buses to Birmingham and Tuscaloosa and Columbus for the season, then barnstorming against pickup teams after that, but I wanted to play football. Eventually, I figured someone had to notice me."

Stofa's method of attracting attention was to throw touchdown passes, 39 during that first season. It didn't get him into the big leagues, but it did earn him a $25-a-game raise for his second season with the Thunderbirds, and he responded by throwing 36 TD passes in 1965.

"Now they start coming around," said Stofa, remembering his lunge for the big time. "Pittsburgh's interested, and the Miami Dolphins are interested. Miami offers me a $1,000 bonus, and I tell 'em Pittsburgh's offered me $3,500. They believe me, and up the offer to $3,500 to sign and $13,500 if I make the team. Hell, that's more than I was making teaching school and coaching the basketball team back in Daytona."

So Stofa resigned his teaching and coaching positions and made the official announcement that he was going to Miami to play professional football for the Dolphins. There was a banquet, of course, fond farewells, a rousing "Give 'em hell, John" from his friends, and he was off. His wife Katie, expecting their second child, remained in Daytona Beach.

The Miami camp to which Stofa reported in July 1966 was in St. Petersburg, and it was Miami's first. The field was fresh sod laid over sand—which held up about as well as one might expect during a scrimmage—and the players stayed in a motel. Since the new organization had limited facilities, the players kept their dirty, sweaty gear in their rooms. They also ate at the motel, feasting on such training-table originals as chicken chow mein. But for Stofa the worst part was that there were four other quarterbacks in camp, all with no-cut contracts.

"I did well," he said modestly. "I was clearly the best-looking quarterback in camp. But I got cut."

His two-week-old AFL career threatened and no job at home, Stofa stayed around camp for four days as the Dolphins tried to find him another place to play. And while Pittsburgh and Oakland showed interest, such arrangements take time to work out.

Time, however, was not on Stofa's side. There was an airline strike, and with football rapidly moving through its training season, he was afraid of getting stuck in south Florida. So he hopped on a bus without knowing his final destination, figuring that he would stop at Daytona Beach, kiss his wife, and make a few phone calls. An hour of telephoning there brought him no offer of a bonus, no commitment, but Pittsburgh finally consented to a $3,000 advance on his salary—which was not decided upon—just in time for him to catch his plane to Atlanta and make the last connection north for three days.

"Things really started off great with the Steelers," he said. "I played well enough for Bill Austin [the Pittsburgh coach] to say he thought I could help them, and I got to be friends with the Rooneys [the club owners]. I was in."

But when the time came to make the final cuts for the season, he was out. Stofa was incredulous.

"It didn't seem possible," he said. "I was sure I was going to make it. We were training in Latrobe, and I'm from Johnstown, just outside. So I sent my brother down to Florida to pick up my car and drive it back."

His brother did just that, and when he returned to Pennsylvania with the loaded car, Stofa got right in and headed back down south.

"Now I'm more determined than ever," he said. "And my inspiration was Eddie Wilson, one of the quarterbacks at Miami. I saw him throw the ball and he was terrible. I said to myself if he can make it in this league for five years I can make it. *I can make it!*"

Before heading back to Daytona Beach, Stofa called his wife and told her of his renewed confidence, and she said she was with him.

"That was important," said Stofa, " 'cause if she'd said she was tired of all this stuff, I've got a real decision to make. But it wasn't that way."

On the road he stopped every couple of hundred miles to check with her, just to see if anyone had been trying to reach him. They had, but no one he was expecting. Richmond, from the Continental Football League, had called him, and Lakeland, in the North American League.

"I drove to Richmond but they really weren't offering very much," said Stofa, "and from there I telephoned Lakeland.

That coach offered me $750 a game. I told him I needed two pair of shoes, and he said fine. So I said goodbye to Richmond and drove to Lakeland."

So John Stofa moved from the Daytona Beach Thunderbirds to the Florida Brahmas, about three hours' drive across the state in Lakeland. Naturally, he planned on moving his family, too.

"My wife and I were driving to Lakeland," said Stofa, "when all of a sudden she starts crying. She doesn't want to move. She's expecting our second child and she doesn't want to leave our home and friends. I felt like a heel."

The solution was simple. The family kept its home in Daytona Beach, and Stofa drove back and forth three days a week to Lakeland.

As quarterback for the Florida Brahmas that season he put on what he calls "Stofa's aerial show," throwing the ball forty, fifty times a game. At the end of seven games he had thrown 28 touchdown passes, and to make sure someone was watching outside of Lakeland he had one of his teammates send newspaper clippings around the league.

It paid off. Toward the end of the AFL season, Miami, suffering quarterback injuries, brought in John Stofa.

The following period of a little less than two seasons with the Dolphins was Stofa's most satisfying in pro football. It was the only time when he felt part of an organization, part of a football family. There were even heroics. At the end of that same 1966 season he directed a last-second, come-from-behind upset of Houston with his fourth touchdown pass of the day.

"Things were really good," recalled Stofa. "The fans were with me, the players were with me. I may not have been the coach's number one choice for quarterback, but I always felt in competition for the job."

After some serious discussion with his wife, Stofa moved his family down to Miami prior to the beginning of the 1967 season. He was that confident.

"Of the quarterbacks in camp, I have to say I was definitely the front runner," he said. "And when Jon Brittenum [one of the other quarterback aspirants] was traded, I took that as a sign. We moved into his apartment. I knew it was going to be my year."

The euphoria was short-lived. Stofa started the first game of that season, against Denver in the Orange Bowl. But after taking the Dolphins down the field for an early touchdown, on the next series of plays he was tackled and broke his right ankle. He spent most of that season on the inactive list, and after the last game he was traded to Cincinnati.

"It was hard to believe," said Stofa. "I had a following in Miami—I even wrote a column in *The Miami News*—and then they traded me."

The trade, however, was not totally demoralizing. The Bengals had given up a first- and second-round draft choice, considered a high price, and Stofa took that as another sign.

"Katie and I decided to drop an anchor," he said. "Cincinnati obviously wanted me badly, and we decided that would be a good place to settle.

"You can't imagine what all that moving and uncertainty does to a family. Planning to be in one place for the season, taking an apartment, then ending up someplace else. Uprooting the kids, uprooting Katie. New apartments, new friends. Our mail always lost in some dead letter office. Cincinnati looked like a good place to make a home. A good place to play and a good place to live."

The only problem was that Paul Brown, principal owner and head coach of the Bengals, hadn't read the new script. And after a rocky 1968 season in which Cincinnati won only three of fourteen games, Stofa spent more time off the roster than on in 1969. It was not a happy situation, and the Bengals began talking trade. A deal with Detroit fell through, and Stofa finally returned to Miami to be the Dolphins' backup quarterback.

But things were changing in Miami. The coach, George Wilson, who liked Stofa, was replaced by Don Shula at the end of the 1969 season. And Bob Griese, the team's number one draft choice in 1967, was developing rapidly.

"Shula was a fair man," said Stofa. "I played some in 1970, and then he brought me into his office early the next season

John Stofa, doing KP at his restaurant in Cincinnati: "Now you know where old quarterbacks go."

PHOTO BY SKIP ROZIN

and told me Bob was going to be his man, and that it might be better for me to go someplace else. He said he'd talked to Lou Sabin at Denver, and that I might be able to start there."

It did not take Stofa long to pack a bag and board a plane for Denver. He was close to thirty years old, and he knew if he was ever going to get his traveling quarterback show rolling he'd better start.

"I should have known things were not going to work out," he said, recalling the flight to Denver. "While in the air my Dolphin watch stopped running."

The watch was prophetic. By the time Stofa reached Denver, Sabin had quit, and Jerry Smith, the new coach, had no thought of using him at quarterback. During the following exhibition season Stofa was released. He talked to Dallas and a few other NFL clubs, but he had decided he'd had enough. Finally, he had given up. He packed his bags, again, headed back to Cincinnati and began concentrating on the rest of his life.

It was there, in Cincinnati, that I found John Stofa. The summer he was cut by the Broncos he had opened up a little fast-food restaurant in one of the shopping centers on the periphery of the city, and the first time I saw him he was there, mopping the floor. As I walked in he waved, swooshing the damp mop in my direction. "Now you know where old quarterbacks go," he said, smiling.

Stofa sits now in one of the booths in his restaurant and talks. It is early afternoon, after the lunch rush has ended and before the early dinner crowd files in, and the place has only a few customers.

"Dallas just didn't sound very sincere," he is saying, talking about his decision to quit after Denver cut him in 1972. "All of a sudden it was winding down. I just didn't have it to pack up and go, and go through it all again."

The restaurant, called The Scoreboard, is one of those little places where you stand in line at the counter, reading the menu on the wall as you wait your turn to order. It is immaculately clean, with comfortable booths and pleasant music piped in through the ceiling.

"Don't get me wrong," says Stofa. "It was fantastic. Especially the times at Miami. After that Houston game I had a real following. I can still remember sitting on the bench in the Orange Bowl and hearing the crowd chanting, 'We want Stofa. We want Stofa.' I swear to goodness I started blushing right there on the sidelines."

His eyes widen as he talks about it. His voice rises to an excited pitch and he pounds his fist on the table. Reliving those times has him bouncing up and down like a teenager.

What must it have been like, that first season out of football?

"That was tough," he says, sitting back in his seat. "I didn't go to many Bengal games. I made excuses, but the truth was I missed it and I couldn't go there and just watch. Even when I wasn't actually playing, I was on the field and I was part of it."

Someone he knows walks in and he stops to say hello, then returns to talk to me. "I made a mistake. I wasn't ready to get it out of my system. I wasn't content to be through. I really missed it, and I knew I could still play."

What did it take to make him realize that?

"It took the World Football League," he says, grinning a broad, silly-looking grin that shows the space between his front teeth. "It took someone offering me another chance."

It was 1973, about a year after Stofa had retired and opened up The Scoreboard, when he received a call from Fran Monaco, a friend he had made while playing for the Dolphins. Monaco, a doctor and businessman in De Land, Florida, was in the process of putting together one of the WFL teams, the Jacksonville Sharks, and he wanted to know if Stofa was interested.

"I don't know if he wanted me to coach or play," says Stofa, "but I talked myself into a playing position."

Stofa's return to football was not the kind of event about which one would dream. The team was poorly coached and underfinanced. There were nine games for which the players were paid, another six games with promises, and it ended with the players ravaging the offices for anything that wasn't part of the foundation or the plumbing.

"It was just what I needed," says Stofa. "I wanted one more chance to play—a chance to start—and I got it. And this time I knew when it was over. Not only did I go, but the whole league went with me."

He sat for a while, talking about the nearly ten years of playing and sitting, of packing and moving, of being cut and going back to try again. He laughed about it and joked, and when the mood settled I asked if he ever felt the players selected over him (the men who remained on the team when he was cut or traded) were better quarterbacks.

"No," he said simply, but in a firm tone. "That would have been giving up on my own ability."

He started talking about the extenuating circumstances, some men being better players in practice than he and some carrying no-cut contracts. That was not exactly the way the question was intended, so I rephrased it and asked it again: In all those years of being cut, traded, and released, in all the seasons he spent on the bench, did he ever feel that someone was trying to tell him that he wasn't good enough to play professional football?

He looked straight ahead for just one second and got very serious.

"I don't know," he said. "I really never thought about it that way." And then he smiled, adding, "Maybe that means something."

It was the only possible response that a man in his position could make. And John Stofa's way of viewing himself and his abilities is the only way for an athlete to see himself: strong, gifted, and, if not unbeatable, surely tough to beat on any given day. And if he were to see himself any other way, he would have gotten out of sports at a much earlier age.

It is the same with almost every average athlete. Regardless of the records and his professional history, he sees himself and his abilities through his own eyes, and therefore perceives his potential more than what he has actually accomplished. He spends his entire career trying to convince himself that he's better than he is, that he can do better, that the success he has always seen for himself waits just around the next release.

5
THE MEN AT THE TOP

It is the second week of June, 1977, and the world is alive with major news events. James Earl Ray, convicted assassin of the Reverend Martin Luther King, has just been captured after his escape from a Tennessee prison. Fifty-three hostages are recovering after Dutch military forces stormed the school and train where they were held captive for nearly three weeks by South Moluccan terrorists. In Spain the first free election in forty-one years is being held. Thirty-five countries are meeting in Helsinki to discuss the rights of human beings. The federal government has told New York City to ban parking in midtown Manhattan.

But the big news in New York is none of these. In every newspaper, on every television and radio station, the number one story is the trading of Tom Seaver, star pitcher of the New York Mets, three-time Cy Young Award winner, and the darling of Gotham since the Mets upset Baltimore in the World Series in 1969.

For days rumors have filled the media. And as the June 15 deadline for trades has approached, the conjecture has in-

FINAL ★★★ **DAILY NEWS**

Sunny, low 80s.
Cloudy tonight, 60s.
Cloudy tomorrow.
Details p. 135

Vol. 58. No. 305 — New York, Thursday, June 16, 1977 — Price: 20 cents

METS TRADE SEAVER TO REDS

Kingman Also Being Swapped

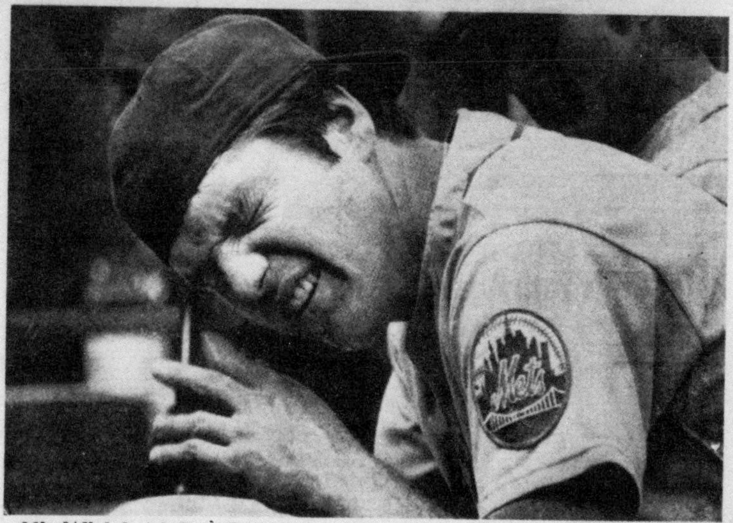

UPI photo

His Wish Is M. Don Granted. Tom Seaver seems to be in terrific anguish as trading deadline neared last night. He was with the Mets for the last time. Today, he's a member of the Cincinnati Reds with a good chance of another World Series trip. A deal for Dave Kingman was also brewing. —*Stories on page 3*

June 16, 1977: Stories of life and death and international morality were moved aside as one thirty-two-year-old pitcher changed uniforms.

creased, with Seaver reported to be heading first for Cincinnati, then for either Atlanta or Los Angeles.

Talk of the trade has grown out of Seaver's direct request to leave New York, not because of any disenchantment with the city or his teammates but because of his quarrel with M. Donald Grant's running of the team. Seaver has wanted the Mets to pursue more vigorously some of the high-priced talent available in the free-agent market—especially hitters to help the club's excellent pitching staff. Grant, chairman of the Mets' board of directors, has signed no one.

But all this is immaterial. The feelings between Seaver and Grant have deteriorated so far that as the trade deadline has approached it's become obvious that, whatever the issue, by Thursday morning—the sixteenth—Tom Seaver would no longer be a Met.

First reports that the trade was consummated came Wednesday night from the wire services: The Associated Press and United Press International. That was about nine o'clock, when the word began leaking out over television and radio. It came in bulletins, sometimes inserted between regularly scheduled programs, and, on some television stations, flashed on the bottom of the screen during the shows. The eleven o'clock news reported the progress of the story, accompanied by denials from the Reds and the Mets.

Not until just before midnight, when the Cincinnati game against Philadelphia had ended, was the news confirmed: Tom Seaver had indeed been traded to Cincinnati, for Pat Zachry, a pitcher, Doug Flynn, a utility infielder, and two minor leaguers, Steve Henderson and Dan Norman.

The response preceded the confirmation by hours. The switchboard at Shea Stadium came alive early in the day with calls of protest, and when it was too late in the evening for that the fans began calling radio and television stations to voice their outrage.

Now, as the city deals with Thursday morning, word of the trade is everywhere. The *Daily News* has a banner headline on page one: METS TRADE SEAVER TO REDS. The headline on the early *Post*—MESSED UP METS FACE FAN REVOLT—leads to interviews with fans throughout the city. Both papers have devoted their entire front pages to the story, pushing national and international news inside. *The New York Times* has kept its front-page play to a picture and story which dominate one of the lower quadrants, but it gives extensive coverage inside, and has an editorial against the trade.

All areas of the media have maintained full coverage, with teams of reporters going out into the streets and to Shea Stadium for fan reaction, into the Mets locker room for the comments of players, and to the Mets ticket manager for his thoughts on how the loss will affect attendance.

One television station, WNBC, days ago assigned its top sportscaster to follow the story as it developed. The result has been a detailed report on Seaver's last thirty-six hours as a Met. The reporter, Dick Schaap, began with a late dinner with Seaver Tuesday in Atlanta, picked up again at breakfast, spoke with Seaver after the game Wednesday night, then followed the story back to New York for the final, tearful press conference as Seaver cleaned out his locker at Shea Stadium.

But the interest in the story has not only been local. Just hours after Seaver returned from Atlanta early this morning he appeared on ABC's "A.M. America" show at eight-thirty, then stayed over for the local talk show which followed. And the coverage will continue. The trade will be reported in all the national news magazines, and it will be featured on the cover of *Sports Illustrated.* Within weeks *People* will run a Tom-and-Nancy Seaver cover, focusing on the couple's adjustment to the big move.

And so it goes, all through this week of the trade and the weeks that follow. The major impact may be in New York—NBC will switch its Saturday baseball game to bring the area Seaver's first Cincinnnati start—but the shock waves are being felt throughout the rest of the country. Stories of life and death, conspiracy and international morality lose America's attention while one thirty-two-year-old pitcher changes uniforms. Even in the world of sports, thirty other transactions on the same day have gone virtually unnoticed. And the only difference is that Tom Seaver is a superstar, the man who in New York they used to call "The Franchise."

The very fact that we have superstars in sports is consistent with our age of inflated superlatives. Ordinary has become inferior. Average is a pejorative. We are all part of an immensely successful sales campaign. Walk through the aisles of your own market (now referred to as a supermarket) and read the labels. No box of detergent is called "small," and few are "regular." They are "giant size" and "king size," "family size" and "jumbo size." And some are even "giant economy."

So it is with athletes. Where once there were athletes and a small cluster of stars, now there is an entire galaxy of stars, and the stars of the stars are called "superstars." Soon there will be so many superstars that a new level will be created for the stars of the superstars.

But athletes are not like boxes of detergent. No bureau of fair packaging exists in sports to require their true size and worth to be printed on the outside. And while we have endless categories of statistics and criteria with which to judge, value can be easily confused. Not just by fans, but by professional observers. When the courts began voiding the reserve clause, many players became free agents and auctioned their talents. And many club owners, eager to buy a winner, paid long-term contracts into the millions of dollars for supposed supertalent.

Disappointing as it has been to the spenders of the big money, none of the athletes bought in the first four years of open bidding fell into the category of bona fide superstars. The closest was Jim Hunter, freed from the Oakland A's by a breach of contract and purchased by the New York Yankees for a multiyear, multimillion-dollar agreement. But most of those freed athletes, like Wayne Garland and John Riggins, Gene Tenace, and the rest, were cashing in on one or two pretty good years and an adroit agent.

Which brings up the most natural next question: What are superstars? The most obvious, direct response is that they are the best athletes in sports. But the matter is not that simple.

The base line for "very good" and "great" athletes is the same. Anyone approaching the superstar class must be able to perform with excellence, and to have done it over a long enough period of time to prove his consistency. It is the old story of the skeptical baseball scout sitting in the stands and watching the local phenom. "Fine," he says after one spectacular play, "but let me see it again." Virtually anyone good enough to be a professional athlete is capable of a great play once in a while. The best do it with regularity.

But in the world of sports today there are many athletes who perform exceptionally day after day. Bob Lanier and Elvin Hayes in basketball; Carlton Fisk and Ted Simmons in baseball; Terry Bradshaw and Otis Armstrong in football—just to name a few. They are all fine athletes. They are all stars, commanding six-figure contracts. But by contemporary standards none is a superstar.

The additional element necessary to make a gifted athlete a superstar is charisma. In sports that can be defined as the ability to win while attracting as much attention as possible, which is most easily accomplished by winning championships. That is why so many clear-cut superstars are in nonteam sports. Jack Nicklaus and Arnold Palmer, Billie Jean King, Muhammad Ali—all are consensus superstars. They are the most visible personalities in sports. They are the endorsers, the people selling products on television. And all transcend their particular sport, so that people unfamiliar with their talent know who they are and what they do. Even as they grow older and their skills diminish, their flair for drama keeps them in the public's attention while younger and often more talented performers are ignored.

The picture in team sports is more fuzzy, but the same rule

exists—superrecognition comes from winning with flair. That is why men like Kareem Abdul-Jabbar and Joe Namath have been two of the major superstars of the last decade. Jabbar has been the single most dominant player in basketball in the 1970s. Namath, a fine quarterback and a flashy and marketable personality, is credited with engineering the Super Bowl upset which established the credibility of the American Football League.

Of these two key factors, charisma often seems the more necessary for superstardom. Consistent winners such as Bob Dandridge, Joe Greene and Mark Belanger, either because of the cities in which they play or their particular assignments in sports—non-scoring players in general, and specifically all football linemen, are considered support players—don't receive a fraction of the attention of a Namath, who, though a good quarterback, was not a "winner" after 1972, yet continued to get excessive press coverage right up until his retirement in 1977. And, at the same time, some players with hardly better than average abilities are able to catapult themselves into star status by their very manner. A prime example is Reggie Jackson, a mediocre outfielder who hits with power, who, in today's market, became a $2.9 million ballplayer when he signed with the New York Yankees for the 1977 season.

Charisma, exposure, and talent—they are the qualities which make a superstar. Only occasionally is pure ability enough, and then only if the athlete is good enough for long enough. Henry Aaron was the greatest home run hitter of modern times. A quiet man who hadn't played on a winner since his Milwaukee Braves were in the World Series in 1957 and 1958, it took his pursuing and breaking Babe Ruth's home run record to bring him stardom. And for Rod Carew, the most consistent hitter since Ted Williams but playing for Minnesota, it took the publicity surrounding his quest for a .400 season to gain him national recognition.

All this is not an attempt to minimize the importance of superstars, only to place them in perspective. They are, to a great extent, created by the media. Good, flamboyant athletes in cities with extensive press coverage are better known nationally than exceptional but quiet athletes in out-of-the-way places. Sometimes it all works out right. Men such as Tom Seaver, Muhammad Ali, and O. J. Simpson are bona fide superstars, and they are—or have been—the best in their sports. But too often the fog of publicity—either too much or too little—hides the true worth of an athlete.

Identifying the best athlete of today is much easier than explaining the claims of superstardom. Tom Seaver and Jim Palmer are and have been the finest pitchers in their respective leagues throughout this decade. Joe Morgan has been the most complete ballplayer in either league. Taking nothing away from Jabbar, Julius Erving is the most spectacular basketball player in the game today. And football, well, football is so heavily specialized that superlatives are difficult. Simpson has certainly been the best running back of the decade. But is he a better running back than Fran Tarkenton is a quarterback, or than Cliff Harris is a safety?

The difference between these athletes and the rest of the players in their sports is as simple as it is complex. The simple part is that they perform better. Through a combination of intense desire and physical ability (which, in addition to things like strength and speed, includes excellent eyesight and reflexes, the ability to heal quickly and endure pain) they play better than others around them, and they do it with consistency, game after game, season after season. It is a self-perpetuating condition, of which the organization of sports is a vital part. Not only are stars given more of a chance than fringe players to weather difficult times such as slumps and injuries, their continued success is helped on a daily basis in competition. Officials are more likely to support stars in tight situations: a Cliff Branch or a Drew Pearson will get the benefit of those questionable in-bounds reception calls, and, when a pitch sails by a Johnny Bench behind the plate, it's more likely to be called a wild pitch than a passed ball. The other differences are more subtle, and are reflected neither in the size of a player's house nor in the price of the car he drives. (So many athletes make so much money today that a Dun and Bradstreet rating tells very little). The true subtleties lie in attitude, commitment, and ego, involving the star's ability to have them interact with his physical talents in such a way as to compel him to play better and better. But it takes more than a glance at a score sheet to uncover this rare relationship.

Baseball is a sport dominated by power pitchers and power hitters. Home runs and strikeouts are the feats which earn the biggest headlines. Tom Seaver and Nolan Ryan, Mike Schmidt and Henry Aaron—they have been among the big names in baseball in recent years. Yet, despite this, the premier performer throughout the same period is a diminutive second baseman who has so effectively developed all of his baseball skills that he is considered the most complete ballplayer in the game.

The man is Joe Leonard Morgan, second baseman for the Cincinnati Reds, and he has earned respect because of one single, indisputable fact: He can do more things to win a ball game than any other player. No one else comes close.

The key to winning in baseball is to score more runs than your opponent. While a man's batting average is considered by many to be the mark of his offensive efficiency, scoring runs or causing them to be scored is closer to the vital point. Every once in a while some student of baseball devises a formula whereby a hitter's effectiveness is evaluated with that in mind. In 1977 Jerry Holtzman, sports columnist for the *Chicago Sun-Times,* devised one system, and in 1976 *Sports Illustrated* used its own. Using both formulas Morgan came out best, showing better than Mike Schmidt, one of the game's most prodigious home run hitters, and Rod Carew, the perennial batting champion.

But Morgan's value to his team does not stop with his offensive capabilities. Defensively, he is the best second baseman in uniform, winner of Golden Gloves at that position from 1973 through 1977, and honored on one all-star team or another in eight different seasons. In 1978 he set a major league record by playing in ninety-one consecutive games at second without making an error.

The man behind all of these professional accolades is a highly complicated individual, fiercely proud and competitive, yet sensitive and very private. He is the kind of man who focuses all of his energies on the perfection of his talent, yet has, when tested, placed personal friendship ahead of his career. He will stress the importance of keeping "outside things" from affecting him, yet work himself into a fury over what he considers the unwarranted attack of a journalist.

In the spring of 1976 Joe Morgan was enjoying the height of his career. That was the spring of the labor dispute between professional baseball and the players' union. The clubs had locked their training camps to their veteran players, and the Reds were working out at a Little League field in Tampa, not far from their own camp at Al Lopez Field.

This was a confused time for baseball. The opening of camps was delayed for three weeks. Players, unsure of what to do, trickled into a dozen makeshift camps around Florida and Arizona. Morgan arrived in Tampa a few days after the bulk of the Cincinnati squad; he showed up one morning wearing a pair of gray baseball pants, a black windbreaker over a T-shirt, and a small-brimmed hat pulled down over his face. He brought with him the tools of his trade—a bat and a fielder's glove.

It wasn't much of a practice. The players ran a lap or two, went through some calisthenics, and briefly took fielding and hitting practice. After the session ended, about noon, Morgan and the rest of the Reds walked leisurely from the field, signing autographs and talking with fans. Watching Morgan, no taller than many of his teenage admirers, you could sense his confidence and good will. He had just won the first of his two Most Valuable Player awards, and he walked in a glow of recognition long deserved. He smiled as he signed one baseball after another, posed for a picture, and chatted with a grinning boy as he autographed the front of his jersey.

But by the middle of that summer some of the attention had turned to abuse. There were articles published which disturbed him, and on one particular day in July he walked into the Cincinnati locker room before a game with a magazine rolled tightly in his fist. The magazine was *Black Sports,* and Morgan was on the cover. The article, he felt, portrayed him as a racist, and he was furious, feeling that he had been wronged. Earlier in his career, while at Houston, he had weathered one serious controversy, but that was a different matter. Friction had developed between Harry Walker, the Astros manager, and Jimmy Wynn, Morgan's friend and roommate. Morgan took Wynn's side, incurring the disfavor of his manager. But that dispute was not a problem for Morgan; he had made a clear choice, one with which he was comfortable. It was all very simple.

"If I had to do it all over again I'd do it the same way," said Morgan, recalling the difficulty at Houston. "Jimmy Wynn is a close friend. Important as baseball is, it's just a stopping point. Jimmy Wynn's going to be my friend long after there's no more baseball."

The situation with the magazine article was anything but simple. A reporter who Morgan said never interviewed him had written a piece which, while generally favorable, did contain quotations attributed to Morgan which he felt reflected a racist attitude.

"I've always believed that people with racial prejudices weren't worth a shit," he said, "and when I read that I'm that way it burns me."

He was walking back and forth in the Cincinnati locker room, waving the magazine. His compact, muscular body jerked with every point that he pressed, as if to give his argument emphasis. And his mouth and eyes, key organs of expression for Morgan, were in constant and abrupt movement as he darted from point to point, asking questions and then answering them in a rapid, run-on monologue:

"Why do they always want to twist things around to make you look like a smart aleck? Because I'm somebody now," he said. "That's not right. I never said the things that had quotes around them. Now people are going to read that and say, 'Well God damn,' and they never get to know me. That bothers me."

There was as much hurt in his voice as there was anger, the hurt of a man who did not understand how someone could take things he did not say and print them in a magazine to present a picture that he felt was not fair or true. He wanted some recourse, some way to make it all go away, or at least to make the perpetrator pay, but his lawyer had told him there was little if any chance of that.

As he paced and talked he was removing his gray suit and beginning to change into his red-and-white baseball uniform. But the effect was more than a change of clothing. The agitation caused by the article was being pushed from his system, and by the time he picked up his glove and headed for the field, though the controversy had not vanished, all evidence of Morgan's involvement with it was gone. It was time for baseball, and nothing could interfere. Morgan hit two singles and a double that night, and dove through the air to stop a line drive headed through the infield, turning it into a double play.

"You can't let outside things upset you," he said. "I never let anything or anyone affect what I do on the field."

This attitude is a guideline for outstanding athletes in all sports. Not only is it necessary for them to have the capabilities to perform well, they must be able to use those capabilities regardless of what is going on in their personal lives. And it is an attitude particularly consistent with the way Morgan plays baseball—with complete concentration and complete dedication. Whether standing at home plate and peering up at the pitcher, moving off first base while measuring his lead, or waiting at his position near second base for the ball to be hit, he is able to concentrate totally on the game.

His involvement with baseball began when he was six years old, playing a game he calls "Army ball" in the schoolyard near his home in Oakland, California. Joe and two of his friends—that was the team. One pitched and one hit and one played the outfield, the rest of the positions played by the schoolhouse wall against which the batter hit the ball.

"We played against the portable wall," said Morgan, describing a portable as a kind of one-room temporary school building. "A hit off one part of the wall was a double, and over the roof was a home run. We'd play all day, from morning until it got dark."

Though playing was always a dream of his when he was young, he never thought to pursue it. He was small as a child and only 5 feet 5 inches tall and 140 pounds when he graduated from high school, considered too small to withstand the rigorous six-month pro season. But the dream persisted, and while he was attending Oakland City College he signed with the Houston Astros when he was nearly twenty.

"Houston, the Mets, and the Yankees contacted me," said Morgan, "but I liked the way the Houston scout talked. He never once mentioned how small I was. He said I was a good player. Those others said I was a good little player. I never thought of my size as a hindrance and I didn't see why they should."

It may appear that Morgan's excellence as a player emerged fully developed when he was traded to the Reds in 1972, but it was the product of years of work which have resulted in steady improvement. He was a major prospect when he entered the league in 1965, was voted Rookie of the Year by *The Sporting News*, and had seven fine if not stellar seasons in Houston. But the trouble with Harry Walker cast his tenure there in shadow and, too, he was playing for a losing ball club.

"I worked hard in Houston, especially my last few years," said Morgan, "improving myself as a hitter, a fielder, and a base runner. I did a lot of things there I do now in Cincinnati, things that didn't get noticed. I'd walk, steal a base, but if no one drove me home it was all for nothing."

Morgan is quick to recognize the importance of being on the right club, of fitting in and having one's talents fit in. He says the things he does were built for the Reds. That, coupled with the natural maturing process and the skills on which he constantly works, has brought him to the top of his sport at the age of thirty-four.

PHOTO BY SKIP ROZIN

Joe Morgan, enjoying the spring between championship seasons: "I don't fantasize anymore about baseball. It's all in front of me now. . . ."

"I have a large ego," he admits, "and that is part of the reason I have accomplished what I have on the baseball field. I think people who don't have large egos don't push themselves enough. I don't see any limits to my game. If I hit .320, I want to hit .325. If I hit 25 home runs, I want to hit 27. People always think I've reached my peak, but they'll see I haven't. Next year will be better."

And when injury threatens to take Morgan out of the lineup, that same dedication keeps him in. At 5 feet 5 inches tall, weighing between 150 and 155 pounds, his enthusiasm and inspired play take a heavy toll. Bruised ribs and spiked arms and legs, pulled muscles and sprained muscles, often bring him to the trainer's room four hours before game time, yet injuries keep him out of the lineup very little.

"You have to play hurt," he says. "I believe you owe something to your teammates and to the people who are paying your salary. If you're going to play only when you're well you're going to miss a heck of a lot of games."

It all fits into the same pattern. Morgan will do anything he can to win a ball game. Hit a single or a home run, steal a base, or knock down a shot through the infield. And if he's hurt and can only give 70 percent, as he says, if his 70 percent is better than 100 percent of the man who'd replace him, he'll play.

"It's simple," he says. "I play the game and I try to get the most out of my ability. I'm not going to let anyone shortchange me. When I quit I don't want to look back and have to say I wish I'd hustled more here or worked harder there. It's too late, then."

This attitude is classic among the greats in any sport—that relentless striving for perfection. They may be pleased with what they've done, but they are never satisfied. They know they are good, they demonstrate it over and over, but instead of growing fat from their success they only hunger for more. It is an emotional quirk, one which separates the good from the great in any area. (The marginal athlete has many of the same feelings about himself and his talent as does the star, but, with no empirical evidence on which to hang them.) Men like Joe Morgan turn success into more success, and their ego and need for perfection only make them want more. They live the dreams of the men on the fringe, and of many of the rest of us.

"I don't fantasize anymore about baseball," says Morgan, who signed a three-year, $1.5 million contract in 1977. "It's all in front of me now, and that's a happy feeling. I'm happy to be able to look back and say that when I was six years old I never thought I'd be as good as I am."

"When I was younger I felt there were all kinds of limits," he said, after pausing for a moment. "Limits to what I could get out of baseball, limits to what I could do in the game. I don't feel that anymore.

"When you're in an all-star game or a World Series, and they introduce you and the people stand and cheer, you feel it all through your body. You never dream about that when you're a kid. Those are somebody else's dreams. Now it's happening to you, and you just want it to go on and on. Well, I think I can make that happen."

After another pause, he says, "I guess that's what being at the top of your game means, feeling you can get anything you set your mind to. I feel that way."

The fame and accompanying fortune that now belong to Joe Morgan came to him relatively late in his career, after seven losing seasons with Houston and the years of building toward a championship at Cincinnati. More often the big names in sports enter their game at the top and remain there. O. J. Simpson was the most famous college football player in the country in 1968, winner of the Heisman Trophy and first pick of the Buffalo Bills, with whom he became the most celebrated running back in pro football. Lew Alcindor was the most sought-after high school basketball player in America before he went to UCLA. There he became the top college player, leading the Bruins to three national championships, and later, as Kareem Abdul-Jabbar, he became a superstar in the NBA.

It is frequently that way with established stars. They seem to burst fully formed from somebody's Jack Armstrong kit. And even when something comes along to interrupt that perfect scenario, rarely does our hero lose control of his career.

Larry Csonka was an all-American fullback at Syracuse University in 1967, broke all of the school's rushing records, and started and was named most valuable player in both the College All-American and College All-Star games. He was the first offensive back drafted in 1968, the first choice of the Miami Dolphins. During the glory years of the Dolphins—three conference championships and two Super Bowl victories in three years—Csonka was the brightest star in their lineup, rushing for over 1,000 yards each of those seasons.

So when Csonka decided to leave the Dolphins after the 1974 season and join Memphis of the WFL, it was big news. It was the kind of coup that could have made the new league competitive with the NFL if it hung on long enough. But it couldn't. And when it folded, following the 1975 season, it was Csonka's reentry into the NFL that made the headlines, nearly as big as when he left the Dolphins.

Unlike O. J. Simpson or Chuck Foreman or some of the other running backs in the league, Csonka does not dazzle you with his footwork. He doesn't run back kicks, he doesn't catch many passes, and in nine pro seasons he has never thrown a pass.

But he does run well with the football tucked under his arm, and rarely are he and the ball separated by force. He runs best in a straight line, and is at his peak running straight ahead—not around the line of scrimmage but through it. He does that very well, running over and through everyone in his way.

This may sound like a very specialized talent, but football is a game of specialties. And since there is a need for someone to do what Csonka does, and because he does it so well, Larry Csonka is a star.

It all seems very neat and easy. Except, of course, that it's harder than it looks. And while Csonka doesn't think that running with a football is brain surgery, it bothers him to hear people dismiss it too lightly.

"A lot of people come up to me and start talking," said Csonka one afternoon before the Giants' camp opened in 1977. "Sooner or later they get around to saying how good they could have been—except for a little piece of bad luck here and there."

Csonka suffered a severe knee injury toward the end of the 1976 season, and had come to the preseason camp at Pleasantville early to continue working into shape. He had just finished lunch at a team hangout in town, and sipped on a Coke as he talked. Periodically, he would stop to shake hands with the people who stopped by the table to say hello.

"That irritates me," he was saying. "I'm not denying there's luck involved. But it's not just sprinkling magic dust here and there and, poof, you're a football player. It takes work. Any profession where you're highly paid takes a long apprenticeship and a lot of development. I've paid my dues; I'm still paying them."

That's straight talk from a man who, at first glance, doesn't look as if verbal communication is one of his strengths. While not as huge as some football players, his appearance is one of pure force in human form—his 237 pounds packed tightly into a 6-foot-3-inch frame, his shoulders thick and strong, his arms and legs rippled with muscles, and his nose so often broken that it flows over his face like the Ohio River at flood stage.

If it doesn't sound as if Csonka is the celebrity type, he isn't, no Joe Namath or Walt Frazier or Tom Seaver, the other stars competing for sports headlines when Csonka reached New York. If they are the city, he is the country. He never finished work toward his degree at Syracuse, and had it not been for football he probably would have gone to work in the same rubber plant in Akron as his father. That shop's still in operation, and many of his friends work there.

But there was football, first at Syracuse, then the Dolphins, the Southmen of the WFL, and finally the Giants, all providing Csonka with a kind of dream life of doing the one thing he enjoys most—playing football.

"I like football and I like the life style," says Csonka. "I like the people I play with and the fun we have. I like throwing a party after a game, I like having my friends around me, and I like getting drunk once in a while. I like being a football player. I like the money I make and I like playing. I like the whole shooting match."

He candidly discusses the series of stages through which his career has progressed, and his changing attitude along the way.

"Football in college was fun," he says, "but those first years at Miami I didn't much care if I played or not. Then I got used to the life style—the money more than anything else—and before long I was playing because I was spending more than I was making. Then I had to play, and that worried me. I felt the pressure every day. I planned out how long I would play—five years, ten years—to maintain my life style. I was buying my life with football."

But then something happened. His career took one more step, and suddenly he was making even more money than before, more than he'd ever dreamed. Suddenly there was no more pressure. Suddenly he was in control.

"For the first time as a pro I felt secure," said Csonka, talking about his latter years with Miami. "I was making a lot of money, more than I needed, and I knew they were paying me because they felt I was worth it. I wasn't worried about losing my job and I wasn't worried about spending myself into a hole. I could concentrate not only on playing football, but on enjoying it. On having fun."

Among the things which football has helped him purchase are a four-hundred-acre farm in central Ohio, and a bar and restaurant converted from a one-hundred-fifty-year-old stagecoach stop. He put his brother to work running the farm, his brother-in-law running the restaurant, called the Pine Tree Inn, and he estimates that he makes as much from them and the rest of his investments as from his salary in football.

"Now I'm back to enjoying football more than I did five or six years ago," said Csonka. "I don't play now because I have to but because I like to."

Csonka is not an athlete who sits and intellectualizes about the game. His attitude toward football is similar to his style of play—hard and direct. He looks back at the years at Miami as good years, and talks about the humor and the frustration so common in sports, dwelling little on the thrill and agony of any single victory or loss. He characterizes the decision to leave the Dolphins and join the WFL as largely a financial one, a chance for financial security in an extremely insecure business.

His arrival in New York was accompanied by great fanfare. As a major star in the NFL and the biggest name first to jump to the WFL and then return, his coming to the Giants was big news. New York made him welcome, even arranging to give him his old Number 39, at the time worn by defensive back Clyde Powers. And there were the conventional trappings that go with being a star: hundreds of kids screaming his name at the training camp; the free Cadillac supplied as part of an advertisement; and the interviews for television, newspapers, and magazines.

Most of what greeted him pleased Csonka, but he was uncomfortable with some of the responsibility.

"I feel I owe the Giants more than good play," he said, "but being a leader is tough for me. I'm just not a captain-type person. I don't know what to say to somebody who isn't doing his job. What I want is to do my job well, and let him learn by my example, but that isn't always enough. About the time I tell somebody else how to do something is when I screw up."

But as Csonka and the Giants progressed through that 1976 football season, it was not the emotional pressures of being a leader or even the myriad requests for personal appearances that proved to be his cross. It was the game itself.

In his seven years with Miami, Csonka had played on just two losing teams, and they were during his first two seasons, when the franchise was in its third and fourth years. From then on it was a steady climb, both for the Dolphins and their star running back. For the next five years Miami never won less than ten games, and Csonka never had a poor season.

But then runners like Csonka are ideal for good football

teams with diversified offenses. His strength—those powerful bursts through the line—can be effectively used on first down, but is more crucial on third down and short yardage, and when the defense is digging in near the goal line to prevent a touchdown. Good, powerful, control football.

There wasn't much of that during the first twelve games of the season in New York. The Giants lost ten of these games, and they were often behind from the first period. Instead of being third and 1 or third and 2, it was third and 8 and third and 12. Not an ideal situation for a runner like Csonka.

"It's a tough time for everyone," he said during the losing streak that lasted through the first nine games. "We all feel the pressure. I know I do. I know they brought me here to help turn things around [four of the club's last five seasons had been losing ones] and it hasn't happened. I don't feel totally to blame for that, but I do assume my share of the responsibility. After all, they paid a lot of money to get me."

Big money in sports is always a point of serious contention, especially when instant dividends are not forthcoming. And through that section of the 1976 season, many people wondered if the million dollars paid Csonka for four years' work might not have been better spent elsewhere. It was a popular subject in the press, and a burden for Csonka, who at one point offered the Giants a chance to renegotiate his contract downward, an offer they refused.

Then, midway through the twelfth game of the season, came the injury, the first serious one he'd sustained since a concussion in his rookie year nearly ended his career.

The incident occurred during the Seattle game at Giants Stadium, when his left foot was pinned against the artificial turf in a pileup and somebody fell across his leg. Csonka limped to the sidelines, knowing that he had been hurt but thinking it was not too serious. Then he reached the bench and had the knee looked at, and the doctor said it would require surgery. Csonka didn't believe him.

"I told that doctor he was full of shit," he recalled. "There

PHOTO BY SKIP ROZIN

Larry Csonka, in training. "I do assume my share of the responsibility. After all, they paid a lot of money to get me."

was a lot of pain but I'd had pain before. Then I got up to walk and I knew. It was sloppy, loose. I could tell that whatever was supposed to hold the knee together was not holding mine."

They examined Csonka's knee the day after the game to determine how bad the damage was, and when the dye and stress tests showed two torn ligaments, they operated immediately.

"I was sweating blood the night before the surgery," he said. "I wasn't scared about my leg, I never doubted I would play again if I got through it. I was scared about dying in the operation."

Recovery from the injury had been slow and tedious. Ever since the surgery he had been on a strenuous program of running, running at home on his farm, running around the track at Giants Stadium across the river in New Jersey. That very morning he had run for over two hours during a heavy rainstorm. When he finally trudged into the locker room, wearing football shoes and shorts, a T-shirt under a plastic rain parka, he looked like a large, wet bear.

"There was nobody there taking pictures this morning," he said. "The money, the glory, that's what people think of pro football, 'cause that's what the papers write. The rest of it, the running and the practice, the working yourself back into shape after an injury, that's not news. But it's football."

It was a tough time for Csonka, and he was uncomfortable with the constant scrutiny. He knew how important a healthy, sound body was to any athlete's career. The ones who set the big records, the Jim Browns and the Henry Aarons and the Wilt Chamberlains, were not only talented but healthy. And lucky. They all avoided serious injury.

"I know what's on their minds," said Csonka, referring to the Giants' front office. "They're worried. They know the recovery rate from this kind of injury is poor. That's why there are five fullbacks in camp."

Though he smiled as he said it, he was serious. Regardless of his past accomplishments, he was a thirty-year-old fullback coming off a knee operation. And though he never used it as an excuse, that situation was made even more precarious because he was playing for the Giants, a team that had not won more than nine games in a season since 1963 and whose greatest problem was its offensive line.

"Those guys give me everything they've got," he said, talking about his line, a vital ingredient to any running back's game, "but they're not the Miami Dolphins of 1972."

He paused for an instant and lowered his voice. "People say I don't run like I used to. What do they expect? I'm not the same player I was five years ago, and this isn't the same team. That's not an excuse. It's just the way it is."

There is a code in the world of sports that the stars, the big men making the big money, silently assume their share of responsibility when things don't go well. Maybe that's fair, since they receive so much praise when things do go well. Larry Csonka's been true to that code at New York. He never offered an excuse when he rushed for 3.6 yards a carry with the Giants instead of the 4.5 he averaged at Miami. (In his three best seasons he averaged over 5 yards each time he rushed with the ball.) And when the press barraged him with questions during the off-season about his worry about his knee or his contribution to the team, he just smiled and told them he was confident about everything. And when they wrote stories about his planning an early retirement, he said it wasn't true.

"I have a place here, a contract, and a job to do," he said. "I plan to do whatever I can to help the Giants win."

Whatever was going on inside of Csonka's mind about his future, the decision would be his. He was still a capable football player, and the Giants showed not the slightest dissatisfaction with their deal. Andy Robustelli, director of operations for the team and the man who negotiated the contract, considered the acquisition a boon at the time, and reaffirmed that feeling two years later.

"Larry Csonka is one of the men with whom this team is going to build back to the greatness it once had," said Robustelli prior to the start of the 1978 season. "He's done everything we've asked of him. As long as he continues that kind of performance he has a place on this team."

That is one of the prime differences between the star and the marginal athlete. Stars, even slightly tarnished, still make most of their own decisions. This is not to suggest that life at the top is without difficulties. But, like everything else in sports, those difficulties are very different from those experienced by the fringe player. Ironically, sometimes the problems of stars are a product of the very success they sought.

The finest professional basketball player in the game throughout the period of the mid-1970s has been Julius Erving. With all proper respect to the established power of the day, Kareem Abdul-Jabbar, and potential power-designate of the future, Bill Walton, their reputations are built on a combination of their talent and the position they play, which is center. Center is the dominant position in pro ball, and led to the crowning of such past powers as Wilt Chamberlain, Bill Russell, and George Mikan. (For fourteen consecutive years, through the 1977–78 season, centers were voted the Most Valuable Player award in the NBA.) All that recognized and accepted, Julius Erving is still The Man.

More than any other American sport, basketball is a game of rhythm and flow. And, as is the case with no other sport, that flow can suddenly be taken over by a strange and inexplicable force. It has been described by those involved as celestial and biological, and occasionally sexual. Suddenly, for no apparent reason, a player will shift his game into a kind of star drive. He will move as if in a dream, speeding past defenders who appear to be moving in sand to complete plays normally executed only in his imagination. He becomes unstoppable. It can happen to almost any player, but more often to those endowed with the greater skills. It is a special thing, which may, with luck, visit some players a few times a season, or in a career. But the man whose game most often approaches this superhuman state, not out of chance or divine guidance but out of planned brilliance, is Julius Erving.

A 6-feet-7-inch forward who began in pro basketball as a rebounder, Erving developed into the most talented scorer in the game gradually, through practice. This is not to say that he scores more points than anyone else—his primary concern has always been winning games, whatever role that requires for him. It does mean that he has more ways of getting the ball into the basket, and can do it in more situations.

He attended the University of Massachusetts, where he led his team to the National Invitation Tournament in the two years he played varsity ball. Following his junior year he signed with the Virginia Squires of the American Basketball Association. In his five years in the ABA, with Virginia and then the New York Nets, he led the league in scoring three times, was the league's Most Valuable Player three times, and twice led the Nets to the league championship. After three seasons with New York, a contract dispute led to his being sold to the Philadelphia 76ers for a reported $6 million—$3 million for the Nets and $3 million in salary for Erving.

From the time he entered the ABA and began making his way through the cities in the league, through Kentucky and Indiana, up to Denver and St. Louis, out to Utah and down to San Antonio, Erving quickly picked up a devoted following. For as the flow of a basketball game can stir the men playing it, so can a crowd of 10,000 spectators, huddled around the hardwood court in an enclosed auditorium, respond to that same charge of electrifying excitement. City by city, Erving turned them on. His "moves" became legend. Every city has its favorite story: his whip-like passes and fingertip steals, and the shots. Guarded and double-teamed, he was still able to score; putting the ball on the floor, dribbling behind his back, then suddenly accelerating, taking off from the foul line, literally flying over a defender, suspended in air, the ball held at arm's length in his right hand, and slamming it through the basket, the backboard left shuddering. It is the kind of excitement fans grew to expect from the man they call The Doctor. And when he arrived in New York, the largest market in the country, his fame spread, so that by the time he moved to Philadelphia and the NBA everybody knew who he was and what he could do.

As a result, Erving is hardly ever alone. They wait for him at the Spectrum in Philadelphia and at the Garden in New York, and at every arena across the country. And when he gives one of his basketball clinics, whether it be at Bishop Ford High School in Brooklyn or City College in Harlem, they wait all morning in lines that stretch around the block. The attention is so intense that Converse, the sporting goods manufacturer that employs Erving and sponsors the clinics as a promotion, has a planned procedure to protect its spokesman. Erving comes in early, while the crowd is still in line. His backdoor departure, after a slam-dunk exhibition has brought four or five thousand kids screaming to their feet, is camouflaged by the raffling off of free sneakers and covered by guards at the door.

Only at home is he safe, in his seventeen-room house in Upper Brookville on Long Island's north shore, or on the south shore, in his hometown of Roosevelt. It was there, at Roosevelt Park, that Erving and I met and talked on a hot July afternoon in 1977.

It was in the middle of a torrid stretch of New York weather (more than a week of days above 90 degrees, with several hitting 100 and over) and Erving had taken his small boys, Cheo, four years old, and Julius III, aged two, to the park, the same park where he had grown up and learned much of his game.

When the four of us reached the fence-enclosed handball court, Julius passed out tennis rackets and balls to each of his boys, then he sat down on the edge of the court, leaned against the chain-link fence, and talked about basketball.

"I had no thoughts of playing basketball as a profession when I was in high school," he said. "I had thoughts about college, about getting into the school of business administration. I played basketball because I loved it."

He gestured with his hands in the air as he talked, huge hands that could hold a basketball from the top when he was in high school. Now, at twenty-eight, he wears size 13½ gloves, the largest made.

Erving was invited to the Olympic development camp as an alternate after his sophomore year, and when a player was hurt he went on to play with the team, both nationally and in the USSR. It was his first big test, and the first time he could measure his abilities against the best young talent in the country.

"I listened to these guys talk about the pros," he said, "about not signing for less than $50,000. I listened to them laying all these plans and I thought they were way over my head. Then we get out there and play, and when it's all over I'm the best player out there. It made me think."

Erving didn't think too much about it the rest of the summer. He returned to school in September, and led Massachusetts again to the NIT. But his team was eliminated early, and he was contacted by an agent for the first time.

"That got the whole thing started," he said. "A few weeks later I reevaluated my priorities and made my decision to leave school and turn pro."

As he talked he kept part of his attention on his two children, who were engrossed in hitting orange tennis balls against the concrete wall. From time to time groups of kids from the park came up to him with questions, and each time he explained that he was busy and would see them when he was finished. Several of them waited.

Erving signed a four-year, no-cut contract with Virginia of the ABA, and went to camp with the Squires as a rebounding forward. He led the team in rebounding that first year, and as he progressed and grew as a ballplayer his scoring skills increased. He worked on those skills, taking advice from Ray Scott and other players in the league, yet never ignoring the other areas of his game: defense, passing, and rebounding.

"My attitude about the game was to develop all 'round so that if any part of my game falters I'd still be on the court playing," he explains. "If I'm just a shooter and my shot goes astray, there's no use my being out there."

He had fond memories of that first season, during which he averaged 27 points and 16 rebounds a game. And especially of the last year with New York, when he led the underdog Nets to the ABA championship while averaging an incredible 34.6 points a game.

The abrupt move to Philadelphia was complicated, but it centered around a dispute between Erving and Roy Boe, the Nets president and principal owner. Erving contends that verbal promises were made concerning his contract, and that conversation to resolve the problem was then cut off. Boe says there were no verbal promises. Regardless, the result was that The Doctor moved his office to Philadelphia, setting up practice with the talented 76ers. And, while it was an eminently successful move financially, there were problems. The team failed to gel properly. That can happen in a game like basketball, where team play and coordination are so vital, and the 76ers were not exactly a team which had grown and matured together. Three of their top players came from the ABA: Erving, George McGinnis, and Caldwell Jones. Their promising young center, Darryl Dawkins, was lured directly from high school by a huge contract. Frequently referred to as the "best team money could buy," the 76ers disappointed their fans and the press by winning only 60 percent of their games, then outraged them by losing the NBA championship to Portland.

For Erving, the move to Philadelphia marked a change in his personal relationship with the game of basketball.

"My early years [as a pro] were very enjoyable for me," he said. "There was a kind of progression throughout those years. Each year demanded more, and each year I gave more. But this year I gave less, because there was less demanded."

He paused for a moment, as if appraising his thoughts, then continued. "The more need there is the more of your skills you can expose, and nothing makes a person happier than using his skills. But there were a lot of times when I didn't get to use all the skills I have, and that made this season less enjoyable."

His mind drifted back to days with the Nets, and he began talking about how clear his role was, and how much he enjoyed filling the role as the team leader. Then he turned his attention to the 76ers.

"I feel like I know what it takes to win," he said. "I know what the easiest way is. And when I'm involved in a situation where guys are constantly trying to do it the hard way, it's frustrating, especially when you try and correct it and you get nowhere."

He interrupted his analysis to settle a minor eruption between his sons. Cheo, the older, husky and all energy, tends to be aggressive. Jay (Julius III), who at two is more slightly built, with wide eyes and fluffy light hair, walks in a dream. But Erving is an attentive father, and gently resolved the matter.

"The situation with the Nets was a good one," he said. "No petty jealousies. We had a good relationship with the coach and the players. I'd call it 90 percent ideal."

About that time Cheo and Jay had finished with their playing. Their father dutifully packed up the balls and rackets into his bag and the tiny caravan moved down the cement path which bisects the lovely, tree-surrounded park. As they walked on toward the tennis court the small gathering of children from the handball court followed, some talking to Erving and others content to follow at a safe distance. One little boy, trailing the rest, carried a scrap of brown paper torn from a grocery bag and half a blue pencil.

Erving stopped at the tennis court and played a few sets with Leon Saunders, a local friend who attended university with him (and who, incidentally, nicknamed him The Doctor) while another friend took the children across the path to the sandbox. Although Erving was stylishly dressed, resplendent in yellowish gold Bermuda shorts, red sneakers, and a blue denim hat, he did not show the same form that had brought him fame in professional basketball.

Then, after the tennis, as if moving toward some planned finale, everybody proceeded toward the end of the path and the basketball court, located right next to the parking lot. It was a big, fence-enclosed complex, similar in that aspect to the handball and tennis courts. It was divided into two sections, each section equipped with four baskets to accommodate four half-court games at a time. And though it was the end of a 100-degree day, all of the courts were in use.

It is nearly six-thirty in the evening and still well over 90 degrees, yet the play on all courts is spirited. At one of the baskets a few boys take random practice shots; at all the others full-blown games are in progress.

"This is the place," says Erving. "Lotta basketball played here."

We are leaning against the fence, watching the play on the courts and talking. The minute Erving entered the complex, the intensity of the games changed noticeably. Though all emotions were contained—a modest wave here, a nod there—

everyone knew The Doctor had arrived, and in their own ways they all wanted to show their best.

"I used to practice by myself," Erving is saying, looking around the court. "That first summer I came back from college I worked here, and when the park was supposed to close at eleven I would blink the lights and get everybody out. Then I'd wait ten or fifteen minutes, turn the lights back on, and play into the night. Sometimes with Leon, and often by myself."

Watching one tall, thin young man hit on an outside jump shot, he talked about coming to a park like this for the first time—or into any new situation and facing new competition. I asked if he was ever so impressed with seeing new players that he was in awe of them and their talent.

"I've never been in awe of another player," he says without a trace of self-consciousness. "I've had respect for them. But anything I've seen anybody do I knew I could do if I wanted to. And if someone outplays me, I can learn from that. I've always been a student of this game. I still am."

He talked about the hours spent practicing his craft, about learning to control the ball when shooting with one hand (he began as a two-handed shooter), about practicing his jump shot from behind a chair so he would jump straight up and not go too far forward, and with a chair behind so he wouldn't lean back, practicing jumping off the balls of his feet without taking time to collect his balance.

I start to ask another question, but he holds up his hand, asks me to remember it, and moves out onto the basketball court.

The game in the near court, which is the one Erving has been watching, is drawing to a close. There is where he wants to play. In the meantime he walks to the basket where the men are taking practice shots. He waits until the ball rebounds in his direction, takes it, bounces it on the court, and then pushes it toward the basket. The ball hits off the rim, the rebound bouncing off in another direction. Erving shows no sign of concern and waits for his next turn. He plays like that for a time, warming up, getting the feel of ball and court, and as the game on the near court ends he moves in to make up one of the teams taking on the winners of the last game.

It's just a simple game of pickup basketball, played on a cement half-court, but it has all the best elements of the schoolyard. The game is fast and rough, the shooting excellent, and while games at the other baskets continue, most of the attention within the fence is on The Doctor. The cement ledge where I sit is lined with spectators, and several people have gathered from the rest of the park and now lean on the fence from the outside. Someone has a large transistor radio, and in the hot July twilight a saxophone mixes jazz with the sound of the basketball hitting off the floor and the sounds of men at serious play.

And then the game is over. There is the slapping of hands, a few comments are passed, and Erving collects his children and heads for the light-brown van with the pastoral scene painted on the side panels.

"That's still fun," he says, "out there, between the lines. I do love to play. I love to get out and work at playing and work up a sweat, to get down and feel loose, and to win."

He loads the kids into the truck. "Winning means a lot," he says. "I can win and not play well and enjoy the winning."

He pauses, thinking, and then grows very serious. "The professional game has changed so much," he says. "The priorities are different. It's such a big business now. Guys are more interested in individual performances, in market value, than in winning. It's obvious. It's rampant throughout the league. Everybody knows there are certain guys who would just as soon get off and have a good game and look good as opposed to winning. It wasn't always that way, but things are different now."

Julius Erving at a basketball clinic in Harlem. "The professional game has changed so much . . . . Guys are more interested in individual performances, in market value, than in winning."

PRO
BASKETBALL SHOES

There was a hint of weariness, almost sadness, to what he had been saying, the sadness of a man who, in a brief period, had seen basketball change from a game to a hard and sometimes ruthless business. His perspective had been changed by all the "dealing and the wheeling that's going on," as he put it. He did not say that he missed the days of his "innocent youth." He just said they were gone, but the implication was clear. It is the kind of realization which comes to all athletes at some point, sooner or later, be they winners or losers. Some are comfortable with it, and some are not. Most mourn the change.

But the star—or even the front-line player, for that matter—can fall back on his sport, and wrap himself in playing and perfecting his game, and in reaping the rewards. Concentration and perfection, they are the obsession of the great in any field. Erving calls himself a "lifetime student of the game," and similar claims have been made by men like Joe Morgan and Tom Seaver, Pete Rose and Rick Barry, John Havlicek and Fran Tarkenton. The contract fights and watching friends cut and traded, the pain and the injuries, all are harsh. But the game—getting down and getting loose—is pure joy.

But for the marginal athlete, it is hard to become obsessed with perfection when bare survival is a daily concern.

6
A POCKETFUL OF GLORY

It is six-thirty in the evening in the great, open-air arena known as the Orange Bowl. Even for Miami in November, it has been an unusually lovely day, warm and clear, and the forecast for tonight's football game between the Hurricanes of the University of Miami and the visiting Maryland Terrapins is good.

This 1958 season has been a disaster for the Hurricanes. Football pundits said Miami would go undefeated if they could just get past their opening game against Wisconsin. Of course they said that in July, back when no one knew that Wisconsin would end up losing only one game en route to a share of the Big Ten title. By the last week in September, when the Badgers blanked Miami, 20–0, they had a better idea. To date, the local heroes stand 1 and 5.

Hardly anyone has arrived at the stadium yet. The lights are on, and a few officials are walking around on the field, but the stands belong to the ushers, a few cops, and the vendors. I am among the vendors, one of the men with the little white jackets who sell peanuts and ice cream, Cokes and beer. As this is twenty years ago and I am but seventeen years old, I am not permitted to sell beer, and so I have taken the next best choice—Cokes. These games attract a lot of serious drinkers; they bring their own liquor and I provide the mixer. And though the crowds have fallen off from the 60,000 who watched the Wisconsin game, those pure fans who have remained faithful buy an inordinate number of Cokes. More, in fact, with each loss.

The fortunes of the University of Miami are in the hands of Fran Curci tonight, as they have been in nearly every game since he came on the scene last year. A short but heady quarterback from a local high school, he so impressed the coaching staff as a sophomore that all the other contenders for his job became instantly less visible. All through his long, painful season the coaches have stuck with Curci, to the displeasure of many of the fans.

Since those who arrive early like to "settle in," as they put it, I do a brisk business even before the teams come onto the field for their ritualistic warmups. During better times I sell only through the warmup and first quarter, then shed my jacket, lose myself in the student section, and enjoy the rest of the evening. (At two cents earned on each cup of Coke sold, I can just about clear expenses and see the game with a diligent ninety minutes of hustle.) Lately, however, I've been working all four periods.

By seven-fifty most of those who are going to show up are here. I have been busy for an hour, and, while I haven't stopped to count my money, I know I've gone back for half-a-dozen trays of Cokes. I stop for the national anthem, but sell through the kickoff, and pause only for a second as Miami takes a 7–0 lead in the first period. I've worked too many games to commit myself for the evening on the strength of one touchdown.

Sure enough, by the end of the half the Terrapins have scored twice and lead, 13–7. Another tough night for Miami, which always works to my advantage. Cokes are going like crazy, and already I've seen a few empty whiskey bottles rolling around under the seats.

Halftimes are busy only if you're working the box and reserved seats. General admission fans go stand in line. I cover the border areas and keep occupied, but not so busy that as the third quarter starts I don't notice the people are getting restless. The game is dull, and Miami is doing nothing. The crowd blames Curci, which isn't totally fair. Still, somewhere around the middle of the period the chant begins for his exit. I can hear them: "We want Yarbrough! We want Yarbrough!" It started in the student section, and now there are little pockets all over the stadium. "We want Yarbrough! We want Yarbrough!"

The man they want is Bonnie Yarbrough, a senior who showed flashes of spectacular play in his sophomore year, but who was never terribly popular with the coaching staff and was completely forgotten when Curci arrived. His position with the fans, however, has remained strong. Whenever Curci has faltered—which has been often this season—the call for Yarbrough has gone up. But even I, who have been selling Cokes as long as Bonnie has been on the bench, have never heard it like this.

Toward the end of the third period I head down under the stands to the concession station for a refill of Cokes. Standing there in line, I hear groans from above. One of the other sellers has a radio and tells me that Maryland has scored again, building its lead to 20–7. I need no play-by-play to know of the crowd's displeasure. I can hear the chanting for Yarbrough grow louder and louder, and feel the steel beams of the huge, skeleton-like structure shake with the sound. Emotion is building; I can feel it here in the inner corridors.

A few more minutes of this as I'm waiting my turn is all I can take. I leave my empty Coke tray in a corner, ditch my uniform in the men's room, and hurry to the student section.

Sitting here now, in the middle of all these chanting students, I am deafened by the sound. All the world seems to be calling for Bonnie Yarbrough. I borrow a pair of glasses from one of the students and train them on the tall, blond quarterback, who now stands in front of the Miami bench. He is motionless, holding his helmet under his arm and watching the game.

Suddenly, as Maryland kicks off to the Hurricanes' 23-

yard-line, the Miami coach motions to Yarbrough and calls him to his side. Seconds pass, Yarbrough listens, and then puts on his helmet. The response is immediate; the place goes wild. People stand and applaud as their hero runs onto the field.

Now the entire stadium is buzzing. The fans watch as Yarbrough calls the play in the huddle, and, as he moves to the line of scrimmage, they begin a new chant: "Bon-*nie*! Bon-*nie*!"

After three periods of Maryland domination, it doesn't seem possible that Miami can turn the game around, but no one seems concerned. The time and the score are lost in the adrenaline pumping through the crowd.

"Bon-*nie*! Bon-*nie*!" they chant. "Bon-*nie*! Bon-*nie*!"

It doesn't take Yarbrough long to respond. On his third play he drops back with his arm cocked. The Miami line, somehow imbued with new strength, holds as the Maryland defenders strain to get by. Yarbrough waits, then unleashes a strong, arcing pass downfield, all the way to the Maryland 44, where a Miami receiver pulls it in over his shoulder and outruns a lone member of the secondary at the 11 to score.

The stadium is going berserk, 26,000 people standing and screaming. Bonnie Yarbrough is back from the graveyard of quarterbacks, and they are all in glory. They stand and they cheer, and they cheer some more for the extra point, which makes the score 20–14.

Now Miami is only six points behind, and the crowd braces for an upset.

The kickoff sails all the way to the Maryland goal line, and the player fielding the ball gets back only to the 15, where he is swarmed over by Miami tacklers. The Terrapins manage to reach midfield before they are stopped, and on fourth down a high, floating punt bounces dead on the Miami 4.

Neither the Hurricanes nor the crowd seems daunted. And as Yarbrough leads the offensive team back onto the field, from all sections of the stands comes the chant: "Bon-*nie*! Bon-*nie*!" Over and over: "Bon-*nie*! Bon-*nie*!"

I take the glasses again and focus on Yarbrough as he calls for quiet and looks over the line. The Miami center, Jim Otto, one of the best players on the team and a classmate of Yarbrough's, looks back just before the quarterback begins to call out the signals. Though it is impossible to see that well even with binoculars, he seems to be smiling. Something very special is happening, and he knows it.

Yarbrough takes the snap and hands off to his left halfback, who bolts off tackle for two yards, and the fans cheer. Then he drops back, fires a pass to his right end, who makes a leaping catch at the 23, and the fans cheer. But two plays later there is an interception. Maryland takes over, moves quickly in to score with seconds remaining, and the rally has died.

But not the dream. All around me people are still cheering. "Bon-*nie*, Bon-*nie*, Bon-*nie*," they shout, unmoved by the fact that the game has ended and Maryland has won. "Bon-*nie*, Bon-*nie*." The chant grows louder and louder.

Out on the field the Miami players are lifting Yarbrough to their shoulders and carrying him across the field, all to a standing ovation by the fans, who refuse to leave.

The whole phenomenon has so confused the Maryland players that they stand there, looking around, as if waiting for some reassurance that they have in fact won.

They have. They won the game, 24–14. But the night, the night belongs to Bonnie Yarbrough and his fans. Though he will go back to the bench for the rest of his brief football career, it doesn't make any difference. This is his night. And many of us who were there will never forget it.

Nothing is more exciting in all of sports than an upset. It draws on an ancient love of underdogs which probably began with David and Goliath. When the 1960 Pirates defeated the lordly Yankees in the World Series, and the 1969 Mets swept the Orioles, when the Jets dumped the Colts in the Super Bowl, and Portland defeated the million-dollar 76ers for the 1977 NBA title, there was never any question which side the people were on. Except for family and local friends, nobody with any soul goes with the favorites. Life is full of the favorites winning. (That's why they're favorites.) The government wins. Con Edison wins. Bell Telephone wins.

This is one of the reasons sports has such spectator appeal. As nowhere else, underdogs have a chance to upset the odds. Nobodies do it all the time to somebodies, and the fans love it. And they love it for a simple reason: It's a little bit of them out there. Finally, a winner.

This is difficult to explain to nonsports fans. The American wife can't understand why her husband, after a hard day at the office, wants to watch a baseball game when his team is not only six runs behind but hopelessly out of the pennant race. Part of the reason is that hard day, because people have been pushing at him and pulling at pieces of his insides since eight o'clock in the morning. And just by being there, by watching that game and sitting on his frustrations for a few hours, he can transfer his personal hopes to nine strangers who are out on a field someplace. And at the core of those hopes: If he couldn't make it all day, they just might make it that night. Twelve games out of first and six runs behind in the eighth inning, it doesn't make any difference. Because it's always possible that they might score seven in the ninth, and go on to win their next fifteen games.

Our lives have grown so complex and cumbersome that the only place underdogs have a consistent chance of pulling a dramatic upset is in a game. Society is far too structured to permit it to happen outside that context. And what spontaneous success stories appear to exist, upon careful examination, are mostly the result of long years of hard, deliberate work, finally culminating in a man's buying the grocery store where he was once the bag boy. Significant, certainly, but not quite the same as a lightly regarded European fighter like Ingemar Johansson knocking out Floyd Patterson in Yankee Stadium and becoming Heavyweight Champion of the World. That's what dreams are made of, the stuff of movies and fairy tales.

The wonderful thing about sports is that it can happen at any time. Though only the true stars are good enough to play brilliantly day in and day out, any athlete good enough to make it to the professional ranks and then to the major leagues in his sport is good enough to be brilliant once in a while—or once in a lifetime. And sports being what it is, a show of drama and excitement, the most unlikely heroes have a way of exceeding their normal capabilities at the most unlikely times.

In the 1956 World Series, the Brooklyn Dodgers won the first two games at home against the New York Yankees, and the Yankees took the next two played at the Stadium. For the fifth game Yankees manager Casey Stengel selected as his starting pitcher a middling right-hander who had lost an impressive 21 games while pitching for Baltimore in 1954, who had lost his only World Series decision, 8–5, to those same Dodgers the year before, and who had started the second game of the '56 Series, lasting only until the second inning. The pitcher was Don Larsen, and all he did on that October afternoon in the Bronx was retire twenty-seven Brooklyn batters in order, giving up no runs and no hits and permitting no batter to reach first base. It was the first perfect game pitched in thirty-four years, the only perfect game or no-hitter ever pitched in a World Series. Larsen played three more years with the Yankees, and in 1960 began traveling, pitching for six different teams in the next seven years, rarely winning as many games as he lost, and finally being released in 1967. He stepped out of nowhere on October 8, 1956, into the spotlight and the record books, and soon after returned to nowhere.

Larsen's perfect game is a historic example, but less spectacular incidents fill the record books. Athletes—good, solid, but very average athletes—performing for one game or one season, or sometimes one play, far beyond their normal capabilities. Four home runs hit in four consecutive times at bat by Art Shamsky, a full-time pinch hitter for Cincinnati in 1966. Tom Dempsey, who has played for six different teams, traded once and released three times in nine years in the NFL, kicking a 63-yard field goal for New Orleans in 1970 to set the existing record. Dale Long, who hit 132 home runs in ten years in the majors, hitting 8 in eight straight games for Pittsburgh in 1956.

And so it goes, in all sports, with surprising frequency. It is truly a world of fantasies endlessly realized. And no possibility is too remote. Just as soon as you concoct some impossible circumstance, a player comes along to prove it's only improbable. The requirements are that he be there, in uniform, playing the game, and that he possess that brand of invincible confidence so necessary in sports.

That confidence is vital equipment, like good eyesight and strong legs. It sounds so right being exuded by a Joe Morgan or a Julius Erving, though it is just as necessary from men on the fringe, and much more difficult to generate. But as you travel from team to team, from league to league, every athlete says the same thing, despite his level of success: "I am a winner. Give me a chance to play and I'll prove it." So long as they still believe that—truly believe it—anything can happen.

In 1957 Bob Hazle was a fading outfielder with the Triple A farm team of the then Milwaukee (and later Atlanta) Braves. A well built six-footer, he had entered professional baseball in 1950, signing with the Cincinnati Reds organization and joining their Columbia team in the old Sally League. He was, as the scouts like to say, an athlete. He had played football and baseball in high school, could run, throw, hit, and field, and seemed to have a bright future.

Though he maintained what he calls "around a .300 average" in the minors, Hazle could not rise above Triple A ball in nearly six years. And when he did get his chance, it was for only six games with the parent Reds at the end of the 1955 season. On that brief visit he hit only .231, and the Reds figured they'd seen enough. In the spring shuffle of 1956 he was traded to the Braves, and relocated with their Triple A farm team in Wichita, Kansas.

And there he played for a season and a half. Languished more than played, for his inability to escape the minors was beginning to wear on him. And by the 1957 season, at twenty-six, he was thinking seriously of quitting.

"I was going bad," said Hazle at his home in Columbia, South Carolina, where he now travels for the Niagra Exercise Manufacturing Company. "I felt like I was tired—my attitude was poor. I knew I could play, but nobody was giving me a chance. I was just about ready to give the game up."

Hazle, who speaks with the accent of a man who was born and spent most of his years in the South, recalled the months leading up to the last week in July 1957.

"I was hitting very poor at the first of the year," he said, "about .216 or .219. I said, 'Hell, I just feel like I give it another year and I be looking around.' But, gradually, I began pulling my average up, till I was at .277 or so. Pride makes that happen. You don't want 'them' taking anything away."

Meanwhile, all through the month of July, the Braves were battling for the National League pennant with Brooklyn, St. Louis, Philadelphia, and Cincinnati. On July 20 three games separated the five teams. The Braves would pull a game or two ahead, then fall back. Up and back, up and back.

Then, about the middle of the month, their outfield was hit by a series of injuries. The fine and speedy Billy Bruton injured his leg and was put on the disabled list. Andy Pafko hurt his back and missed some games. And there were other injuries, less serious but always lowering the overall effectiveness of the team. None of the outfielders seemed immune. It got so bad at one point that Del Crandall, the Milwaukee catcher, played some games in left field.

To deal with the problem the Braves turned to their farm team in Wichita. And while he was not the best fielder on the club or the man with the highest average, Robert Sidney Hazle was the man they brought up to replace Bruton on the roster.

"I was happy to be up," recalled Hazle, "but I was no dumb-dumb. I knew it was for a cup of coffee, and when it got cold, goodbye. So I figure if I'm going to play, what's the difference? Swing the stick."

Hazle arrived in Milwaukee in time for the game on Sunday, July 28, but he did not play. The following game he was sent up to bat in the fifth inning for Dave Jolly, the pitcher, in a bunting situation. He advanced the runner, then sat out the next game.

"I started my first game that next day in right field," said Hazle. "I remember lining a double down the left-field line my first time up."

As he talked, his mind sliding back over twenty years, he apologized for his poor memory, then injected that it was a curve that he hit for the double, and that he then sat out the next two games while the Braves dropped into second place, trailing St. Louis by .002. Listening to him, you felt it all could have happened the day before.

Then on August 4 he was back in the lineup and got a single, a double, and a sacrifice fly. The next game he went three-for-three, and two days later four-for-five with a home run.

"It just went on from there," said Hazle. "It seemed like every game I was in it was one-for-three, two-for-three, three-for-four, on like that."

It was an incredible stretch, for Bob Hazle and the Milwaukee Braves. From August 4 to August 15 the Braves won 10 straight games and pulled ahead of the pack by 8½ games. And in the time he was there—forty-one games—Hazle hit an amazing .403, helping Milwaukee make a joke out of the pennant race, which they won by eight full games over the Dodgers.

"It was something," said Hazle. "The guys kidded me, Del Crandall, and them, saying how they couldn't believe it. But it kept going. And I never enjoyed anything more. It was the best time of my life."

The honeymoon lasted until after the World Series, which the Braves won over the Yankees, 4 games to 3. Hazle was voted a two-thirds share of the Series money, and, while he felt he deserved a full share, he wasn't too upset. The real problem concerned his salary.

He remembers when he came up from Wichita that he was

making the major league minimum which was then $6,000. Once he began hitting so well and it was obvious he was going to stick with the club, he suggested to the general manager, John Quinn, that he might be entitled to a raise.

"He kept telling me he'd take care of me," said Hazle. "Over and over, he said he'd take care of me. He said he didn't want to jinx me. 'You're going great, you're going great,' he said 'and I'm gonna take care of you.' So I didn't argue with him."

Hazle remembers conversations with Quinn going on all through the pennant race, but his salary stayed the same.

"He finally got around to taking care of me," said Hazle. "He called me into his office after the Series and offered me a great big bonus—he offered me $1,000. I gave it back to him and went on home to Columbia."

The dispute between Hazle and Quinn concerning the check continued during the off-season and while Hazle played winter ball in the Dominican Republic, and it was replaced by a dispute during contract negotiations before the 1958 season, but that's all incidental. For with the end of the 1957 World Series came the end of a very special episode in Hazle's life. The magic that had visited him those months with Milwaukee was gone, and soon so was Bob Hazle. After twenty games of the 1958 season, hitting .179, he was sold to Detroit, where he spent most of that year sitting on the bench. He spent 1959 back in Triple A, and within a year was out of baseball and home selling monuments. ("The granite," he says, referring to the trade name, adding, "no, don't call it no dead business.")

In explaining the remarkable stretch of hitting, Hazle, who's added seven or eight pounds to his 1957 playing weight and whose thick black hair is flecked with gray, just smiles and shrugs. He talks about the hits that fell in, about the luck, and sums up by saying that he always did like to swing the bat.

"It was the best," he said, "and I think about it a lot. I don't mean I drag out my scrapbook or anything. It's in the bottom of my trunk up in the attic and I don't even look at it. But I still wear my World Series ring—I wouldn't take it off to bathe. And of course I have these."

Bob Hazle's glory lives in these postcards, ordered in 1957, now stored in boxes: "It was the only time in my life I was on top. I tell you that was the best."

He was sitting at his desk and reached over to pick up one of the black-and-white postcards that he had made up that summer in Milwaukee. It was when things were good, when he was leading the Braves to the pennant, when he felt he'd made it in baseball. So there in the midst of his glory he ordered a thousand cards with a picture on the front of him in uniform, kneeling with his trusty bat. He was going to send them out, to friends and fans all over the country, but by the time they were ready the season was over. Then came the trade and the minors, and he didn't feel like sending them anywhere. So they sat, in the boxes they came in.

"I've started using them now," he said. "Every once in a while some kid writes and asks for a picture, and I send him one. It really makes you feel good when somebody asks."

He stopped for a moment and fondled the twenty-year-old postcard. "I'm a quiet guy most of the time," he said. "I don't sit in bars telling people who I was and what I did, but it's nice when they remember. One of our announcers from the Braves was doing a film for television, *Summer, 1957*, and he talked to Aaron down in Atlanta, and to Lew Burdette. And he came up here to see me. It was nice. I never did see the film, though. I sure wish they'd run it here—show people what it was like."

He put the card down on the desk and talked about old timers' days, those nostalgic gatherings of old baseball teams held during the summer prior to regularly scheduled games.

"I don't get to go much," he said. "We gathered one time years back down in Atlanta, and it was wonderful, seeing all the boys and talking about those days. I was really thinking last year they might pull the twentieth anniversary of the World Series team together, but nobody ever called me. That really surprised me.

"I wouldn't take anything for that time. It was the only time in my life I was on top. I tell you that was the best."

The best for Bob Hazle, who earned the nickname "Hurricane" that summer, lasted for two months. The best two months of his professional career—of his life. Two months during which he performed the way he always dreamed that he could. Ten years of professional baseball, justified by two months.

Stars don't have to look to isolated periods for their satisfaction. Their worth rests not with the extraordinary but with the ordinary. Consistent play makes them what they are—predictable excellence, game after game. Their moments of additional brilliance are almost expected: Wilt Chamberlain's 100-point game; O. J. Simpson's rushing for 250 yards; Tom Seaver's striking out 19 batters. Impressive as such figures are, the reputations of these men come from bigger feats: Seaver, striking out 200 or more batters a year eight straight times; Simpson, rushing for 1,000 yards or more a season five times; Chamberlain, scoring 65 points or more a game fifteen times. Consistency, it is the true measure of greatness.

But for the marginal player, there is no such consistency, and that moment of glory—infrequently as it occurs and at whatever level—is crucial. It is what helps him to continue to believe in himself. Years of performing below his expectations cause frustration and even make an athlete doubt his own ability. He hungers for the opportunity to show the world that the potential he exhibited at sixteen was no illusion.

Sometimes that moment sets a record, as it did with Long and Dempsey. Sometimes it creates only a mild stir, as when Dick Bosman, a second-line pitcher for his seven years in the majors, pitched a no-hitter during the final season of his otherwise mediocre career. And sometimes it isn't noticed except by those persons directly affected, as when a reserve player gets the opportunity to start, plays three or four games over his head, and then quietly goes back to the bench. No headlines mark the occasion. No one not involved with the game even knows it happened. But the player knows, and it's important as a piece of tangible evidence on his side.

The New York Knicks carried such a reserve on their squad through the 1976–77 season. His name was Mo Layton. A walk-on to the Knicks rookie camp in September, Layton had played and was cut at Phoenix and Portland in his three previous seasons in the league, and had spent a year playing semi-pro ball before getting his tryout with New York. While he played very little through the first part of the season, Layton, a streetwise competitor from urban Newark, was given a chance to start several games while New York's star guard, Walt Frazier, was out of the lineup. Over a two-week period he scored 14 points a game, and in one game led the Knicks with 24 points.

During that period Layton was floating. A tough-looking hustler with narrow eyes and a piece chipped from one of his front teeth, he walked those weeks with a swagger, head up, like a gambler on a winning streak. One night before a game, as he entered the Knicks locker room, dressed in a light tan jump suit and matching wedgies, he was greeted by a stack of mail sitting on the stool by his locker.

"Oooh weee," he exclaimed when he saw the mail. "Will you look at that? I'm getting more fan mail than Clyde [Frazier]. Well, maybe not *more* than Clyde," he said in mock seriousness, picking up the first letter, "but more than Earl [Monroe]. Surely more than Earl."

To the coaching staff it was a fluke, and Layton returned to obscurity when Frazier was again available. But there was nothing surprising about it to Layton, who had been trying to make a place for himself in the NBA since being drafted out of Southern Cal in 1971.

"Listen," he said after the stretch had ended and he had returned to his customary position on the bench, "when I'm playing good steady time, I'm one of the best shooters in this league. I mean one of the ten best, and there are some shooters around here."

Layton did not consider his performance to be that exceptional. He viewed it as an indication of his true ability. Maybe he couldn't average 24 points a game, but he felt the man on the floor that night was closer to the real Mo Layton than the man who spent most of his time sitting down. All he wanted was a chance to prove it.

"That's the kind of ball I play," he said. "I penetrate and I shoot and I score. I've had big games before. I scored 37 points one night for Phoenix. I can do it. I've done it before. But I've got to be playing. I need time. Good, steady time."

It is a familiar refrain, not so different from what Bob Hazle said as he left Detroit and the majors. While he never suggested he was a .403 hitter, he felt that given a chance to play regularly he could have hit .300.

"I proved I could hit major league pitching," he said, "and I coulda done it again if they gave me the chance."

While the odds are stacked against such an athlete coming

up with a headline-making performance, it happens just often enough to give every survivor in every sport hope. Every time a Bob Hazle or a Don Larsen comes out of nowhere for a moment of glory, it strengthens the belief of every fringe player that it could happen to him. And it could.

In that respect the marginal athlete is not so different from many of the rest of us. Stories like *Rocky* feed his fantasies just as they feed ours. And, like us, he plays the old spectator game: Sitting in the stands or on the sidelines, or even at home watching television, he sees established pros performing and he knows he could do at least as well. Like us, he performs magnificently in his mind and knows he could make that happen in a game. The difference between him and us, of course, is that sports is his life. That fantasy, while amusing and even rewarding to us, is a key part of his professional sustenance. It is often what got him into the game in the first place.

When Gary Cuozzo was a junior in college he was one of those people sitting in the stands, comparing his ability to that of the men on the field. At the time he was a premed student at the University of Virginia and quarterback for the football team.

"Playing football was always a dream of mine," said Cuozzo. "I just loved the game, and I wanted to play. But it wasn't like it was for some other guys, guys hungry for the game, hungry to make it. They were born underdogs. I came from a comfortable family situation. I just loved to play."

With his father and brother already practicing dentistry, and Cuozzo headed in the same direction, his life seemed set. Whatever fantasies he held about professional football were just that, overzealous extensions of his imagination. While he loved the game and played well, the pros were never a realistic consideration to him, not since he had seen his first game while a child visiting New York.

"I can still remember it," said Cuozzo. "I was just a kid and my dad took me to see the Giants play the Bears when they had great games with the Bears. Everybody looked so big and so good. The whole thing looked so spectacular that I didn't think

I could ever play. But I was a kid, and I saw it through the eyes of a kid."

He carried that image of pro football all the way through grade school and high school, until his junior year at Virginia, when everything changed.

"I went to a pro game in Washington, the Redskins playing the Colts," said Cuozzo recently. "I saw the guys in warmups and I realized I could throw the ball like that. All those years I had thought there was something different about them, but for the first time I saw them up close, through the eyes of an adult, and I realized there wasn't."

He hesitated for just an instant. "That was the turning point. I could see myself out there, competing for a job as a pro. Suddenly it wasn't a fantasy anymore. It was all real."

From then on pro football became a more active part of Cuozzo's thinking. He still planned on pursuing medicine (he had been accepted at Yale) but he had a secondary plan which focused on football. He was applying to the University of Tennessee, which had a part-time program in medicine. And while the pragmatic part of his mind was occupied with a sound, stable future, he was preparing for any fantasy eventualities which might develop by perfecting his craft on the football field. He was doing pretty well. While at Virginia he completed 98 of 181 passes, earning an invitation to the Blue-Gray and Senior Bowl games.

"I had talked with several teams and expected to be drafted," said Cuozzo. "Then after the regular season I was in New York for the Hall of Fame Scholarship dinner, and Terry Baker's agent came in and said he'd been drafted number one by the Rams. My agent didn't exist, so I went out and bought a newspaper. The first ten rounds were there and I wasn't listed in any of them."

Cuozzo was disappointed. He didn't understand being passed over in the first ten rounds, but he contained his feelings and went out the next day for another paper to see where he would be playing as a pro.

"I couldn't believe it," he said, remembering his shock as he scanned the draft choices in the paper. "All twenty rounds were listed and I wasn't there."

Cuozzo reestablished contact with the Baltimore Colts, one of the clubs with whom he had previously talked, and ended up signing as a free agent. Along with four other quarterbacks, he attended the Colts rookie camp in 1963, confident but careful. ("I wasn't so confident that I gave up my place at Yale," he recalls.) But he was the only one invited back to the full camp in July. And when the season opened Baltimore had two quarterbacks, John Unitas, the all-pro veteran, and Gary Cuozzo, the rookie free agent.

That was the beginning of ten years in the NFL for Cuozzo, nine of which were spent as a reserve quarterback.

"It's a tremendous tearing at your insides," said Cuozzo, "because to play means that somebody else has got to be hurt. You don't particularly want other people to get hurt, but you want to play. You're torn between the team aspect and the personal aspect. It's very difficult."

It was a conflict which accompanied Cuozzo throughout most of his career, through all four years at Baltimore, his one season with the expansion New Orleans Saints, three of his four seasons with Minnesota, and his final year, with the St. Louis Cardinals. So he waited because, like every other reserve, he knew that when he got his chance he could make things happen.

Gary Cuozzo sits in the waiting room of his office in Sea Girt, New Jersey. For eight years he attended dental school during the off season at the University of Tennessee and now, four years after his retirement from football, he is a successful orthodontist.

It is after hours, and the office is closed. Behind Cuozzo's desk are team pictures, a wall of them representing the four different teams with which he played during his ten-year career. And as he leans back on the bench usually occupied by waiting patients, he recalls those years.

"Mostly it was a wonderful experience," he says, "the playing and the camaraderie—the whole hoopla. Being involved. And I really felt like part of the team, even when I wasn't playing."

In the fraction of a second between the end of his last sentence and the beginning of the next one, his mood changes and his voice lowers.

"Still, a lot of it was tough," he says. "After the game was over—that's the hardest part. The victory is yours and you're really not part of it. You really want to be dirty and you really want to be sore and you really want to play."

He stops and looks around at the pictures by the door which leads to the receptionist's desk and the functioning part of the office. They are shots of Cuozzo in uniform, fading back for a pass. He has changed since leaving the game. At thirty-six he is still tall and straight and suntanned, but he has picked up a few pounds over the 195 of his playing days and has abandoned crew-cut hair for a longer, more modern style.

As quickly as his mood had changed before, it now changes again. He smiles as he begins to remember. "I probably never was great," he says. "I never could run that well. Maybe I wasn't as good a passer as I thought. But somehow I was able to make it all work when the pressure was on. I was always at my best coming off the bench."

Cuozzo's biggest call off the bench came in 1965 in a game against the Minnesota Vikings. It was his third year with the Colts, and until then he had played very little, mostly during the summer in Baltimore's early exhibition games, and occasionally late in some games during the regular season. But never, in nearly three full seasons, had he started.

"Then in '65 John [Unitas] hurt his back," recalls Cuozzo. "He'd been hurt before, but he'd always played. But the night before the game Shula [Don Shula, Baltimore coach] came in and said he couldn't go. I would have to start.

"I was scared," he says, grinning. "It was like my first game when I was in the ninth grade. The other team came onto the field and I looked up at my friends in the stands and thought, What am I doing down here? I felt sick. It was the same at Minnesota. I was in a different league, but the body was the same."

The Minnesota game, played in the November cold of Bloomington, began slowly, and it looked as if it was going to be a rout for the home team. The Vikings scored first and threatened repeatedly. The Colts relied on their defense, then managed a 17-yard field goal and a late touchdown to take a 10–7 halftime lead into the locker room.

"I hadn't played very well—nobody had," says Cuozzo. "Then in the second half we went out and everything went right. Everybody came open. The lanes were clear. I never got thrown for a loss. Suddenly I couldn't do anything wrong."

Cuozzo led the Colts on an 80-yard drive at the beginning of the third period, climaxed by a 22-yard touchdown pass. Minnesota responded with a scoring drive of its own, but after that it was all Cuozzo and the Colts. In the course of the afternoon he threw for five touchdowns—still a club record for Baltimore—en route to a 41–21 rout. The young quarterback was thrilled; the 47,426 in Bloomington were shocked. And Norm van Brocklin, the Vikings coach, quit the next day.

"It was a biggie," says Cuozzo, smiling. "Just like a dream. Pro football was always a dream to me, and that's what that was like. I had made it. I was there."

But glory is short-lived for reserve quarterbacks. The official line from the coach is that his starting quarterback is his starting quarterback until he proves that he can't do the job.

"I went out to practice the next week knowing I was going to start," recalls Cuozzo. "I'd set a record the week before. But there was John, bad back and all. And he played well that week against Philadelphia. I just sat there charting the plays. But there was no doubt that I had to go."

Cuozzo was traded to New Orleans after the following season, but he had difficulty behind the first-year team's young

Gary Cuozzo, on his final season with St. Louis: "I just wasn't hungry enough. Guys like Unitas . . . they were always hungry."

offensive line. From there he went to Minnesota, for what he calls the most satisfying four years of his career.

"Though I was only the Viking starter for one season," he says, "I always felt I was in contention for the job. Those were the best four years for me."

Still, looking back over his ten years in the NFL, Cuozzo's great successes were not long stretches of solid, consistent leadership. They were those spot games, apparently coming out of nowhere, when he was almost unstoppable. There were several of them. The Minnesota game in 1965, a game against the Chiefs in 1970 after Kansas City had defeated the Vikings in the previous Super Bowl, another game against the Vikings when he was playing for St. Louis, and others. But always special games, one here and one there, and often years apart.

"That's discouraging," he says. "I thought I was better than that, but the truth is I didn't have that consistency. I was the kind of guy who really had to psych himself up. Then I could do it. But I just wasn't hungry enough. Guys like Unitas were different. They were always hungry."

He stops for a moment, crosses one leg over the other, then uncrosses it. He is a thoughtful man, and religious. Around the office, beside the memorabilia from the NFL, are little stacks of pamphlets explaining and praising different facets of Christianity. When he begins again to talk it is slow and deliberate.

"I probaby wasn't that great that they would go with me, day in and day out," he says. "You never like to admit you're not as good as you think you are. You keep waiting for that right moment. Well, circumstances are important, but if you're really good, eventually it will come out. I guess I just wasn't that good."

Gary Cuozzo is more forthright than most about the limited successes he enjoyed throughout his career, and painfully candid about his ability. But he in no way minimizes his feelings for the game.

"I did love it, despite all the frustration," he said. "You can't imagine that feeling of being part of something like a team. It's taken me four years to even start to want to compete at anything. Everything was so nothing after football. I played golf, tennis. They were nothing. I'm just now getting back to the point where I can hit a tennis ball against the wall and enjoy it."

He looked around the room, and his eyes fixed on the last team picture, that of the 1972 St. Louis Cardinals.

"That last summer was painful," he said, referring to his return to the St. Louis camp in 1973. "It was clear that I wasn't welcome. I had a contract, but I could tell they didn't want me. They ignored me. They were treating me like I'd seen other quarterbacks treated when I was coming up and phasing them out. But now it was happening to me. It was horrible."

He shifted awkwardly in his seat. "If that hadn't happened I'd never have quit. That and having orthodontics waiting for me got me out of football, but it would have been easy for me to stick it out. I'm thirty-six. I'd be out there now, someplace, sitting on the bench, waiting for my chance. I loved it that much.

"I may not have been as good as I thought I was, but I could make sparks fly when the pressure was on, in situations when I got charged up. And there's something about the thrill of winning those games that you just can't replace."

A handful of games out of a ten-year career, a dozen quarters of football when everything went right. Moments, when an athlete strikes fire with his talent. But how were they different from all the rest? What is it like when suddenly everything works?

"It's a very strange thing," said Cuozzo. "The pressure and the tension are enormous. You're scared. And then something happens. There's this click, and it's like the camera goes from fast to slow. You start seeing everything, just like it's in practice. Sometimes it's all going so fast you don't see anything—you're looking but you don't see. And then sometimes, sometimes you're the only one going fast. Everybody else is in slow motion."

A good, sound explanation, the product of the kind of reasoning that earned Cuozzo his Phi Beta Kappa in premed. And, if you listen to it carefully, it is not so different from the words of Julius Erving on the same subject. The main difference, perhaps, is that it is a subject with which Erving is infinitely more comfortable. And, like an old friend, he speaks of it with more familiarity.

"Well, I think," he said, laughing, "it probably has something to do with the sun and the moon and the stars and the tides, all coming together at that point on that one particular evening. You let it [the ball] go, and gravity takes it right through the hoop.

"It's something that happens and when it does you gotta enjoy it," he said, more serious now. "You try to savor the moment."

Then he smiled and added, "Anyhow, that's not you out there. That's somebody else."

7
THE LOWEST HILL

Bob Oliver leans against the batting cage and watches the newest prodigy on the Columbus Clippers swing the bat. It is about two hours before game time in this Ohio city, and the home team is taking its customary turn at infield and batting practice.

Oliver, an imposing figure of a man who carries 220 pounds on his 6-foot-3-inch frame, had been in the field shagging balls, and now he waits his turn at bat. He is the Clippers' first baseman and senior man on the team, and he says nothing as he stands and peers into the cage at the young player taking his cuts.

The player is Dale Berra, youngest son of Yogi Berra of New York Yankees fame. He plays third base for the Clippers, the Triple A farm team of the Pittsburgh Pirates in the International League, and is considered by the organization as a "prospect." Young Berra leads the team in home runs, and has not missed a game since making the jump from the Western Carolina League in Class A before the season.

Oliver, squinting into the afternoon sun, watches him loft an arcing fly ball over the center-field wall. "Ten years ago that was me in there," he says. "In 1967 I was on my way up."

Bob Oliver isn't on the way up anymore. He is listed as a

PHOTO BY SKIP ROZIN

Bob Oliver, briefly with Chicago on the way back down. "I had a good spring . . . but Cleon [Jones] was having an exceptional spring, and that was that."

player-coach on the Clippers 1977 roster, the property of the same Pirates organization that signed him out of junior college in 1963. Since then he has spent six years in the minors coming up, seven years in the majors with four different clubs, and two more years in the minors on the way back down.

Oliver had been invited to the White Sox camp in Sarasota in the spring of 1976 as a free agent. Along with Cleon Jones, another major leaguer in camp as a free agent, he was fighting for a designated hitter's job. The Sox decided to keep Jones, who once hit .340 with the New York Mets. That day in March when Chicago sent him down to their minor league complex was the last time Oliver had on a major league uniform.

"I had a good spring, I was hitting the ball good," he explains, "but Cleon was having an exceptional spring, and that was that."

Though it was a disappointment for Oliver, it was not his first in baseball. Trying to struggle up through the Pirates system in the mid-1960s was not easy. On the big club there were Roberto Clemente and Willie Stargell, Donn Clendenon, Bill Virdon, and Matty Alou. As a result, Oliver played his games in ball parks in Gastonia and Kingston, in Asheville, Columbus, and Macon, not in Pittsburgh.

"I had good years in the minors," Oliver had said when we talked in Sarasota, "always hitting around .300. But my position was first base, and because I could play other positions I was always getting shifted around for some kid who could hit and only play first. So I became a jack of all trades, and a master of none."

While coming up through the minors, Oliver played every position except catcher—even pitching an inning in his second season. Finally, at the end of 1967, he was traded out of the Pittsburgh organization to Minnesota, and a year later he was selected by the new Kansas City Royals in the expansion draft.

That was a break. The healthy part of Bob Oliver's professional career occurred in the next six years. He spent three good seasons with Kansas City and then nearly three more with California. While never a star, he played regularly, knocking in as many as 99 runs in one season and hitting around .260. But in his third season with the Angels something happened. The word "something" is appropriate because exactly what happened is hard to explain. Not even Oliver is sure.

"My career was going along just fine," he says. "I had good years in Kansas City, and I came over to California and did real good there. I led the team in home runs and RBIs in 1972, and had another good season in '73. But in 1974 I lost my job. I don't know why. Just like that, it ended."

Oliver came to camp overweight in 1974, and even after getting down to 217 pounds he could not seem to find the niche where he had prospered the previous two years. The Angels, themselves struggling, replaced manager Bobby Winkles with Dick Williams midway through that season, and somewhere around there Oliver got lost in the traffic.

"Dick Williams' dealings with me were very horseshit," he recalls with anger. "After the season I had in 1973 I deserved to play every day in '74 to get myself together. But it didn't happen. Williams didn't give me a chance to play and he never told me why. I just sat."

From then on the disintegration of his career was rapid. He was released on waivers to Baltimore with three weeks left in the 1974 season, and during the winter was sold to the Yankees. After a good spring he sat during the season, appearing in just eighteen games through mid-July, and was released. Not until the following spring did he even get a shot with another club, and then it was for one short month with the White Sox.

"When Chicago sent me down they said they wanted me to play with their Triple A club, and I said okay," recalls Oliver. "I went over there and hit the shit out of the ball, but they said they had too many prospects and released me. I found a place on the Philadelphia Triple A team in Oklahoma, and there is where I spent the season."

Oliver hit .325 for Oklahoma City in 1976, and, at the Phillies' suggestion, played winter ball in Venezuela. It was just after returning from South America that Philadelphia released him.

Without a job and without prospects, Oliver began making phone calls. Someone, he thought, could use a right-handed ballplayer who could field, hit, and hit with power. He called Minnesota and Cleveland, and the two expansion teams, Seattle and Toronto. And then he started on the National League, finally getting enough of a response from Pittsburgh to land a spot on their Columbus team. No talk about a future, but a job.

Now, at thirty-four, he stands and watches as if it were his own youth before him, running and hitting, sliding into bases and making the double play, reaching for the glory he never found.

"It was tough going back to the minors that first time," he says, still standing behind the batting cage, "and it's tough being here. I have so much more at stake than these kids. They're in their primes, their whole careers before them."

He watches as Berra reaches after an outside pitch and, getting just the end of the bat on the ball, sends it sailing out to right-center field.

"Now they've made me a player-coach," says Oliver, scratching his head. "I do a lot of work with these kids. I've helped Berra, here. We talk about fielding balls and about throwing balls.

"This is great. If I can be a good coach here on the Triple A level, then one day I can be a halfway decent manager in the minor leagues. And everybody knows, managing in the minors is really important to get a big league coaching job. That's what all this is about.

"But you see what's happening. They've got me thinking about coaching instead of playing. It's gotten all turned around. Suddenly my job's to help these kids make it, instead of my only concern being making it myself. That's not the way I want to be thinking. I've had a good year, good enough that they could give me a shot at the big leagues. That's where I want to be. In the big leagues, playing. Not here, teaching."

Johnny Lipon, the Clippers manager, stops behind the cage and speaks to Oliver about one of the other players on the team, a man who's been in a long batting slump. He wants his coach to work with him. Oliver agrees and then returns to what he's been saying.

"Baseball's a funny game. Maybe the Pirates don't need me, but maybe somebody else does." He pauses and his eyes narrow into a stare. "Hey, I'm not through. I'll be the first one to say when I can't do it anymore. I'll hang it up. But I can play. I'm leading this club in RBIs, and second in home runs. I can still play."

It is Oliver's turn to hit. Just as he enters the batting cage, Mike Easler, one of the young Clippers with whom he has worked, stops to ask a question. As always, Oliver answers patiently and thoroughly. But by the time he has finished, one of the other players has jumped into the cage and is hitting.

Within a few weeks, at the end of the International League season, the Pirates will call up five players from the Clippers. One will be Dale Berra; another will be Mike Easler. About that time Bob Oliver will pack up his family and take them back to California, another season having ended.

The career of the marginal athlete forms the lowest of hills. No sooner has he managed to get to the top when, to his shock and surprise, he finds himself on the way down. The trip up is filled with hard work and enthusiasm. The way back down is filled only with pain.

No athlete can remain at his peak forever. That is a simple enough truth. Even for the superstars, there is that point at which things begin to change. Skills diminish. The body begins to fail. Suddenly, what yesterday was second nature becomes a supreme effort. Tomorrow it will be impossible.

For an elite few in sports that first indication is enough. A step lost. A split second's reflexes. Nothing more. It was enough to drive Joe DiMaggio from his game. Jim Brown, Sandy Koufax, a few others. They saw things begin to change—or felt the change inside—and moved on with their lives.

But quitting at that point is hard. A genuine superstar who

loses 10 or 15 percent of his game is still a superior performer to most of the men around him. Only personal pride can force him out at such a time. And for almost every athlete, while pride is important, staying in his sport is more important. It has been his primary concern for so long that the thought of filling his life without it is terrifying. Turning away from his sport, the style of living it has permitted him, and his friends—the men with whom he's shared joy and suffering. Walking away from the excitement of being a professional athlete and into the anonymity of a nine-to-five job. Those are painful prospects. So it's not surprising that when the first call to retire comes, most athletes ignore it.

The good ones pull it off, at least for a while. It isn't that hard. They have a built-in cushion, a few years during which they can rely on superior skill and reputation to ease themselves out. Hank Aaron and Mickey Mantle, Oscar Robertson, Johnny Unitas, Willie Mays. We have all watched them in what sportswriters like to call the "twilight" of their careers, performing far below the levels that earned them their fame. They saw their careers take that inevitable turn downward, then decided to play on for a few more seasons before retiring. And why not? They're entitled. We look at them and shake our heads. We remember them in their prime, and feel compassion for them. But we don't have to face that short, lonely walk out of the spotlight and into the darkness.

Still, those capable of gradually, if not gracefully, exiting from sports form a small, select group. Most athletes are not given the opportunity. From the point where their careers change direction, what was already a shaky pursuit of survival becomes a losing effort. Slow enough at the start, it gains momentum, until the athlete becomes a solitary figure, standing defiantly in the path of the onrushing wall of time. He may resist, but soon he must be swept away.

That change, that reverse in the direction from being a good, steady performer to being expendable is usually very subtle. Few recognize that it's occurred. Often it takes the perspective of time to see just what happened and where. Sometimes it is a matter of remembering when things were good and when they were bad, and identifying the crucial period of transition as the space in between. Even then, one's reaction to it is likely to be disbelief.

For nine seasons Mike Riordan was a player in the NBA. Drafted in the twelfth round out of Providence by the New York Knicks in 1967, he came to rookie camp with the likes of Bill Bradley and Walt Frazier, and, as one might expect of a late-round pick with an established team, he got cut.

"I wasn't surprised," said Riordan, a gutsy kid out of Holy Cross High School in New York City. "I didn't really expect to get that far. In fact, I had planned on going on for my master's, and had lined up a coaching job."

But all that was before he got to camp. Just being there, wearing a uniform and working out with established NBA players, can turn the head of the most pragmatic of men. And Riordan, who had played in the shadow of Jimmy Walker at Providence and was accustomed to having his value minimized, was suddenly very committed to basketball.

"I was physically prepared for camp," he recalled, "but I didn't think I had much of a chance. Then when I got there and started playing, it all felt right. And when I lasted to the very end, I knew I could make it. Even if I couldn't play for the Knicks, I knew I could play someplace."

With the Knicks's assistance he played that 1967 season with Allentown in the Eastern league, served in the National Guard where they placed him (the draft was still very active at that time) and "had a little extra money thrown" his way. And, when he came back the next fall, he made the team.

"At first I just played a little," he said, recalling that first season in the NBA. "I'd come in to give fouls and stuff. I got a lot of ribbing from the fans [they used to call him a goon and a thug] but I didn't mind. I was just happy to be there. But you keep raising your goals. The next year I wasn't satisfied just to be there. I wanted to play. And after a while, I wanted to start. You always want more."

Riordan, at 6 feet 4 inches tall, was between guard and forward, not quite right for either in size, but what he lacked in natural ability and height he made up in energy and determination. And when he was traded in 1972 to Baltimore he got his first real chance to play regularly, first as a third guard, and even for a few happy though shaky seasons in the starting lineup at what the Bullets called "small forward."

"The years starting were super," said Riordan, a friendly, polite man who nonetheless carried the look of potential violence, as if the wrong question could provoke a punch in the mouth. "I played my best basketball as a starter, even though I always felt a need to be looking over my shoulder."

Then midway through the 1975–76 season it happened. He was platooned with Nick Weatherspoon, a forward three inches taller than Riordan and five years younger. As the season drew to an end, Riordan's playing time diminished.

"I really didn't understand what was happening when they began to platoon me," he said during that season, his eighth in the league. "I figured it was just a bad period—I had been through others—and I would come out of it."

But he didn't. Things just got worse. The following year was Riordan's most difficult in the league. He played in only forty-nine games, even fewer than during his first season with New York.

"When the season started I knew things were different," he recalled. "But I figured, okay, this is the beginning of a prolonged phase of playing part time. I could handle that for a few years. The next step after that was being out of the game. I knew that—it had to come. But I figured it would be years."

As the season wore on, however, Riordan played less and less.

"It's a terrible thing to go through," he said after one of the many Bullets games that season in which he saw no action at all. "And I still don't know how it happened. One season I was part of things; now, suddenly, I'm not. I'm still here, but I'm not."

PHOTO COURTESY WASHINGTON BULLETS

Mike Riordan, racing toward the end: "One season I was part of things; now, suddenly, I'm not."

In less than two seasons with the Bullets he passed through all the stages of his basketball career, like a drowning man watching his life pass before him.

"I thought of going in and talking to the coach," said Riordan, referring to Dick Motta, then in his first season with the Bullets, "but I think that would be unproductive. He would tell me his reasons, and there would be nothing I could counter with. It's a subjective thing. All he could say is that if I'm not happy here I could . . ." and his voice trailed off.

"No matter what the situation is," he said, "I'm still on a team. I'm not going to start bitching and start trouble."

So he sat, and watched his teammates play the game he'd loved since he was a child.

"Being part of it is still fun," he said. "The traveling, the locker room camaraderie—that's still fun. But it culminates in nothing. Games are no fun, and they were always the best part. Now all my games are played in practice."

Not only did Riordan's point production diminish with his reduced playing time, so did his effectiveness. Starting from 1972 to 1974, he hit close to 50 percent of his shots from the field, while scoring 18.1 and 15.9 points a game. Coming off the bench in the 1975–76 season his percentage dropped to .440 and his scoring average to 8.4. The following season he hit on only 36 percent of his shots, and scored only 1.6 points a game.

"It's tough coming in and being cold," he said, echoing the words of so many part-time players. "By the time you get warm you're out of the game. But I guess it's something I'm going to have to get used to."

It was not an easy adjustment. Where basketball had always been a very physical experience, that season it became an intellectual exercise.

"While you're still on the bench you try and stay in the game mentally," he said, "following the flow and making decisions on each play along the way. But your mind strays. You wonder why you're not out there. And you know, inside, that you can still play."

But the torment was not restricted to the basketball court. It rarely is. Whatever is going on in an athlete's sport spills over into his personal life. Riordan, married and with three children, learned that all too well.

"Mostly you're thinking about yourself, about how it's affecting you personally," he said, reflecting back on those last two painful years. "Then you begin to see how it's affecting the people around you. You'd have to be blind not to see it."

He talked about the pressure on his family, how the mood throughout the household changed as his role on the court changed, falling from productive, active athlete to a man helpless to stem the slipping away of his career.

"There are a lot of down periods and you're not any fun to be around," he said. "It affects every aspect of your life. Your wife hangs with you. She knows how important it is and she can see what's happening. But even that gets tough; a person can only take so much. But it's much worse with the kids. They know something's wrong—they can see it in you. But there's no way they can understand what it is.

"You see all this happening and you want to ignore it, but you just can't. So you try and restrict the down periods to your basketball. That's hard. It makes an already difficult thing harder, and you can only keep it up for so long."

The problem did not continue that long. At the end of the 1976–77 season Riordan talked with the Bullets front office to see what their plans for him were for the coming season. As Riordan put it, "They had none."

"I've been talking to people [on other teams]," he said during that off-season, "but there doesn't seem to be a market for me. I'm still running and keeping in shape, but soon I'll have to make a decision. Either I go full time in working out, or I just give it up."

He sighed, "It just doesn't seem possible that it's all over."

Mike Riordan's surprise at how quickly his career turned around is a familiar reaction. Most athletes wonder where it all went. They know they did not suddenly get old or lose their skill. They too feel that, given a chance, they could still play.

They probably could. But somewhere along the way, from one season to the next, something changed. Maybe it was that one year they added. Riordan was thirty-two that season, his ninth in the league. The Bullets might have figured it was time to start moving someone younger into his spot. Or maybe it's a change in administration, the departure of one coach who knows a man's special value and the arrival of another coach who only knows the record book. The Bullets changed coaches before that season, and that could have hurt. It could be almost anything that does it, turning a happy, reliable athlete into a man on the edge. It happens every day, and few men know how.

Only those players whose careers turn on an injury don't have to wonder. For men like Wayne Mulligan, the center for the Jets, there is no difficulty spotting where and how the end began. It is clearly documented in medical charts and operating reports. And should they forget, for even one moment, they have the scars as handy reminders, scars on the mind as well as the body. For not only do serious injuries rob an athlete of his strength, speed, and agility, they attack his spirit and confidence which, as much as muscles and ligaments, are the fibers that hold his career together.

Ron Blomberg started the 1976 baseball season with the Yankees full of hope and enthusiasm. He had injured his shoulder during the previous season, but had worked hard to regain his previous form and fight his way back into the Yankees lineup. That form had gotten him selected first in all of baseball in the 1967 free agent draft, and it had moved him quickly through the New York farm system.

He was a quiet, sensitive young man who maintained a close relationship with his mother and father back in Atlanta even after signing with the Yankees and making it to the big leagues, often calling home long distance for their support. But he covered his private insecurity with a public façade of bravado, giving the appearance of being gregarious, confident, and occasionally even loud—the "jock" image.

While not known for great defensive ability, Blomberg was

an excellent hitter from the start, with special success against right-handed pitchers. He had some trouble with lefties, especially those with a good curve ball. While he was playing Triple A ball—the level where serious coaching takes place—the emphasis was on winning games instead of teaching young players, and so he was platooned and ended up watching most of his left-handed opposition from the dugout.

Somewhat handicapped, Blomberg still proved to be a valuable player for New York over his first five seasons. Playing mostly against right-handed pitchers, he carried a lifetime average of .302 into the spring of 1976. He had begun as a first baseman, was switched to the outfield, and back to first base. Finally he settled in as the Yankees' designated hitter—officially the first in the majors—and was perfectly happy. Hitting was always what he most enjoyed.

In the days before the opening of the Yankees' Fort Lauderdale camp in 1976, Blomberg—nicknamed The Boomer—felt everything was working for him. He had avoided a serious operation after his injury in 1975, and with apparent success. Meanwhile, he was carrying on a love affair with New York and with baseball. He talked about being part of the city, about being involved with many facets of the community, about the work he did for the Yankees, and about the special relationship between him and the fans, especially the Jewish fans in the metropolitan area.

"The Jewish people sort of look up to me as an idol," he said, "because there are not too many Jewish athletes. I do a lot of charity work, and I meet a lot of influential people. That's important to me, being part of the community. I respond to the fans and they respond to me."

He recalled with emotion how, after he had been out with a leg injury in 1973, a crowd of 50,000 at Yankee Stadium stood and cheered his first pinch-hitting appearance. He was a man living the American Dream.

"Athletes are something special in this country," he said before the beginning of spring training. "Actors and politicians, they all want athletes to be their friends. I was in Califor-

PHOTO COURTESY UPI, INC.

Ron Blomberg, as a rookie in 1967, between Yankee veterans Joe Pepitone (left) and Tom Tresh. "God gave me the ability to hit a baseball. . . ."

nia and Milton Berle came up and asked me for my autograph. Uncle Milty! It wiped me out for a year.

"Some people can maybe field better than me," he said, shifting subjects, "but God gave me the ability to hit a baseball, and I don't think anyone can hit a baseball better than me."

He felt good about himself and about the Yankees. Tanned and healthy looking from being south for the winter, he was looking forward to the new season. He was only twenty-seven and, despite a history of nagging if not debilitating injuries and the look of worry that often accompanies a man losing his hair, he was confident about the future.

"I have a fantasy," he said, lowering his voice. "I see Phil Rizzuto announcing my name at an old-timers day in fifteen or twenty years, and the people going nuts. And when I get out to the outfield, I have a monument out there next to Ruth and Gehrig."

It was a good, honest fantasy, dreamed by a man who felt he was within reaching distance of anything he wanted. But soon after that things started to go sour for Ronald Mark Blomberg.

Midway through the exhibition season, while swinging a bat, he reinjured the shoulder that had given him trouble in the previous season. This time there was little question. Surgery would be necessary, and Blomberg would miss virtually all of the season.

While he worked hard to get himself back into shape after the operation, exercising at the Stadium and at a gym near his home in Riverdale, he began to feel more and more removed from his team and his sport.

The Yankees won the pennant in 1976, but Blomberg had no part in it. And though he received a full share of playoff and World Series money, only Elliott Maddox among his teammates called to see how he was progressing, and no one from the organization called to invite him to any of the games. As the date drew closer for the expansion draft in the American League, the rumors were that Blomberg would not be protected.

"Mentally I've already left this club," he said before the draft took place. "When I cleaned out my locker after the last game, I tore up my yearbook and put 1976 out of my mind. I don't know where I'll be next season, but I'm sure it won't be New York. It hurts, but that's how it is."

But Blomberg was damaged goods, and he was not selected in the draft by either Toronto or Seattle. And while he tried to concentrate his attention on the 1977 season, his old enthusiasm was not there.

"I came down here [to Fort Lauderdale] five weeks early to get ready," he said during spring training. "I know I want to play, but I don't know where I'll be. I never thought I'd be saying that, but I've changed. I've been educated."

Blomberg knew he would be fighting for a job that spring, the Yankees roster having been beefed up with such established names as Reggie Jackson, Paul Blair, Jim Wynn, and Carlos May. And there was the attitude of the Yankees owner, George Steinbrenner, who let it be known that Blomberg's position with the team was precarious.

Blomberg, who always tended to press, reacted by pressing even harder. He was determined to prove he was as good as ever. And while he started off well, there came that fateful afternoon in an exhibition game when a line drive took off over his head. For years he had heard the taunts about his poor fielding, taunts that hurt him deeply, and he raced for the ball at full speed, glove outstretched. There should have been a warning from the centerfielder that he was nearing the wall, but if it came he never heard it, and he crashed into the fortified cement, shattering his knee on impact and then crumpling to the ground.

The name of Ron Blomberg slipped from the Yankees vocabulary after that. There were cruel jokes by some of the newer players about his "dogging it" while picking up his $50,000 salary, and indifference expressed by the front office. While his number "12" was not issued to any of the thirty-eight men who wore pinstripes that season, his locker was used by the batboys—"while I was still in the hospital," says Blomberg—and later issued to one of the young players up from Syracuse in the International League. So Blomberg became a ghost, drifting further and further out of the organization consciousness.

At precisely what point the process was completed it is hard to say. It probably began when he suffered his first injury. The odds against an athlete's completely recovering from serious surgery are always high. The instant such an operation is scheduled a red light goes on in the brain of the organization. At some point Ron Blomberg stopped being the team's desig-

Ron Blomberg, after signing with the White Sox in 1978. "It was like being brought back from the dead."

PHOTO BY SKIP ROZIN

nated hitter in recuperation and became a name being dutifully carried on the injured reserve list, a name all but forgotten. Exactly when that happened is not only impossible to learn, it is immaterial. The important fact is that within two and a half years, while going to bat just twice, an athlete saw his career and his life make a complete turnaround, one from which few are able to recover.

Fortunately for Ron Blomberg, the current situation in baseball in general plus one sensitive individual in particular combined to offer him an additional chance. Declaring himself a free agent in the 1978 reentry draft, he was selected by Bill Veeck of the White Sox—a man with one leg, who seems to have a special understanding for men fighting their way back from injury. Chicago signed Blomberg to a four-year, $600,000 contract.

"It was like being brought back from the dead," said Blomberg after he signed. "I thought my baseball career was over, and now I feel like a rookie again."

Still, he was nearly three years out of the game, a difficult absence to ignore. And as the middle of the 1978 season approached, The Boomer was still a man looking for his timing.

"I'm struggling," he said, hitting at just .203 into June. "I know that. But they've given me a chance, and I'm going to make it back."

Most players are not so fortunate as Ron Blomberg was to get such an opportunity. Usually that crippling injury that removes a player from the scene for a season or more also costs him his career. The story of Blomberg and the Yankees is far from unique. The names change from team to team and sport to sport, but the story is repeated, over and over.

Often, however, there are no signposts: no day in practice when a knee popped, no game in which a collision resulted in a torn shoulder muscle. Sometimes, strange as it seems, dramatic reversals in the direction of a man's career take place somewhere beyond natural vision, quietly, in the middle of some dark night. *Shazam!* One instant you have a strong young athlete, capable of exceptional performances, and the next instant you don't. Unlike the case of Mike Riordan, age is not a factor. The same man is there, but his talent is gone.

Perhaps such occurrences are more a mystery to us than they should be. The skills of sports—throwing a baseball to a prescribed point, hitting the pitched ball, tossing a basketball into a hoop while not looking, catching a football in midair amidst a crowd of defenders—are so precise that they almost amount to God-given abilities. And as they are given, so can they be taken away.

One such victim was Sammy Ellis, who in the mid-1960s was one of the best young pitchers in baseball. He came up with the Cincinnati Reds, and, while working mostly as a relief pitcher in his rookie season of 1964, compiled an impressive

10–3 record while giving up just 2.58 earned runs a game. The following year, as a starter, he was 22–10.

"It all seemed so easy," said Ellis, who was working as a minor league pitching coach in the summer of 1977. "I always worked hard at what I did, but everything just fell into place at the beginning. I was on top of the world."

Then, suddenly and without any reason that Ellis could explain, his world came apart. He got off to a horrendous start in 1966, losing 11 of his first thirteen games. Glimpses of his old form appeared from time to time (he won five straight games in the middle of the summer) but the overall season was a disaster. And the next year was worse.

"I just couldn't seem to put it back together," Ellis tried to explain. "I was okay for a game or two, then I'd go back for three or four games. I was healthy; my arm was sound. I don't think it was a head thing; I wasn't going crazy. I just couldn't pitch."

He was traded in 1968 to the California Angels, where he was 9–10, and in 1969, with the Chicago White Sox, he was 0–3. He spent part of 1969 in the minor leagues, pitching poorly in Triple A with Portland, and even worse with Tulsa in 1970. In 1971 he dropped down to the old Dixie Association with Birmingham in Double A. And there, his career having become a down escalator, he got off.

In 1977 Samuel Joseph Ellis was employed by the Fort Lauderdale Yankees, New York's Class A team in the Florida State League. Since he had had such vast experience with pitching problems, he felt he would be a good pitching coach. The Yankees agreed.

Sammy Ellis sits in the home dugout of the young Yankees while the team works out in the field. He is a tall, attractive man just past his thirty-sixth birthday, and obviously in good condition. Earlier, at the beginning of practice, he was out on the field, running, keeping in shape. Now he sits on the long, slatted bench, dressed in baseball pants and shirt and a blue windbreaker. In his right hand he holds a baseball, which he continually moves back and forth in a pitching motion.

"It's hard to explain," he says, talking about the mysterious phenomenon which cost him his career. "I just seemed to lose my rhythm. Something was wrong mechanically and I couldn't figure out what it was."

As he sat there, talking, it was easy to remember Ellis when he came up with the Reds. He was strong and confident, almost cocky, with a blazing fastball to support his ego. He had light brown hair then, and his 179 pounds were tight on his 6-feet-1-inch frame. Now his hair is mixed with gray, he seems more fidgety, and though he is within five pounds of his old playing weight, twenty pounds of excess have come off since he arrived in camp in the spring.

"The strange thing was that as late as 1971," he is saying, "I could go to the outfield and throw the ball as hard and as far and with as much life as I could when I was twenty years old. But on the mound I just couldn't throw."

Even now, six years after he gave up pitching, there is a tone of disbelief in his voice, as if he's still asking how it could have happened. He describes his feelings when suddenly, without warning, he could no longer do the one thing he had done so naturally for so long, and there is pain in his words.

"It was horrible," he says. "I got to the point where it 'bout drove me up a tree. I came close at times to having a nervous breakdown. I couldn't keep my mind on anything else. You've got to understand. When you're a pitcher, when your life is based on how well you throw a baseball, and all of a sudden you just can't do it, it dumps you upside down."

He stops and looks at the ball in his right hand, then watches himself go through the motion of pitching.

"I even threw all winter, twice, trying to get that feel back," he says. "I had a few movies at home, and I looked at those till I damn near wore them out. But I couldn't find that one intangible that would make it all fall back into place."

He interrupts himself to point out one of the young Fort

Lauderdale pitchers with whom he has been working, taking pride in his progress. He mentions some of the pitching coaches who had worked with him (Jim Turner, Bob Lemon, Warren Spahn, and others) and adds that he should be an expert by now at dealing with pitching problems.

"The White Sox traded me to Cleveland," he says, "and Cleveland sent me down to Portland, saying that if I was okay they'd bring me back. My arm was still sound, and I knew if I could put it back together I'd be okay."

But he didn't. He had a rough half-season in Portland, and at spring training with the Indians in 1970 he was released.

"That was the first time it really stood up and slapped me in the face," he says. "I knew I was in trouble. I hooked on with the Cardinals, and they sent me to Tulsa. It wasn't even good down there. I just couldn't seem to find it. There I was, back in the minors, and I still couldn't put it together. I was embarrassed and I was confused. I kept asking myself, *Where did it all go?* After six weeks in Tulsa I was released."

Ellis sat out the rest of the summer, then signed with Oakland's Double A team in Birmingham for the 1971 season. He pitched well enough to win there but, as he says, "I was doing it with experience." He still didn't feel right.

"But my arm was sound," he says again, and the words come out as an echo. "I never gave up the idea that I would be okay. Every time I dropped down a level I thought to myself, *It went away—it'll come back.* But it never did."

Ellis never found an explanation for what happened to his pitching skill. He now thinks, looking back, that it was some little change in his arm action that threw off his rhythm. He thinks that if he'd known that ten years ago he might have saved his career. That, of course, is conjecture. All Ellis knows for certain is that when he finally quit after Birmingham he'd had it. He was tired and humiliated. He wanted out of baseball.

Back home in Tampa, he got involved in the real estate

Sammy Ellis, now a coach helping young pitchers with their problems, recalls his own horror: "I thought to myself, *It went away—it'll come back.* But it never did."

business and was quite successful. But as the years passed and the pain of his lost career eased, his love for the game returned. He started playing ball again—just for recreation—and then came the longing to get back in uniform, in any capacity.

"I missed being outside in the sunshine and I missed being in shape," he said. "I missed wearing a uniform and talking with other players. I missed it all."

He missed it so much that he got in touch with the Yankees and asked for a job.

"I've felt great since I been back," he said. "I'm in shape, and I can pitch better today than I did when I was released that last time. I feel good out there," and he pointed to the mound.

Does that mean he might consider a comeback effort?

"I wouldn't go through that again for anything in the world," he said. "I wouldn't go out there and embarrass myself again. Not for anything."

Sammy Ellis' story is special because the change was so abrupt. One year he was getting batters out with ease, and the next year he wasn't getting them out at all. He won 22 games in 1965, and lost 19 in 1966. It has happened to others. Steve Blass won two World Series games for Pittsburgh in 1971, won 19 games with a 2.49 ERA in 1972, and couldn't find home plate a year later. John Brockington, who rushed for more than 1,000 yards in each of his first three seasons with Green Bay and a total of 4,159 from 1971 through 1974, was waived by the Packers after the 1976 season and remained unclaimed by any other NFL team for the $100 waiver price.

In none of these cases could an injury be blamed for the collapse. Suddenly the man found that he could no longer do what he had done before. It would be easy to sit back and hypothesize that it's the pressure that finally gets to him, that at some point all the tension of performing before packed gymnasiums and ball parks takes its toll, and that the place where it breaks through is in his ability to perform. It's possible, even plausible, but also conjecture. The only certain thing is that it's gone. And with it goes his career.

Once that process begins, it's almost impossible to reverse. Even *if* an athlete could find whatever key he lost to his talent, getting someone to believe in him would take a Herculean effort. For once he drops from the active consciousness of the establishment of sports, he's just another phone call on somebody's callback list. And in this business nobody ever seems to call back.

Any interruption in the career of the average athlete—caused by an off-season or an injury, or maybe a trade to a team where he just doesn't fit—and, before he has an opportunity to recover, he is likely to discover it's too late. Visibility of talent and consistent performance—at whatever level—are crucial, especially to the fringe player. A star's talents are more special, and any lapse in their obvious presence elicits patience. But once a marginal athlete gives any reason for doubt about his ability to compete successfully for his job, professional sports has little use for him. All the hoopla and the huge salaries are predicated on one constant: the athlete's being able to perform better than the others contending for his job.

This is one of the most uncompromising realities in sports. "Loyalty," a popular term, is commonly used by front offices when decrying a player's demands for more money or to be traded. Rarely does it come up when an aging or recuperating player wants time to work himself back into his game. And though these are the ground rules—rules everyone knows—living through them can be tragic. An athlete who is on the downside of his career remembers the pampering in high school and college, the scouts who came to his home and bought his mother a new stove, the draft and the generous contract he signed, and all of the years of pandering when he was playing well. Then, suddenly, an off-season or two, and no one knows his name. It's a shock.

It took Nate Colbert five years to work his way through the minor leagues and establish himself as the first baseman for the San Diego Padres. Once there, he did a good job with the expansion team. He was a better than average fielder, and he hit with power. Noticeable power. In his six years with the Padres he averaged 80 runs batted in and 30 home runs a season. Twice he hit 38 homers and he still holds the club records for singles, doubles, home runs, runs scored and runs batted in—virtually all offensive categories.

But in 1974 San Diego picked up Willie McCovey from San Francisco, a west coast favorite and major draw, and Colbert was relegated to the outfield and pinch-hitting duties. At the end of the season he was traded to Detroit.

"When I went to Detroit [in 1975] I said, 'Give me time, just give me time,' " he said later. "No matter how hard I work, I always get off to a slow start. It takes me about 200 at-bats before I get rolling. But they said they didn't have that much time."

After a disappointing season in Detroit, his worst in the

majors, Colbert was sold to Montreal midway through June and the following year was released. He signed with Oakland for the club's Triple A team in Tucson, and there he dropped out of sight.

"It's the strangest thing," said Colbert, a huge man with a thick black mustache that covers much of his face, "but sometimes baseball stops recognizing that a player exists. That's what happened to me. They just wiped what I was and what I did away."

He was talking in the visiting dugout of the Toronto Blue Jays one afternoon in the spring of 1977. Colbert had been invited to the expansion team's new camp as a free agent, offered a chance to make the team.

"I've seen it happen before," he said. "Guys just disappear. I saw it with Roy Foster, once Rookie of the Year in the American League. The next season he hit .270, then he was traded, and then he went to the minors. Just like that—gone."

He was sitting on the bench, holding onto his personally designed model Louisville Slugger bat as if someone were going to take it away.

"You don't forget how to hit overnight," he said. "If I was good enough to play regular for six years, getting off to one bad season shouldn't change all that. But I guess they figure those good years were a fluke, and I'm getting down to my level now."

It was after Colbert lost his job in San Diego, and went through two years of bouncing around to three different clubs in three different leagues, that he decided he might be better off making a deal for himself. So he became a free agent at the end of the 1976 season, along with players like Reggie Jackson and Don Gullett and Joe Rudi, entering his name in the reentry draft of that November.

But while thirteen different clubs elected to bid for the services of Jackson, Gullett, and Rudi, no team selected the name of Nate Colbert. Of the twenty-four men involved in the draft, only he and Willie McCovey were not drafted. And when

McCovey signed with San Francisco, Colbert became the only man not to end up with a team.

"The day of the draft I was waiting by the phone to see who drafted me," said Colbert. "The only call I got was from a reporter asking how it felt to be one of only two players not picked."

He tried to smile but couldn't. "I really couldn't believe it. My lawyer made some phone calls and sent out some résumés—you hear that, résumés, asking for a job—and all we got back were feelers for pinch-hitting spots. Hell, I should be at my peak, but nobody wants to give me a chance to prove it."

Apparently Toronto was being very cautious about giving him that chance. Just before opening camp they traded one of their young prospects, Mike Weathers, and $30,000 to Oakland for Ron Fairly, a veteran best suited for the same first base/designated hitter role for which Colbert was competing. Their investment was in Fairly, and in the young players who would be their future. After a spring in which Colbert played in only eight games he was released, though he was hitting .316 at the time, higher than anyone else contending for the job. But Colbert was a question mark, a man who had not played in the majors in a year and not played well in three. Despite what he had done before and what he showed that spring, whatever talent he still possessed was simply not visible enough.

What happened to Colbert is a classic example of the way a sports organization treats an athlete who may be qualified for a particular job, but in whom that organization has no interest. It is as if they feel an obligation to invite him to camp to demonstrate their open-mindedness, but then they proceed to ignore him. It happens with appalling regularity: a young athlete drafted or invited to camp by a team already amply supplied with his particular talent; an older athlete brought in "for a look-see" when it is already known what he can and cannot do. It may be a necessary lesson for the rookie—better that he should learn early what the game is about. But for the older player it takes on a quality of tragedy. Listen as Gary Cuozzo describes his last confrontation with pro football, at the St. Louis Cardinals camp prior to the 1973 season:

"It was clear that I wasn't welcome," he said. "It was the first time I ever got the sense of being invisible. The coaches don't talk to you like they used to. If you make a mistake, they don't seem to care."

Not only would a player's time be better spent with a team that actively was looking for someone with his abilities, but the experience of being brought into camp and then ignored is painful and humiliating.

"I really felt good when Peter Bavasi [Blue Jays general manager] invited me to camp," said Nate Colbert. "But from the time I got there I knew they'd already made a decision. They weren't looking at me. I'd play a game as the DH or at first, get my hits, then sit while someone else played the next two days. Nobody talked to me, nobody made me feel like I was part of the team."

Colbert was talking from his home in Encinitas, California. It was the fall of 1977, eight months after he had been released by Toronto. He had given up baseball and was working as a stockbroker.

"I walked around like a ghost," he said. "Nothing I did in a game seemed to make any difference. From the record that spring you'd think I won a job. But how could I when I was never really there?"

He could have gone back down to the minors, hoping for another chance to make it back. But he had done that once, and it isn't an easy road. The poor playing conditions, the low pay, the cheaper and older equipment, the hand-me-down uniforms, they're all light years away from the excitement and glory of the major leagues. And those who do choose that path know it's tough to reverse their direction. The major leaguers of all sports have a poignant way of characterizing that particular adjustment. I remember Steve Kline, who had pitched in the big leagues with New York and Cleveland, as he sat on the floor of the Toledo Mud Hens locker room and opened a packet of letters sent down from the Indians. He looked at the front of one envelope and read aloud what was written there. "Steve Kline, Cleveland Indians, Cleveland, Ohio."

Kline smiled as he opened the letter. "I guess they don't know I died."

Death. That's how they see it. Just a flip expression, but it does convey the disappointment of being sent down. Still, most go, at least for the first time. Because whatever chance they have of making it back lies there. The structure of baseball is very helpful in that way. So long as a man can still play and so long as his ego doesn't get in the way, there is always a team somewhere that will give him a job.

Veteran players exercise the option all the time. Ten years after the Washington Senators released him, Minnie Minoso, at the age of fifty, was still playing baseball in the Mexican League. And there are plenty of others, especially in the Mexican and Pacific Coast leagues. Just looking through the 1978 edition of the *Baseball Guide*, names like Dick Selma, Diego Segui, Hal King, Clay Kirby, and Horacio Pina appeared. Among the leaders in the Pacific and Central leagues of Japan that same year were Leron Lee, Roger Repoz, and Hal Breeden. All are baseball players long out of the majors. Out then, but not necessarily forever. For as long as they're in uniform, somewhere, there is always a chance. And every once in a while one of them makes it back. For their pennant drive in 1977 the Dodgers reached into the Mexican League and picked up Vic Davalillo, then thirty-eight years old and out of the majors since 1974.

While similar kinds of opportunities do exist in other American sports, baseball's minor leagues—and the game's great popularity in Japan—make finding a place much easier. A professional football or basketball player being pushed out of his job has no choice but to leave the country if he hopes to find a well-structured and well-financed league other than our own majors. Canada has a thriving professional football league where many Americans play when they can't make it in the NFL. For basketball players, it's a longer trip. The only place where anything resembling major pro basketball is played besides the NBA is across the Atlantic, where leagues in Britain and Scandinavia and on the Continent provide jobs for hundreds of Americans each year. (About ninety Americans played on the 240 basketball teams in France alone during the 1977–78 season.)

But if a player wants to remain in the United States, he has fewer options. All he can hope for is to find another team, one less rich in talent than the team he's leaving, someplace where the abilities he has left will be appreciated for a while.

Some players adjust to this reasonably well. Their careers fall into two distinct parts. The first part is usually spent with their first team, in their prime, and the second as nomads, fitting in wherever they are needed. Dave Bing was drafted first by Detroit of the NBA and spent nine seasons with the Pistons, but since 1975 he has changed teams three times. Pat Toomay, who was drafted by and spent five fine seasons as a defensive end with the Dallas Cowboys, spent 1975, 1976, and 1977 with three different teams.

Other plays don't adjust that well. For some, the shock of that first trade is terminal. For others it takes longer, but the effect is similar. One with whom it finally caught up was Neal Walk, who was the second basketball player drafted out of college in 1969, signing with the Phoenix Suns. Walk, who was big (6 feet 10 inches tall and 230 pounds) and aggressive when he entered the league, put in five top seasons with the Suns, averaging 20.2 points a game and pulling down 1,006 rebounds in his finest season, 1972–73.

Then in 1974 he was traded to New Orleans, and in 1975 on to the New York Knicks, and when he arrived at the Knicks training camp for his second season there he had the feeling he was going to be moving again.

"I feel added pressure this season," he said when he arrived in camp, referring to the influx of rookies and new players from the defunct ABA. "But I've prepared. I ran twice a day and I lifted weights once a day, six days a week. I've worked hard because I want to make this team. I want to stay here."

It was all to no avail. Soon after the season opened, and

after playing very little in either the exhibition season or the first few games of the real season, Walk was cut. But a man of his size, ability, and age (he was just twenty-eight at the time) needn't go long without work in the NBA. He was contacted by Detroit, a team in need of a backup center.

Walk, however, never fit into any of the conventional athlete stereotypes. Born in Cleveland, he grew up in a prosperous section of Miami Beach, then went on to star at the University of Florida. And despite his fine team play on the court, he was an individualist bordering on being a loner. He liked to talk in metaphysical terms that drove the press crazy, and permitted no meat in his diet. When the call from Detroit came, he was not pleased.

"I love basketball," he said from inside the thick growth of black beard which encases his face. But I don't want to go to Detroit. The people seem serious enough, and they've made me a reasonable offer. But I just don't want to go there."

He was sitting in a restaurant on the upper West Side of Manhattan, sipping from a glass of beer in between sentences and trying to get comfortable in a chair designed for a person considerably smaller.

"They tell me that if I don't play in Detroit now I'll never play basketball again," he said without explaining who "they" were. "I don't want to hear that stuff. That's a threat, and I don't like being threatened. Besides, I don't believe it. I'll sit out a year and try some camp next season. I'm not quitting. I still want to play. But I'm tired of being forced to go play where and when I don't want to."

He drained one glass of beer and ordered a second, and while he waited for it he began munching on a large bowl of salad.

"This is my third team," he said, "and I'm tired of being shuffled around. I'd begun to like it here. I've got a place in Connecticut, and I've got some friends. And my dog likes it here too. Detroit's not a bad place. I just don't particularly like it, and I don't want to spend seven months of the year there. I should have some say about where I live and work."

Neal Walk's attitude is unusual among athletes. Sports is a business not well suited to free thinkers. The game is played by the rules, and owners and general managers make those rules. Players who insist upon challenging them—unless they are recognized superstars—suffer.

"We're just meat on the hook," said Walk, bending his index finger into the shape of a hook. "I just don't know if I want to live like that anymore."

It isn't a pleasant image, but neither is it far from the truth. Athletes are properties, commodities to be bought, sold, traded, and, occasionally, disposed of. Players frequently discuss this inhumanity, but rarely do they defy the system. What they usually do is try and take as much advantage of it as they can while they are young and in their prime, demanding as much salary as the market will allow. They all know that soon enough whatever leverage they have will be lost, gone with the passage of time and their own diminished skills. And they know that if they want to remain in their sport the only way is to accept whatever job is offered under whatever conditions. Some, like Neal Walk, refuse to be forced into situations that they consider unsatisfactory. Curt Flood was another, a player who, when facing a trade at the end of his career, simply refused to leave his home and play where he did not want to. His actions eventually resulted in the loosening of the owners' iron control of their players, but it drove Flood from baseball. Most athletes aren't willing to go that far. They take whatever situations are available to them, and make the best of it.

One of the better adjusters in sports was Norman Bailey Snead, who could make the best out of almost any situation. In 1976 Snead played in his sixteenth season in the NFL. Only Earl Morrall and Jim Marshall had more seniority that year. But on the subject of longevity—and the price and the rewards of a player's hanging on past his prime—no one in the league could hold the floor against the gentleman quarterback from Wake Forest.

"Frankly, there have been times when it didn't seem worth it," he said during that 1976 season. "In 1974 with the Giants

I had made a home in Connecticut—wife, kids, house, everything. Then the Giants traded me. When that happens you think about quitting. Then the next day in San Francisco you throw a 50-yard touchdown pass and it's the greatest thrill you could possibly feel and you say, God, yes, it's worth it.

"You know, when you throw that thing in the air and see it caught, see the guy cross the goal line, and the official's arms go into the air, the goosepimples go up and down your back. I'm not comparing it to sex or anything, but it's something."

It's easy to tell from talking to Snead that he enjoyed most of his years in the NFL. Despite his "advanced" age of thirty-seven, he was one of the true children of sports. A quiet man with a broad, lively smile, he might grant an interview one day, answering each question with thoughtful, intelligent answers in his gentle Southern accent, and another day, deciding he preferred not to talk, go running out of the locker room, leaping over benches and laughing all the way.

Whether or not that's the way Snead was before he began playing football is hard to say. Constant, daily insecurity over a prolonged period can have a residual effect. And while he played the bulk of his career for just two teams—Washington and Philadelphia—he was not known as a winner. In fact, he was involved in just one winning season out of his first ten as a pro.

"I've worried about being cut since my first day with Washington," said Snead, "and I'm still worried about it. You never get used to that. When it's cut day you just wait for that guy to come around and knock on your door. I've seen men weep. What it's like is dying."

Though Snead never got accustomed to the feeling, he had lots of practice. In the last seven years of his career he was cut or traded five times.

"You get to know the signs," he said. "There's always some young quarterback on the squad, and suddenly one day he isn't making any mistakes. Usually when there's a young guy he makes mistakes and they can turn to the older guy and say,

'Look, this is how you do it.' But then that day comes when they don't do that, and you say, 'Oh, oh, here it comes.'

"When you're cut you ask what the reasons are. They say first of all you're too old and second you make too much money. Then you ask, 'Does that mean I can't play?' They say, 'No, no, you can still play,' and you feel better. That old 'Yeah, I can still do it.' Silly, but you feel better. You've got no job, but you feel better."

He was talking in the New York Giants locker room, at their camp in Pleasantville, New York, in 1976, before the new facilities in New Jersey were ready. It was eight o'clock in the morning, before anyone else had arrived for the day's practice. That was during his second stint with the Giants. He had been traded to San Francisco midway through the 1974 season, and when the 49ers cut him in '76 New York picked him up.

"I wish people understood what living under that pressure is like," he said. "Abilities are so close, and you never know who they're going to keep and who they're going to cut. I've seen more guys crack under the emotional and psychological trauma than the physical thing."

At the time the Giants were in the midst of a nine-game losing streak, and Snead talked about the pressure on Craig Morton, the starting quarterback. He talked about the feeling of hearing 60,000 people booing, and the pressure of being told you're not going to play anymore.

"The pressure," said Snead, "is that you've got to take that and play with it. The booing and the abuse, the fans calling you a son-of-a-bitch with your wife and kids sitting right there. And when they cut you and tell you you can't do it, you've got to go someplace else and prove that you can."

If there is so much emotional strain and physical abuse (Snead had three knee operations) what makes it worth playing?

"I love it," he said, smiling. "I love the game and I love the people in it. I love all the craziness, the going to bars and drinking beer and telling stories. I love this locker room."

He stopped and looked around the room, which was begin-

PHOTO COURTESY NEW YORK GIANTS

Norman Snead, in his customary pose, waiting. "I understand that if I want to stay in football that is the job open to me."

ning to fill with players getting ready for practice. There didn't seem to be much to love. Fifty or so lockers, a couple of couches, and some empty laundry hampers awaiting the dirty uniforms, socks, and jockstraps. But there was a life to this place that had been so quiet only moments before, an energy all its own. Radios and tape decks played, men sang and joked as they dressed, and, every once in a while, on the way to the trainer's room or the toilet, one of his teammates would stop and pass some comment to Snead.

"I'll never forget when I was in college we played in a hurricane one day," he said, leaning back on the couch. "The locker room stunk with sweat after the game and a ninety-year-old alumnus of Wake Forest came in and was introduced as a tackle on the team of 1907 or 1909 or something. This frail old man stood there, closed his eyes, and breathed. 'God,' he said, 'I've waited fifty years to breathe that again.' That's what it's about."

By then the locker room was full of players, and it was time for Snead to get ready for practice. His locker was on the far wall, across the room from Morton and Larry Csonka and the rest of the starting backfield.

Surely it must be difficult, being a backup player after so many seasons as a starter.

"I've made that adjustment," he said. "I understand that if I want to stay in football that is the job open to me."

He looked over to Morton, who was getting on his uniform, and lowered his voice. "It's a lot harder on him than it is on me," he said. "I'm the savior, standing on the sidelines. I just wait, and in the back of my mind that old ego's saying if they call on me they'll see something great—I can turn this whole thing around. It's a bunch of bullshit, but that's what I tell myself." And, smiling, he headed out to practice.

Two weeks later Morton was sidelined with an elbow injury, and Snead was called upon to start the game against Washington. The aging quarterback engineered a quiet but steady upset for the Giants' first win of the long season.

I walked into the locker room that following week of practice, and found Snead sitting in front of his locker, cutting the tapes from his ankles. When he saw me he smiled, and I walked over and shook his hand.

"Congratulations," I said.

"It's nice to win," he said, and after a moment of silence added, "I been benched," and burst out laughing. "How quick they forget."

It was a simple matter. Craig Morton was the starting quarterback, and Snead played only while he was hurt. Those were the rules, and he knew them. And, as he had said, it was just one of the adjustments he had made to play another season.

Later, after he'd gotten dressed, I asked him how long he was going to keep this up.

"Hard to say," he said. "I've always said there were several factors that would contribute to my decision to keep playing: As long as I'm not a detriment to my family; if I'm physically able; and so long as I feel I can do someone some good. Well, I'm still doing the Giants some good and I feel okay, but I have five kids and they're of the age that moving them just isn't right. This is the first season I don't have them with me, and that is a problem for me."

It was a quiet, thoughtful moment for Snead, and the words that he offered seemed even to surprise him with their serious tone. But it quickly passed, and when he looked up again there was a broad smile on his face.

"Listen, they begged me to play in the first place," he said, referring to his college days. "They pampered me at Wake Forest, drafted me number one, and have burped me and given me yearly raises ever since. I guess they'll have to beg me to stop."

He got up to leave, pausing at the large open door of the locker room.

"My wife is concerned about how I'm going to be when I'm fifty," he said. "I couldn't care less. I don't care if I'm crippled. This is worth it."

8
THE JAGGED EDGE OF OBSCURITY

It is October 18, 1971, in a packed and noisy Municipal Stadium in Kansas City, and the Chiefs are playing the Pittsburgh Steelers. On a third-down play early in the fourth period, Steelers' quarterback Terry Bradshaw drops back to midfield and lofts a long pass downfield to his wide receiver, Dave Smith, a speedy second-year man from Indiana State. Smith pulls the ball in, clutches it close to his breast, eludes one tackler, and races for the end zone. But as he crosses the five-yard line, apparently thinking it is the goal line, he lifts the ball high over his head in a sign of victory—styling, the players call it—and lets it fall from his hands. It bounces into the end zone, is fallen on by one of the Chiefs, and what was about to be a touchdown and six points for Pittsburgh becomes a touchback.

A freak play, a mistake in an otherwise fine season for the young receiver, but it will be the one event with which people associate the name of Dave Smith.

Now it is almost five years later. We switch from Kansas City to New York, from the excitement and jubilation of a jammed stadium to the solemn calm of an almost deserted practice field. It is nine o'clock in the morning, and a light rain falls over the quiet complex. Though it is still summer, late in August, the overcast skies and gray light which filter down have the look of winter. There is no cheer here today, just the sober tone of judgment.

Three men, football coaches wearing blue rain jackets, stand in the middle of the wet field. One of them holds a stopwatch, one a clipboard, and the third a football. Off to one side there is a fourth man, a player, dressed only in gray shorts and a T-shirt cut off at the waist, involved in a series of exercises. Before he was standing with his legs apart, bending, stretching first toward one foot and then the other, and now he is beginning to jog around the field, loosening his legs.

"Do whatever you have to to get yourself ready," says one of the coaches to the man in shorts, "then tell us."

After running a few short sprints, the player jogs over to the three coaches and says he is ready. His voice is firm enough, but there is a look of anxiety on his face.

First they have him run a 40-yard sprint, noting his time on the clipboard. Then they clock him as he zigzags his way through 30 yards of staggered hurdles, urging him to cut as close to each as he can without hitting it. Once he slips on the wet grass, sliding into one of the small barricades, and the pain of anger and fear flashes across his face. He quickly regains his composure and finishes the course.

"Can I do that again?" he asks, and the man with the stopwatch nods. He runs it again, this time without a flaw.

Just as he finishes the group is joined on the field by a second player, also in shorts and T-shirt. He talks briefly to the coaches, takes the football for a few practice tosses, then sets up to throw to the first player. Three passes are perfectly timed, and the first player gracefully catches them, but a fourth slips through his fingers and bounces on the wet field. Again pain flashes across his face.

That the place is the Giant's preseason camp in Pleasantville is not important. That the man running pass patterns is the same Dave Smith who once started for Pittsburgh is not even important. What the scene represents, however, is important. We are watching a man who has fallen out of the normal apparatus of sports try to rejoin that exclusive club. It is a common effort, because sports has a way of expelling so many of its members, and the same element is always present: Regardless if the man is a free agent coming to an opening camp or, like Dave Smith, is showing up by himself, he is on the outside trying to get back in. In an occupation composed of men performing in groups, he is a man alone.

Most often it is an older player (young players out of positions rarely have the credentials even to warrant conversation) who has always been able to perform in the past. Somewhere, at some point in his career, he was good enough to play. Maybe someone decided he couldn't do it anymore; maybe it was his own decision. Now he wants back in.

Dave Smith has been out of the NFL for three years, and out of football for two. After two-and-a-half seasons with Pittsburgh, the eighth-round pick was traded to Houston in 1972. He logged some time in 1973 with Kansas City, and in 1974 played in the WFL with Birmingham and then Chicago. And then he gave up. Or they gave up on him. Though he was still young, still strong and without impediments, teams stopped answering his phone calls. He would call, ask for the general manager or the director of operations, leave his name and number, and no one would call back. And then he stopped calling.

"Lotta people laying a lotta shit on me," he says, remembering the difficult times that followed his departure from Pittsburgh. "Lotta people say I'm a troublemaker, and I just got tired of bucking it."

He is an attractive young man with a warm face, who smiles even when he discusses adversity. His body, 6 feet tall and 205 pounds, is a good size for a receiver, and he has obviously stayed in condition. His thighs are large and well developed, his chest broad, his stomach tight and hard. And his wind is good. Within minutes of catching his last pass, he is again breathing normally.

He has been living in Pittsburgh these last years since he stopped playing, working with kids in the city's youth program and, for some time now, employed by a local radio station, WAMO, where he takes phone calls on the air from people who want to talk about sports. It's good work and he likes it, but it isn't football, and that's turned out to be a problem.

"I blew it," he says. "I had it and I blew it. I don't mean I did anything I'm ashamed of. I just mean I had it and I walked away from it. That was dumb. I miss the excitement and I miss the prestige. And, man, I miss the money. A lotta stuff I shoulda had I haven't got."

He began working out at Three Rivers Stadium, and developed a program of running up and down the hills of the city. He knew he couldn't get back with the Steelers. They had built a championship team since he was there, and you just don't walk back in and present yourself as the prodigal son to a team like that. But his relations with the organization have remained good, and through their help he got a tryout with New York.

"This is the thing I've got to do," he says now, following by a few yards the group of coaches as they head into the weight room for the next test. "I'm a wreck at home. My wife's about to throw me out. And the kids in the program, they really get to me. They come up to me and say, 'Hey, Dave, you were there once, how come you ain't there no more?' I've got no answer."

A few minutes of working out with the weights, and it's all over. The whole thing takes about thirty-five minutes. Having gotten up at dawn in Pittsburgh, caught a flight to New York, dressed, and "showed my stuff," as he put it, now all that is left is to wait.

"This is the year for me," he says, heading toward the dormitory where the football players are housed during the preseason. "This is going to be it. If they bust me this year, I'm really through."

He walks slowly, with his head down, keeping the morning drizzle out of his eyes. He knows that no immediate decision will be made about him. If they've paid his way here, they'll at least keep him here through the week to practice. He brought his bicycle in on the plane, and even in the rain he will pedal over the narrow, twisting back roads around the training camp, keeping his body fit and in tune. Hopefully, he'll be able to play in the exhibition game that weekend. It happens to be against Pittsburgh, and he wants to be ready.

"Once you're there you gotta hang tight," he says, " 'cause if you make a mistake you'll be gone before you know it. That's all it takes—one mistake—and you're gone. And once you're gone . . ."

He never finishes his sentence, but walks off into the rainy morning, up the hill toward the dormitory.

For most Americans retirement is a cherished goal. Plumbers, schoolteachers, policemen, engineers plan with great anticipation for the day when they are no longer slaves to alarm clocks. They plan for their leisure years in places like Florida and Arizona, looking forward to afternoons of fishing and puttering around in their gardens. The years spent on the assembly line or at the office, the years of regimentation and monotony—they lead to retirement. It is the heaven for which the good Christian lives his good, dull life.

It is different for the professional athlete. His sport has not only been his means of making a living, it has been the nucleus of his life, the point around which all decisions have been made. While we see a thirty-three-year-old baseball or basketball player and compute that if he turned pro at twenty-one that makes a twelve-year habit he's got to break, this is an unrealistic picture. That relationship between a man and his sport, which begins somewhere in early childhood, has been making serious sounds since the first coach or scout started talking about "the big time." If making it were not an obsession before that point, it was thereafter. And once he signed with a pro team, at least half—and usually two-thirds—of every year has been spent living with his sport and his teammates.

The result is that sports has dominated his life. It has become either his passion or his curse, depending on how his career has gone. His highs, his lows, his depressions, his joys are more often experienced within his sport than anyplace else. Talk to any athlete and the response is likely to be the same: The feeling of making a great play, whether it's throwing a touchdown pass or turning a double play, is the supreme feeling of excitement and fulfillment. And the rejection of being benched or cut causes a depression from which he thinks he will never climb out.

Are the highs worth the crashing? His presence in uniform testifies that they are. With that he becomes the most precious of mortals—an athlete. Sought after by children and celebrities, chased by women who consider time spent with him a trophy, paid exorbitant salaries, given preferential treatment wherever he goes, forgiven for whatever social graces he may occasionally ignore, he enjoys all the benefits of being special. Most of all, he is envied by a vast percentage of the male public. He belongs to that exclusive group who share great mystical secrets of which the rest of us have been denied knowledge. He's on the inside of the joke told at the batting cage, the casual remark that has those players bent in laughter, and we are shut out.

There is an additional dividend: So long as the athlete remains in his sport, he retains some degree of the youth he had when he started. Aside from crippling injury, aging is his most feared enemy. Despite reminders all around him, teammates and friends growing older and leaving the game, he somehow refuses to accept that it can happen to him. If youth is a preoccupation in the civilian world, it is an obsession in sports. Players dress young and act young. They lie about their age, dye their hair, and even get hair transplants. They are caught in a dialectic bind: Staying in sports keeps them young; aging shortens their career. And all the while, time passes.

It is fair to view a career in sports as a separate little lifetime all its own. The people within it, the language used, the pace, the values, the life style, they are all alien to the world outside. The athlete enters as an infant, callow and naive to the professional's ways. His early years are filled with learning, and he grows to become a hardened, educated veteran. When his career is heading toward an end, that end has a firm look of finality. In his book *Life on the Run,* published just before the beginning of his final season with the New York Knicks, Bill Bradley wrote:

"He [the athlete] approaches the end of his playing days the way old people approach death. He puts his finances in order. He reminisces easily. He offers advice to the young. But the athlete differs from an old person in that he must continue living."

The end of which Bradley speaks is inevitable. From the first day an athlete puts on his uniform he knows that someday he will either retire or be released, yet it is an eventuality for which few plan. He may talk about it, but he seems not to accept it. The conversation is an intellectual exercise, like the young man who talks bravely about death. When he is close to seventy he clings to every breath.

As Bill Bradley entered his final season of basketball, having decided it would be his final season, having explored the possibilities of a life in politics, and having set down his memoirs and agreed to be the subject of a television documentary, another Knick entered that same 1976 season knowing that he too was approaching the end of his career. The player was Jim Barnett, and he was not so well prepared, even though he was well aware of the mounting pressure.

"I look at the numbers," said Barnett, who at 6 feet 4 inches tall and 175 pounds seemed remarkably frail for a professional athlete. "I look around at how many players are on no-cut contracts and how many young guards are up from the rookie camp. I know things are gonna be tough."

Barnett, a talented running guard during his ten years in the NBA, was accustomed to moving around. He had played for six different clubs, none for longer than three seasons and one, New Orleans, for only forty-five games. As he stood on the court that first day of the veteran camp, the gym full of television and newspaper reporters, he talked about the mental adjustment he'd made during that off-season.

"I've made up my mind not to worry about it," he said.

"I've tried to align my life this summer and plan for the future so that I would go out—if I have to—with a little bit more positive aspect and not a bad taste in my mouth."

He spoke directly and slowly, pronouncing each word carefully, as if firming it up in his mind at the same time, and added that completing ten years in the league was an important accomplishment for him. "That old pride factor," he called it.

"But perspectives change," he said. "Quite frankly, it doesn't mean as much as it used to. Basketball was a live-and-die situation. I don't know what I would have done three years ago, four years ago, five years ago, had I been released. Now I'm ready for it."

It was a positive attitude for a thirty-two-year-old veteran who had seen the end come for many of his teammates over the years. He understood what was happening. In addition to putting in extra time working out over the off-season, getting in shape, he had also talked with people in and around his home in California, and he had job prospects. Nothing firm, but prospects. He has resolved to his own satisfaction the end of his career, he said, and he felt he could handle the necessary adjustment.

But of course that was the first day of camp, and Barnett had spent months preparing for this day and the questions that would be asked. Actually being there adds another dimension. The experience might support his fears; he might see that he is in fact overmatched, and feel that he's just too old to cope. Or, just possibly, it could work the other way. The smell of sweat and the sound of sneakers on a hardwood floor, the feeling of a perfectly thrown pass, the joking with old friends—it can turn a man's head. It can even make him think he's a kid again.

"I feel terrific," Barnett was saying by the second week. "I guess all that working out paid off. I can feel my game coming back."

As the preseason continued and Barnett practiced more with the team, sharpening his skills, conditioning his body back to the ryhthm of basketball, running and again becoming part of the mechanism of the game, he became more confident.

PHOTO COURTESY NEW YORK KNICKS

Jim Barnett, the pragmatist. "I can be gone in less than half-an-hour."

Some of the younger guards were released, there were injuries to others, and he could see a situation developing where the Knicks would have to call on him.

"I want to make this team," he said after one of the early exhibition games. "And if I don't make it here, I think I can find someplace else. I've got three bags with me. I can be gone in less than half-an-hour. And I'd be willing to go. I want to play."

Then, about midway into the exhibition season, Barnett suffered a leg injury during an intersquad game. That placed him in a position from which he could not be cut from the team until he was healthy, but from which it was impossible to fight for his job.

"It happened at a bad time for me," he said. "We had just started running, and that is great for me. It complements my game. It's a chance to show them what I can do to help the team."

The injury, a muscle tear that occurred when one of his teammates collided with him from the rear, kept Barnett off the court throughout the rest of the exhibition season. His basketball life consisted of the slow, tedious process of getting the leg back into shape, spending his time in the trainer's room, in and out of the whirlpool, and all the while watching other men fighting for his position on the team.

And while he watched and waited for the final Wednesday when the squad would be cut to the regulation twelve men, he evaluated his position, planning on the way to best assure his own survival.

"The way things are going," he said, "I don't know if I'd make it or not. So even if I were well I wouldn't go out there on Wednesday. I get well Wednesday and they say, 'Okay, you're well—cut.' No chance to make the club. No money. You wait till Thursday and they've got to put you on the injured list. That's five games. You've got a chance, and five games' salary. It's as simple as that. Black and white. I'm not going to be ready, but I certainly wouldn't go out there Wednesday and give them the chance to cut me. They'd love that."

He smiled, checking again to make certain he wasn't being overheard. "It woulda been great if I'da really wrecked my leg, if I'da torn it up and gotten it in a cast or something and not been able to play till December 1, then I'd get my whole year's salary. But unfortunately it wasn't that severe."

There was a wide grin on his face as he spoke, signaling his intention to weight his comments with a liberal portion of salt. But the progression of his reasoning is not pure fantasy. While possibly not common practice, it is often considered by athletes facing extinction. Some players have been known to hide on the injured list for as long as half a season, fearing that when they were finally activated they were sure to be cut. But most, like Barnett, only want to be certain they are healthy enough to fight for their jobs before being activated. Sometimes it works, but not too often.

Barnett remained on the injured reserve list for eleven games of the regular season, and once he recovered he was released. But he did not announce his retirement as he had discussed that first day. He went home to Orinda, California, where his wife was expecting their first child, and took care of her while staying close to the telephone.

"I've talked with several teams," he said, "and I keep an eye on the newspapers. I know who's being traded and I know when someone gets hurt. That's probably my best chance now, moving in when someone gets injured. I can still help somebody. I'll just wait it out for a while."

When most of us think of professional athletes, the image that immediately rushes to mind is of a batter standing at home plate in Yankee Stadium or Riverfront Stadium, 50,000 people cheering as he sends a pitch deep over the outfield wall. Or we envision Doctor J, floating through the air to stuff a basketball through the hoop, or Tom Seaver leading the victorious Mets in a ticker-tape parade through Manhattan. Far more common than any of these is the image of Jim Barnett, sitting at home by the telephone, waiting for someone to call and salvage a piece of his career. You can easily substitute Nate Colbert or Dave Smith or a hundred other athletes. Everyone who leaves his game, regardless how firm his decision to go and whatever his plans, wants someone to ask him to stay. They all want that phone to ring with an offer of one more season.

When it comes to taking or avoiding that final step, it is often easier for an average player to find a place for himself on a team than for a faded star. A respectable hitter, past his prime but still capable of entering a game during the late innings and delivering a timely pinch hit, can usually find a spot as the twenty-fourth or twenty-fifth man on a club. Many a good, durable football player has scratched out a few extra years because some team was willing to buy whatever limited services he could offer. A former star doesn't fit that easily into a corner. His pride probably won't let him take a part-time position, and even if it would, he would not accept the commensurate pay cut. No team can afford to pay a spot player an all star's salary.

It is probably fair to say that Brooks Robinson played three years past the time when he should have quit. The great third baseman for the Baltimore Orioles, one of the best ever to play that position, had a decent season in 1974, but slumped badly the following year, and played only sparingly in 1976. Many thought that he would end his twenty-two-year career after the last game in 1976, but Robinson decided otherwise. He had been an athlete most of his life, he insisted, and he felt he was still an athlete.

"If I got to the point where I embarrassed myself, I would hang it up," he said during the off-season. "But that isn't the case. Defensively, I'm as good as anybody in the game. It comes down to how much Brooks Robinson can hit. I had some problems last year, but I think I've worked 'em out. I'm ready to play ball."

That put the Orioles in a spot. Seeing Robinson's steady decline, they had been grooming a new third baseman for four seasons, Doug DeCinces, and he was ready. But Robinson was a hero in Baltimore, a legend, and could not be pushed out. So the Orioles waited, and so did their fans. Several times throughout the '76 season groups had asked about a special Brooks Robinson Night, an opportunity to honor the man who

Brooks Robinson, starting his twenty-third season. "If I got to the point where I embarrassed myself, I would hang it up. But that isn't the case."

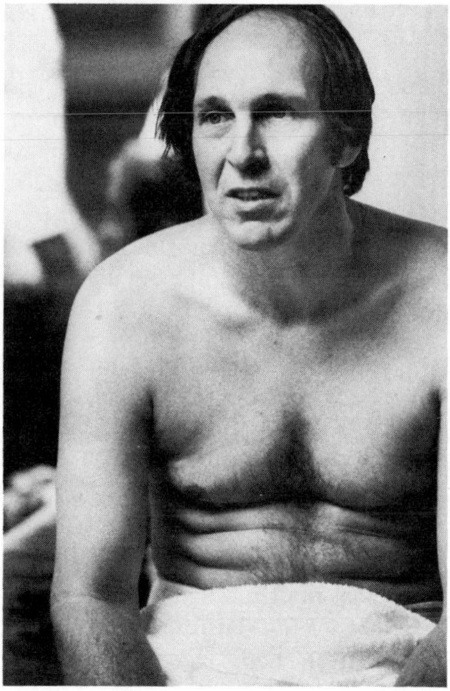

NEW YORK POST PHOTOGRAPH BY JOCOBELLIS.

had won sixteen consecutive Golden Glove awards at third base. And then on the last night of the season the Oriole faithful, feeling it was their last time to see him in uniform, gave Robinson a standing ovation as he came to bat in the eighth inning. When he lined a single to center they cheered some more, and continued as he was replaced by a pinch runner. They refused to stop when he reached the dugout. They chanted "We Want Brooks, We Want Brooks," and the game was held up for Robinson to come out for one more bow, one more burst of thunderous, emotional applause.

But it did not end with this Hollywood finish. When spring training arrived the following February, there was Robinson, an old man at thirty-nine, his hair thinly spread over the top of his head, his middle thick, clinging to his number "5" uniform as if it were a life raft.

"I love this game," he said that first day in camp in Miami, "and I'm hanging on till it's all over. People ask me if I'm afraid I'll tarnish my image. That never enters my mind. People say they hope I don't hang on like Willie Mays did. Hell, nobody remembers Mays's last days. They remember that catch he made in the '54 World Series."

He looked especially tired that spring, due partly to the burden of carrrying batting averages of .201 and .211 over his last two seasons, and due partly to those incessant questions from the press about his retirement.

"In professional sports, there's always a hurry to get guys in and out," he said in answer to one question. "But being a big league player has been a lifelong dream for Brooks Robinson. I'm in no hurry to relinquish that title."

Baltimore, a team in contention for the pennant, wasn't the best place for Robinson to be ending his career. The pressure was great on each of the twenty-five men on the club. He had talked with several teams, especially the two expansion teams, Seattle and Toronto, hoping one of them would sign him to a two-year contract, something to make moving his home and family worthwhile. Neither team would agree, not for a man his age, and in his salary range, estimated at $120,000 a year. He could have worked out a deal for one year and less money, but he refused.

So Brooks Robinson began the 1977 season as a player-coach for the Orioles, spending most of his time in the bullpen. Then, toward the end of August, having gotten just seven hits in the twenty-three games in which he'd appeared, he officially retired.

Such determination and tenacity, applauded by organized sports when exhibited in young athletes, is an embarrassment when it comes to aging stars. The Orioles would have liked Robinson to quit at the end of 1976, with pride, as they might say. That's front office thinking. They like things neat. There is discomfort with the messiness of having "to deal" with an over-the-hill star who will not exit gracefully. It's even worse if they have to cut him, there before the eyes of the world. That was the case with George Blanda, who was unhappy with the Oakland Raiders' decision to give his place-kicking job to a rookie at the beginning of the 1976 NFL preseason. Blanda, then forty-eight and the holder of most career records for longevity and place kicking, dressed every day for camp anyhow, and was finally released just before the start of the season.

"You don't like to see that kind of thing," said Andy Robustelli of the New York Giants, talking about athletes' refusing to accept the inevitable. "You like to see a man realize when his time has come. You like to see him get out—cleanly—instead of fighting through camp, trying to squeeze out that one more year. It's uncomfortable for everyone."

He meant it's embarrassing. When you've got a player who's going to end up in the Hall of Fame, everybody's watching. All that attention, plus the burden of a six-figure salary, makes aging stars a delicate commodity.

That is one problem the fringe player does not have. No one is watching when a team invites a thirty-five-year-old part-time player to camp. And if he works out, he can be quietly and cheaply added to the squad. Sometimes anonymity is a blessing.

About the same time Brooks Robinson's career was taking an abrupt turn downhill, Ray Sadecki had been dealing with the same problem as a matter of course for several seasons. He had signed with St. Louis right out of high school in 1958, and managed to win more than fourteen games only once in his nearly eighteen-year major league career. That was 1964, when he won 20 and lost 11. Other than that year he mostly lost as many as he won. But he could be counted on to turn in two or three innings of strong relief work each time he pitched, and, while not a starter since 1969, he always seemed to have a job.

"If you look carefully at the statistics," said Sadecki in 1976 when he was pitching for Milwaukee, "you'll see that .500 isn't that bad. It isn't exciting—it won't make you rich—but it's the guys who can't break even who are out of the game."

He was sitting on a stool before a game, chainsmoking cigarettes, philosophizing about his up-and-down career. He isn't a very big man, just under six feet and weighing 190 pounds, but he looked to be in good condition, suntanned and healthy, and he had been spared any serious arm trouble. He had been with Milwaukee most of that 1976 season, having been released by Kansas City, and was doing his usual creditable if not spectacular job.

"Somebody can always use a good left-handed reliever," he said in his slow midwestern accent. "I do my job and I don't cause any trouble, and that keeps me working."

Sadecki, who credited expansion with extending his career, was later released by the Brewers, after the season. The following February found him in camp with the Mets, and when the 1977 season opened he was again a working pitcher.

"Money's another thing that keeps me working," said the thirty-five-year-old pitcher. "A lot of people price themselves right out of this game. My not being in a high-money bracket has helped me survive. I never planned it that way, you understand, but that's how it's worked out."

Survival. Trying to find a place to play. Sooner or later, in the life of almost every athlete, it gets down to that. Often it is something over which a player has no control. When a man is cut and nobody calls, there is little he can do. There are no free-lance basketball players. No spectator is going to pay $5 to watch a former second-string catcher field balls fired into the air by the popup machine. But often it is a matter of how badly he wants to stay in the game. Just what will he do, and how little money will he take to do it? For some athletes with a great deal of ego or the financial responsibility of a large family, their standards are too high for their position. Others will take whatever they can get. Sometimes that means part-time play, and sometimes playing in foreign countries or in cities and towns far from their homes and families.

But most men keep looking for a place. As tough and frustrating as it sometimes gets, the years spent in their sport represent a part of their lives separate from everything else. For many—stars and fringe players alike—it is the best part, the only time when they feel they are something special. Like the ex-fighter played by Brando in *On the Waterfront,* it is a chance to be "somebody."

In June 1978 Rob Gardner was a fireman for the city of Binghamton, New York. This meant that he sometimes rode in one of the city's big yellow fire engines, helped fight fires, occasionally pulled people out of burning buildings, and administered first aid. It also meant that he sat around the fire station, did his share of KP, mopped the floor, cleaned equipment, and, more than anything else, played cards to pass the time.

But all that was new. Until March 1976 Rob Gardner had been a baseball player, a left-handed pitcher who showed some fine moments during his thirteen-year pro career. Some, but not a lot. More often, he showed only determination and potential. Those are essential ingredients in an athlete's life. One keeps him going; and the other keeps people interested in him and gives him a place to play.

He had been a local hero in Binghamton, an uninspiring town of about 60,000 people in the south-central part of the state. He had been a star in Little League and a star in high school, and when he graduated in 1963 the Minnesota Twins paid him $12,000 to become a baseball player, which was what Gardner thought was his destiny.

"It was always what I wanted to do, but nobody'd believe me," said Gardner, who, like most professional athletes, was shorter and lighter than the figures given in the record books. The book listed him at 6 feet 2 inches tall and 175 pounds, but he was closer to 6 feet and 160 pounds. "My counselor in school would ask me what I wanted to do," he recalled, "and I'd say I want to play baseball. He'd laugh, like I said I want to be a cowboy, and ask me what I *really* want to be. But then I signed with the Twins and it was a big story in the paper. Nobody laughed then."

Unfortunately, he never fulfilled the potential that he or the Twins saw. He bounced around the minors for his first two

Rob Gardner, with the Yankees in 1972. "Even when it was bad it was good. It was still baseball."

PHOTO COURTESY NEW YORK YANKEES

seasons, then came to the big leagues with the Mets in 1966. After two seasons there he pitched for the Cubs in 1967 and Cleveland in 1968, spent '70 through '73 shuffling back and forth beween the Yankees, the minors, and Oakland, and it was with the A's that arm trouble signaled the beginning of the end of his sputtering career.

"I wouldn't trade it for anything," he said one recent spring day in Binghamton. "Even when it was bad, it was good. Do you know what I mean? It was still baseball. It was fun. It was a game, and I loved it. The fact that I was getting paid just made it better."

It was about noon, and Gardner was taking a little time off from his duties around the fire station. A heavy rain had been falling all day, and the town and the mountains surrounding it were drenched. There is a lot of rain in that part of the state, which may be one reason the Binghamton Fire Department is so quiet. The only excitement that morning had been generated by one false alarm.

"I see my life as being lived in two different worlds," said Gardner, leaning back on the couch in the station's lounge. "There's baseball, and then there's the rest. Don't get me wrong. I like what I'm doing. But baseball, that was something else."

He started to talk about his early years in the Twins organization, about driving to Florida for his first camp. He had bought a new car with his bonus money, but he was just eighteen, had never been away from home before, and had no idea how to get to Florida. An old friend, one of his coaches, went along as a guide.

"I remember my first time in Minnesota," he said. "After the game I went downtown to where they told me to stay, but they didn't have any rooms. They said they were full. I told 'em the Twins'd told me to come there and they said, 'Oh, oh, are you with the Twins? Of course we have a room for you.' Then my TV didn't work, and I called downstairs very sheepishly to ask if something could be done. I didn't get the phone hung up before there was this guy at the door with a new TV." He laughed as he recalled the incident, and slapped his hands together. "This is great, I said. I can't wait. What an introduction to being a ballplayer. I'm gonna love it."

A nice-looking man, trim and still firm at thirty-three, with wavy brown hair, he spoke in a full, enthusiastic voice that rose and fell as he discussed his career, which was played out in twenty-three different cities, eighteen of them in the minor leagues—six of those the first two years.

"Those early years were really exciting," he said. "Every place I turned there were players I'd read about as a kid and seen on TV. My first time with Minnesota they lockered me next to Vic Wertz. *Vic Wertz.* I had been a Cleveland fan and I remembered him from the Series. I got all excited. I told him I remembered when he did this, when he did that. He was really nice. Great guy. Super guy. It was terrific."

Not all encounters with his boyhood heroes were so rewarding. There was the time he was shagging balls in spring training. Who should he find himself next to but Duke Snider—one of Gardner's favorite players as a child.

"I got to talking with him," he said, "and I told him I remembered when he hit four home runs in the World Series, and he smiled. Then I told him that I had his baseball card, and he told me to get the hell away from him. I was crushed."

While he talked, remembering the good times (like being mobbed by fans outside Yankee Stadium after a double header) and the bad times (like being sent down to the minors on any one of numerous occasions, being traded, or, worse, released), on the floor below the rest of the department went about the daily chores of maintaining the station and killing time until the next call. Few of his fellow firemen were baseball fans, so there was little talk of it around the station. But there were times, family gatherings and such, when people would talk to him about his years as a pitcher, and ask his opinion about one ballplayer or another. And, every once in a while, some reporter would call to talk, just to see how he was adjusting to civilian life. It was all very different from when he was playing, when baseball comprised the majority of his conversation and the local papers ran stories regularly about his progress.

"Baseball's an ego trip," said Gardner, who lives there in his hometown with his wife Kitty and their two children, Amy and David. "You get a feeling when somebody asks what you do and you tell 'em you play baseball. You get a feeling when you put on the uniform and run out into a stadium with 40,000 people. You get a feeling when you're on the mound challenging a Willie Mays or a Henry Aaron. You just don't get that feeling anyplace else. And just to have done it—to have been part of it—is something that changes your life. You never lose having done it."

Arm trouble got Gardner released from the A's in 1973. ("One day on the mound there was this terrible pain in my elbow," he said. "I had pains before, and so it didn't bother me. But this time it didn't get better.") In 1974 he signed with Evansville in the American Association, but by then he was pitching in severe and steady pain, and soon he was released again.

The doctors told him his arm needed rest, so he sat out the rest of 1974. With free time, he wrote to everyone he knew in baseball. He was looking for a coaching job, just a little something to keep him in the game until his arm was better. The Yankees responded, sending him to Syracuse for the 1975 season as the pitching coach for their Triple A club.

That was a difficult time for Gardner. He liked coaching but he missed pitching, and during the winter he had an operation by the Syracuse team surgeon. A spur was taken off the elbow itself, bone chips removed and scar tissue scraped from the tendon. It seemed successful, until he threw in a game the next spring and the arm hurt worse than ever. That was it. Though the Yankees offered him a coaching job, he turned it down.

"If I couldn't pitch," he said, "I figured I might as well hang it up. I couldn't sit there and watch someone else doing what I wanted to do. I just couldn't."

That still bothered Gardner in 1978, two years out of baseball. He did not play ball for recreation, and only went to see games in which his ten-year-old son was playing. He could not stand to watch a game on television.

"If I said I could watch a game I'd be lying," he said. "I'm envious. I see guys I played with or guys that I coached, and I feel that I'm better than they are. But they're there and I'm here. It kills me because I know I should be there, too."

Gardner insists that he's comfortable with his decision to retire, and adds, touching the six-inch-long scar on the back of his left elbow, that he had little choice. Even when he's out in the backyard playing catch with his son and his arm feels great, he pushes any thought of a comeback out of his mind.

"I'm pretty happy," he said. "I'm spending time with my family and I've got a job with security. That's new for me. I'll never get rich as a fireman, but I won't starve, either."

It was after two o'clock and past time for him to attend to his share of the chores around the fire station. He didn't want anyone to think he was shirking his portion of the "housework," as if being an ex-ballplayer placed him above such tasks. He was careful to avoid that impression. He stood up and started to walk toward the stairs.

"Sometimes when I'm on my hands and knees, cleaning floors, I really miss baseball," he said, and joked about fantasies of walking through "beautiful downtown Cleveland."

Then he got serious.

"But the tough part comes in February," he said. "I used to really look forward to getting my shit together and driving on out of here with the snow up to the windshield"—he gestured with his hand up to his forehead. "I miss heading down to Florida, and seeing old friends. I miss pitching—standing on the mound and seeing if I can send this hitter walking away carrying his bat."

He stopped on the stairs for a moment, wanting to finish the conversation before joining the other firemen. "When I used to have some kind of job in the off-season," he said, "it never bothered me, no matter what it was. I knew that come February I'd be heading out to play baseball. And when people asked me

Rob Gardner, with his fire engine: "If I were eighteen years old again and knew what it was going to be like, I'd do it all over again."

PHOTO BY SKIP ROZIN

what I did, I never told 'em I corrected smudges on blueprints [one of his off-season jobs]. I told 'em I was a baseball player, 'cause that's what I was."

Rob Gardner never had a secure day in baseball in thirteen years. He never played on a championship team, never played in an all-star game, and the only way he got to the Hall of Fame in Cooperstown was when he took his kids. Still, he had eagerly committed his youth to the game. He had even eagerly risked surgery on his elbow that last season to stay in it.

"If I were eighteen years old again and knew what it was going to be like," he swore, "I'd do it all over again. Even if somebody offered me a $60,000-a-year job out here, I'd tell 'em I'd rather be a pitcher."

That's a strong commitment, so strong that his adjustment since leaving the game has been difficult. He will adjust, he says, but two years is just not long enough. Someday he'll be able to watch a game on television, and maybe even play a little on Sundays.

His comment is not unique, and neither is his difficulty in adjusting to the real world so rare. Both are shared by most athletes leaving their game; it has been with them too long, and has meant too much. When it's all over, when the last pay check is cashed and the sound of the last cheer fades from their memory, a lot of men are in trouble. It isn't something that former athletes like to talk about. What they do is try their best to adjust, sometimes with the aid of their families, but more often than not by themselves.

This is a big part of the problem. Getting out is the one thing in sports a man handles all alone. For as diligent and thorough as professional sports is in finding and testing players and getting them into uniform, its method of getting them out is as barbaric as putting an old Eskimo out to sea in a kayak to die.

It is a problem that every athlete faces, sooner or later, regardless of how illustrious or disappointing his career.

For fourteen seasons Nick Buoniconti was a professional football player. For half that time he played for the Miami Dolphins, anchoring the defense that led them to three consecutive Super Bowls. But in July 1976 he retired. It was not his idea. The Dolphins told the thirty-five-year-old linebacker that he was no longer needed. He could come to camp if he wanted, but it wouldn't make any difference. He was through.

Buoniconti, a lawyer practicing in Miami, was incensed. He openly split with the Dolphins and their head coach, Don Shula, on the handling of the matter.

"I don't care if it's a Nick Buoniconti or anybody else, you have to let the guy lose the job," he had said. "You don't take a job away from a man. Let someone beat him out, but don't just take his job away. It's embarrassing. It's humiliating, and it doesn't do the team any good. If you do it to one guy, you can do it to anyone."

Obviously, Buoniconti's no pushover. Bright and articulate,

he could handle himself on a football field as well as he could in a courtroom. His pride would not let him go in and discuss the situation with Shula ("That would be even more humiliating," he said) but he was angry and hurt. And on that July day in his plush law office on Flagler Street, when he was to announce his retirement at a press conference, he was an unhappy man. Unhappy, and concerned.

It is early afternoon and hot in downtown Miami. Outside the temperature is close to 90. But here, inside Nick Buoniconti's office, it is cool and comfortable. The office is beautifully furnished in contemporary Mediterranean, and a thick carpet in a rich gold covers the floor. Behind Buoniconti, who led the Miami defense to two Super Bowl victories and one perfect season, are the books of his more civilized trade, shelves of handsomely bound law books: the series of *Martindale-Hubbell* on the first shelf, the *Supreme Court Digest* on the second, and the *Cyclopedia of Trial Practice* on the third.

Soon, when the press conference begins, the room will be strewn with cables, floodlit with television lights, and jammed shoulder to shoulder with reporters either scribbling their notes or trying to get a microphone close to the desk. But for now it is quiet. None of the reporters has arrived. Buoniconti, neatly dressed in a brown suit, leans back in his plush, high-backed chair and talks. He seems relaxed, but he is very sober.

"I'm not worried about making a living," he says, and motions around the room. "I'm gonna do just fine. But there are 300,000 lawyers in this country, and just 600 football players. Tomorrow I'm gonna be one of those 300,000—just another guy who's a lawyer—and I don't know if I can handle that."

He leans forward in his chair and clasps his hands before him on the desk. The ring finger of his right hand is noticeably bent and there are scars on the side of his hand, the result of injuries suffered while playing football. One of them cost him his last season with the Dolphins.

"This is an exclusive fraternity," he says, speaking slowly and distinctly. "Every year some join and some fall away. And once you leave, you can never get back. I don't mind saying it: I don't want to leave."

There is a troubled look in Buoniconti's dark eyes as he speaks; clearly he is taking leaving football hard. But that's understandable. He fought to play for Notre Dame, and fought to make the Boston Patriots when they drafted him in 1962. He wasn't big for a linebacker—5 feet 11 inches tall and 210 pounds—and it was a struggle all the way. Then, when Boston gave up on him and traded him to Miami in 1969, he fought to make his place there. Now, fourteen years after it started, they have taken his job without permitting him to fight.

"I love this game," he is saying. "I love every aspect of it. I love sweating in the locker room before the game. I love running into the Orange Bowl with 75,000 people there. And I love getting up there hearing the national anthem, thinking about the game, the butterflies in my stomach, wondering what I'm going to do, how I'm going to stop the opponent. I love every bit of it. I love the pressure, and I don't want to leave it."

He stops to compose himself, then begins talking about other players he knows who've gotten out and the trouble they've had.

"The problem is the psyche of the individual athlete," he says. "When it's time to quit the game the majority are not ready to make that transition from professional athlete to average citizen who's no longer in the limelight and no longer treated as someone special. There is a tremendous letdown. Many guys never adjust. Their marriages break up, they move from job to job, looking for something to replace their sport—they have real emotional problems."

There is a sincere, almost impassioned tone in his voice, which is clear and strong. He makes no attempt to hide that he is projecting his own fears into his conversation. He has played football all of his adult life, and his first year away from it concerns him.

"I know that it's difficult to go on the wagon," he says

adding that he has agreed to provide color commentary for CBS, partially to help himself with the adjustment. "There's too much about football that I love."

When he had finished, Buoniconti stood up and walked to the door of his office. Already outside were several people from the local media, loaded with equipment for the scheduled news conference. Soon, within an hour, he would make the announcement that every football fan in south Florida expected to hear.

"I've been in football since I was nine years old," he said, talking about the contract to work for CBS. "I don't want to make a clean break. I'm not one of those heroes who just walks away. I don't know if I can, so I've protected myself by keeping my hand in."

Buoniconti didn't even walk as far as he'd planned. It was soon after he'd announced his retirement that the Dolphins ran into linebacker difficulty and asked him to return. And he did, for that one more season. The law practice would wait, and he gambled that CBS would wait. He knew he was not avoiding the problems that lay in retirement, only evading them temporarily. But that was enough.

"I'm going to be retired for a long time," he said, discussing his decision. "I owe this to myself. Being thrown out of the game hurt—and that's what it was. I'd rather leave under my own power, walking out the way I came in, as a player."

One more season. Fourteen more games in which to better prepare for becoming just another lawyer among hundreds of thousands of lawyers. Prepare for it, and avoid it.

"That's the coldest part of the game," said Buoniconti, talking about getting out. "There is an endless supply of interchangeable parts, and the machine just keeps on working. When they're finished with Nick Buoniconti, football player, they pull him out and drop him into society. Then they take some other guy and shove him into the slot. Nobody cares

Nick Buoniconti, in his law office in Miami: "I'm not one of those heroes who just walks away. I don't know if I can. . . ."

about the man they've discarded, so long as the machine keeps working."

The idea of Nick Buoniconti delaying full-time law practice and risking a lucrative television contract to return to football for one more season is strange to many on the outside of sports, just as are his fears about adjusting to civilian society. It does not fit the stereotype that we have of the aging athlete. We know some have difficulty when they leave sports, but assume it is because they cannot do anything else, because they are not particularly smart or are not capable of dealing with the real world.

The truth is that athletes are pretty much like the rest of us. Some are bright and some are not. But there is one quality which most share, one trait common to them as a group, and that is their commitment to their sport. It is not so different from the commitment which an artist has for his art—very deep and very personal. The time and effort required simply to survive, year after year, the physical abuse and emotional pressure, they drop it all into a little compartment and go on performing, wherever and for however long they can. But unlike an artist, all that energy runs into a stone wall somewhere about the time of life when most of us are approaching our prime.

The drive does not turn off easily. It is a devastating defeat for a player to resign himself to the fact that his dream has ended and that he can no longer play. Confronted with this inevitability, many compensate in their personal lives. Some begin drinking excessively, while others sublimate their fears in more physical directions. The wife of one player with whom I had spent considerable time talked with me for hours about the change in her husband's behavior as he approached what was to be his last season.

"He's screwing every woman in sight," she said. "We've had a good marriage—I know that. But this off-season he's just gone crazy. I know what he's afraid of. I know the pressures confronting him in camp this season. But can I just sit by and watch what's happening? It's humiliating to me. Even worse, it's forming wounds that may never heal."

For most, however, the reaction to the impending end of a professional career is to ignore it. And when it finally happens, to refuse to accept it. Cut by one team, they try again someplace else. Cut there, they go on and try elsewhere. It all sounds so masochistic—a teacher who can't find a job will usually do something else—but it is not just an occupation these men are clinging to. It is their manhood and their youth. They need to go on playing their game.

That is why it is so difficult for athletes to retire. They love their sport and they have devoted their lives to doing it well, and they don't want that to end. They wrestle with the decision toward the end of an unusually bad season, finally announcing their retirement, then go away haunted by what they have done. And once they've thought it over and realized the finality of their new state, the fact that, like Nick Buoniconti, they are "going to be retired for a long time," many come back and try again. One more try, for one more season.

And so for many that final step out comes not at the end of a season, as might be expected, but in the middle of preseason training camp. Especially for the marginal athlete, that is the arena of final judgment. The time off after the regular season heals the body and the spirit. It softens the memory of hours spent with ice packs and whirlpools, of nights trying to sleep in an airplane seat, of games before hostile fans, and of the embarrassment of sitting on the bench for a last-place team. Two-a-day drills have the power to bring all that back. If more is necessary, the sight of children—teenagers, actual children—competing for their jobs adds a further shock. For the player who still refuses to surrender, it becomes the club's job to step in and explain that the end has come. For some, even that jolt doesn't last. They go away, think it over, and after a season (sometimes even longer) they question their decision. Most ignore those twinges to try it again. Most, but not all.

No one can say that Ron Swoboda didn't have his time in baseball. He came up with the Mets in 1965, played with New York into the 1971 season when he was traded to Montreal, then went on to the Yankees until 1973. Those nine seasons, while mostly inconsequential, included the 1969 World Series with the Mets in which he not only batted .400, but made a running, skidding, rolling catch of a sinking line drive by Brooks Robinson that saved the fourth game for New York. It was a brilliant catch, maybe one of the best ever made in a Series, and it won a piece of immortality for Swoboda. Not a big piece—not Bobby Thomson size. But a little, and what more can a .242 hitter ask?

They started breaking up the World Champion Mets soon after that magic year, and it took them until midway through the 1971 season to reach Swoboda. Then, around Christmas of 1973, after two and a half seasons with the Yankees, he was released.

"I didn't think I was done," Swoboda recalled. "I figured I'd hear from somebody. I did. Atlanta called. And with the Braves that spring I thought I was doing a real major league job. I thought I looked like an athlete."

But toward the end of spring training in 1974 Eddie Mathews, then the Atlanta manager, called Swoboda into his office and told him he was being released.

"That buried me," said Swoboda. "Right down to my shoes, that shocked me. It was an awful experience, to know that at that point in my career, at twenty-nine, that was it. I remember wandering around for days, searching my soul, wondering what the hell I was going to do."

About two days later he received a call from WCBS-TV in New York. They had heard he'd been released and were looking for a sportscaster for their early news show. Swoboda had a choice: WCBS or the minors. He had a wife, two kids, and a house on Long Island, so he went on television.

"Ever since I made that choice I've wondered what would have happened if I'd tried," he said. "I like doing television, but there are no thrills in this business like playing. And not knowing if I could was like living with a ghost."

That was the summer of 1977. Swoboda was sitting in a spare office at WCBS's broadcasting studio on West 57th Street in New York. It wasn't much of an office: a cubicle with a desk and two chairs. He sat behind the desk and tried to act cool about what he was saying. But Swoboda is not a cool guy. He is a kid trapped in a man's body. He gets excited when he's having fun, and everybody knows when he's angry or in trouble. Sitting there, wearing his current favorite uniform of slacks and a knit golf shirt, there was love in his face as he talked about playing baseball.

"There's no feeling in this world like playing," he was saying. "Getting a big hit is the biggest thrill. That's super macho shit. I beat this guy out there trying to throw this ball by me to the catcher. I beat him. And when you're a .240 hitter you know they've been beating you a hell of a lot more than you've been beating them."

In the two years since he joined WCBS, first with their 6:00 P.M. news show and then on the late news, the question hovered in his mind. Did he give up too easily? Could he have made it back? Then, before spring training of 1976, he contacted M. Donald Grant of the Mets and asked if he could come to camp. No contract. No promises. Just a try.

He leaned back in his chair and began talking about men who'd tried comebacks, some relatively successful and others not. He talked about Frank Gifford of the New York football Giants, who came back after retiring in 1960. And he talked about Jim Bouton, who, after retiring, had worked at the same television station as Swoboda, but who, at that very moment, was out there in Double A at the age of thirty-eight, trying to find a knuckleball effective enough to carry him back to the majors.

"I knew I was an average ballplayer before," said Swoboda, "and all I wanted to do was go back and see if I could be an average ballplayer again. I knew if I was ever going to try, that was the time."

There is no fairy-tale ending to this story. When Swoboda climbed back into a uniform for the first time in two years he discovered what he suspected all along. Time had taken its toll. He didn't play badly, but he didn't play up to the men fighting for outfield jobs on that team, up to Del Unser or Dave Kingman, or even Mike Vail or Bruce Boisclair.

"I knew I would be a thirty-two-year-old ballplayer when I got out there," he said, "but maturity sometimes means more than reflexes. I was older, but I was smarter. I thought that counted for more than it did."

Six years before, when Swoboda had played for New York, he was a young twenty-six-year-old. Full of energy and spunk, he was a main contributor to that image of the upstart Mets

PHOTO COURTESY WIDE WORLD PHOTOS

Ron Swoboda, on trying to come back in 1976: "To be perfectly honest, taking batting practice is more exciting than running the eleven o'clock news."

who upset the heavily favored Orioles in the World Series. But sitting there, analyzing his own needs and emotions, was a mature man with a strong sense of himself and what it is to be a professional athlete.

"There were times when I thought I was going to make it," he said, "when I thought I could show 'em I could play. There were moments when I really thought I had a chance. But it wasn't there. I just didn't have it. I couldn't make the big play. They knew it, and so did I. It wasn't a matter of being too old. It was being away. I'd been away from it too long."

So it ended. On a Monday morning in April Ron Swoboda was released for the final, final time. That quickly he was changed back again from a ballplayer to the man who reports the sports on the eleven o'clock news.

"It was a good thing to do," he said. "I laid it to rest. Hopefully, now it won't be a problem anymore. You can never be a hundred percent sure. But I'm close."

Would he have left WCBS, where he was making more money than he ever made in baseball?

"I would have had to show them one hell of a lot more than I did," he said. "But yeah, I'd have gone back. That's why I was there."

He stopped for a moment, pushing himself away from the desk he'd been borrowing for the last two hours. "I may have been just an average ballplayer," he said, "but being an average ballplayer to me is a hell of a lot more exciting than being the greatest sportscaster who ever lived. To be perfectly honest, taking batting practice is more exciting than running the eleven o'clock news."

A CLOSING SCENE

It is half past eleven, and the morning practice at the Tampa Bay Buccaneers' camp is over. None too soon. Everyone is feeling the tension. After ten days of two-a-days, the frequency of cuts is beginning to increase. Today at breakfast another player was released, the fifteenth so far. Few here had even gotten to know his name. Now he is gone.

The field has less the look of a place for games and more of the site of a battle just passed. Scattered randomly on the scarred and chewed turf are the casualties, men dressed in outrageous uniforms of orange and white, stretched out and exhausted from the morning's workout. They do not seem to breathe. They just lie there, helmets by their sides, enjoying the absence of abuse to their bodies.

It was a particularly hard, long scrimmage, running well over the usual two-hour limit. Two or three players were hurt and had to be helped into the trainer's room. Another, Charlie Evans, the veteran running back, was clotheslined by an ambitious rookie at the end of a play, and a fight erupted. There have been others over the first ten days, some the result of tension, many more caused by men just trying to get the coach's attention, showing him something—anything, even pure savagery—before being cut. They are the signs of pressure, as anxiety rapidly builds toward anguish. Each man finds his own way of hanging on. One, John Andrews, a tall, handsome tight end who came into camp with a pulled leg muscle, jogs delicately around the field, still nursing the injury. Each day the coach asks if he's ready to practice, and each day he shakes his head. Ten days on a muscle pull. He won't be able to hide much longer.

Slowly, with observable pain, the men begin to move. One by one they pull themselves to their feet. Pete Duranko, big and tired and wet with perspiration, drags himself toward the locker room. Council Rudolph, late to report and fighting to get in shape, lumbers across the field. As if responding to some inner clock, the half-dozen or so who flopped where they were when the scrimmage ended rally their strength and head in for a shower and some lunch. Within three hours they'll have to be back here to do it all over again.

Now the field is clear. Only one player remains outside the air-conditioned complex, sitting up by the door, leaning against the wall there amidst the scraps of white tape, the few small rolls and the odd strips, wads and balls pulled from ankles and pads. The man is Mike Current, one of the few players reasonably assured of making the team. He is an offensive tackle who's been drafted from Denver, and before undergoing knee surgery during the 1975 season he had been a starter for the Broncos for eight years.

Right now, however, he seems sure of nothing, and that includes his ability to get up and walk into the locker room. He sits against the wall, eyes closed, head tilted up at the clear blue sky. Beside him on the ground, his shoes, jersey, shoulder pads, and helmet are gathered in a pile of disarray.

He is a large hulk of a man, his pale shoulders and chest broad and massively developed the way an offensive lineman's must be, his thick arms powerful enough to keep the oncharging enemy at bay. But as he sits there, so peacefully, with his boyish face and blond hair, it is difficult to imagine his being aggressive toward anyone.

"I almost quit yesterday," he says, looking down at his left knee. "It always hurts, but yesterday morning was the worst. It was so stiff, so swollen that I couldn't bend it and I couldn't straighten it out. It was locked somewhere in between."

Then he shrugs, adding, "But I'm still here."

He sits there with his legs stretched out and talks about the knee injury, a cartilage damaged years before and constantly beaten on, splintered, and worn away until there was nothing but bone rubbing against bone at the joint, and then they operated. He talks about lying in the hospital bed in Denver and wondering if he'd ever play again, and about the Broncos giving up on him.

"The day I was operated on John Ralston [Denver's coach] wanted a walkie-talkie hooked up from my operating table to his office," says Current. "Then, as soon as they cut my leg open, they could radio back that he could go ahead and get another tackle. That's the kind of coldness I had seen happen to hundreds of guys before, but all of a sudden was upon me."

That was the end at Denver. By mutual agreement Current was left unprotected in the expansion draft, and Tampa selected him in an early round.

"If I were not to play this year I don't know how I'd handle it," he says. "I really want to play. Someone has said, 'Hey, I don't want you.' Denver said that, and I want to prove they're wrong."

Having someone say he wasn't wanted was not a new experience for Current. Denver drafted him out of Ohio State in the third round in 1967, then cut him after eight weeks. Miami picked him up, played him for a game, cut him, brought him back in two weeks for another game, then cut him again. He called Denver and they told him to come on back, activated him for one game, and then cut him for the fourth time in less than half a season.

"I fell apart," recalls Current. "I'd come from Ohio State where they told us we were the greatest for four years, and now someone was telling me I wasn't good enough to play on their team. I went home [to Toledo] and stayed with my parents for a while and had my mom tell me how wrong they were and how right I was, and when I finally got tired of that I started lifting weights and running—and running and running and running."

He returned to Denver for the 1968 season and, after some extra work on pass blocking ("Coming from Ohio State," he says, "I never heard of a dropback pass"), he started the first of 105 straight games, the streak interrupted only by the knee surgery after seven games of the 1975 season. Even before the operation was performed, the Broncos decided that they no longer had a place for Current.

"They said I couldn't do it anymore," he says, "but I'm here."

Current openly admits that part of the reason he's here is the money and the life style that football offers him. He's a man with responsibilities: he has a wife and a baby on the way, and two sons by a former marriage; his wife's daughter by a previous marriage lives with them, and so does her sister. Current happily welcomes them all under his wing, but he wants to pay the bills his way. He likes working at his sport for six months and fishing for six months, and he can't think of anyplace else where he'd be paid $75,000 to do that. But the main attraction is the game. Not only is it the only thing that he knows well, it is the only thing that makes him happy.

"I love Sundays," he says. "I hate practice but I love playing on Sunday. I love going out there and knocking somebody on his ass. I love putting a good move on somebody, or having somebody put a good move on me. And I love helping my team score. That's the greatest feeling in the world. Money gets me from Monday to Saturday. Sunday takes care of itself."

With all of those factors in support of his playing football, the obvious question is what brought him so close to quitting.

"It was a bad morning, and I was in a lot of pain," he says. "I thought about the pain and the bad blocks. I knew what was necessary to make it better, but I didn't know if it was worth it. You look ahead, and you wonder how many more mornings like that there'll be."

He talks about his own game and how the surgery has limited his mobility. He doesn't have the speed he once had, he says. His pass blocking is still good, but he can't "get out and motor" like he used to, and it bothers him when he can't do the things on the field that people expect of him. ("Some days I just can't do it, no matter how hard I try.")

He has nine years of experience in the league, and no one in the Bucs camp has more. It has earned him the tag of "old man," and that is a burden. It means he must go out every day and prove it isn't so.

"I've always got to be wondering if the Bucs are going to go to a youth movement," he says. "Am I expendable because I'm thirty years old? And what about next year? Then I'll be thirty-one! Listen, there's never been any security in this business for me—no one's ever given me a no-cut contract. I know damn well that if I don't do the job my ass is gonna be on the street, and it can happen at any time. But that's the way this business is. It's one of the reasons we're making this kind of money for however long we last."

It's nearly noon. Current struggles to his feet, using his helmet for leverage. Yesterday it took a combination of sound, ice, and heat to control the swelling and the stiffness in his knee. Today it is better, but there is still pain. The pain never leaves.

The conversation comes full circle. If there's so much pain and the insecurity takes such a toll, why go on playing?

"For Sunday," he says. "I really and truly enjoy Sunday afternoon. I may never go to a football game after it's over because I'll miss it so much."

He picks up his helmet and pads and the rest of his gear and starts to head in. "They call me old man and they burn my ass," he says, "but I'm here."

PHOTO BY SKIP ROZIN

Mike Current, sweaty, tired and hurting: ". . . but I'm here."

EPILOGUE

Some of the athletes with whom we have spent time require no further word in the context of our story. Steve Mix is still the third forward with the Philadelphia 76ers; Sammy Ellis is still the pitching coach for the Fort Lauderdale Yankees. For others, whose lives have significantly changed, the following current information is offered.

An Opening Scene

It might surprise no one that the only player introduced at that very first camp of the Tampa Bay Buccaneers who survived the first season and returned for the second was John McKay, Jr., son of the head coach. Of the ninety-six men in camp that first day, only twenty-two made it through the season. In all, during those fourteen games (of which the Bucs won none) 142 different men saw playing time.

Chapter One

Donn Seidholz, the minor league baseball player, bounced back and forth between Double A in the Southern League and

Triple A in the American Association in 1977, and is currently playing Double A ball in Knoxville.

Tommy Davis played most of that 1976 season with the California Angels, then was traded toward the end of the season to Kansas City. He was released by the Royals prior to spring training the following February and officially retired; he is now working in national promotion for Casablanca Records in Los Angeles, California.

Chapter Two

Bernard King left the University of Tennessee after his junior year, and was taken in the hardship draft of 1977 by the New York Nets, who later that summer moved to New Jersey. He was one of the few bright spots for the Nets in that 1977–78 season, scoring 24.2 points a game, tenth best in the league.

Lonnie Shelton continued to establish himself as one of the good young men in the NBA, and by 1978 was a popular fixture with the Knicks.

Rick Bullock went into temporary seclusion after being cut by the Knicks in 1976, but then talked with other clubs. He was invited to the San Antonio camp the following September but was cut before the season began. "That's it," he said from his home in San Antonio. "No more. I'm doing like my father said I shoulda done all along. I'm back in school in business, and I'm gonna get a job. I wish it was different, but that's how it is."

Phil Jackson seemed ready to retire from basketball after the last game of the 1977–78 season, but in a postseason trade he went to the Nets and signed a multiyear contract.

Chapter Three

Larry Foster was finally freed from his bondage to the Knox Sox. He was traded to the Kansas City organization at the end of the 1977 season, went to camp with the Royals in '78, and was assigned to their Triple A club in Omaha.

Fred Norton never found another club to sign him; he now

plays softball for recreation and works as a mason in Mill Run, Pennsylvania.

Kevin Bell, playing with the White Sox in June 1977, was injured in a collision at home while trying to score. The recuperation time for his injury, a torn rear ligament in the left knee, was projected by the Sox as one year. "We're not going to rush any player that valuable," said Chicago vice president Roland Hemond. "He's got a future."

Carl Giosa, the minor league football player, carried out his plan in 1977. He studied the rosters before trying another NFL free agent camp. Then he tried the Colts again, and then the Giants in 1978. Each time he was cut and each time he returned to catching passes for the Jersey Oaks. He helped them win the league championship in 1977.

Charlie Criss not only played all of the 1977–1978 season with the Hawks, participating in seventy-seven of their eighty-two games, but he finished as the team's third-highest scorer, averaging 11.4 points a game. Atlanta rewarded him with a new, multiyear contract. During the summer of 1978, naturally, he could be found playing basketball in the city leagues in and around New York.

Chapter Four

Pete Varney did pull himself together after being sent to the minors in 1976. But when he went through most of the 1977 season hitting over .300 and still the Braves did not bring him up to Atlanta, he tried to work out his own deal as a free agent. "My lawyer talked to every team in both leagues," said Varney, who was twenty-eight in 1977, "and they all said I was too old." Varney figured he'd given baseball all he could at that point. He retired and is now living with his wife and two children in the Boston area, pursuing his master's in education at Boston University and working as a baseball coach.

Jim Foote's quest for his dream ended when the Houston Oilers released him prior to the 1977 season. He now runs a discotheque, The Orchard Club, in Houston.

Duane Carrell, who thought he'd finally found a home punting for the Jets in 1976, was cut at the end of their 1977 training camp, then signed with St. Louis for the season. "I feel terrific here," he said midway through that season. "I feel like I'm part of something permanent." Carrell's security lasted until the college draft during that off-season, when the Cardinals' first choice was Steve Little, a punter out of Arkansas.

Lenny Randle is considered by most baseball people to be a lucky man. After his fight with Texas manager Frank Lucchesi in the spring of 1977—a fight which sent Lucchesi to the hospital—Randle was traded to the Mets, and has played well there. Baseball, a conservative sport, has been known to banish players for less radical behavior.

Dave Gallagher is now attending medical school at the University of Michigan.

Wayne Mulligan is retired from football, and works as a sales representative for Industrial Coatings, Incorporated, in Baltimore.

Chapter Five

The status of stars rarely changes. All of the athletes in this chapter are still playing with their respective teams, and seem happy with things that way.

Chapter Six

The whereabouts of Bonnie Yarbrough is a mystery, but all information indicates that his football career ended after the University of Miami's last game in 1958.

Mo Layton was cut by the Knicks after training camp prior to the 1977–78 season. He signed with San Antonio, spending that season as a reserve guard with the Spurs.

Chapter Seven

Bob Oliver decided over the winter of 1977 that he really did not want to be a teacher of baseball players; he only wanted to be a ballplayer. So he signed with Puebla in the Mexican League; as of the first week of June, 1978, he is hitting a healthy .339.

Mike Riordan retired from basketball at the end of the 1976–77 season when no NBA club expressed interest in him. He now operates Riordan's Saloon in Annapolis, Maryland.

Neal Walk never did sign with the Detroit Pistons. Instead, he accepted a lucrative offer to play in Italy, and spent the 1977–78 season with the basketball team based in Venice.

Norman Snead retired from professional football when the Giants did not invite him to camp for the 1977 season. He returned to his home in Yorktown, Virginia, to work for the Newport News Shipbuilding and Dry Dock Company as a recruitment coordinator and coach of their football team. When asked if he missed football after sixteen seasons as a pro, he replied, "No," then, "but if the Giants find they need a quarterback, I think I know where to find a good one."

Chapter Eight

Dave Smith was cut by the Giants before the beginning of the 1976 season; he returned to Pittsburgh, where he continues to work with the youth of the area and to run his radio talk show on sports.

Jim Barnett finally heard from someone in the NBA. Midway through the 1976 season he signed with the Philadelphia 76ers, filling in for the injured Doug Collins. When Collins returned in April, Barnett retired for good; now he works for Jack Nadel, Incorporated, a specialty advertising firm selling promotional items.

Brooks Robinson is employed by Crown Central Petroleum, mostly in a promotional capacity, and provides color commentary for the Orioles' televised games.

Ray Sadecki lasted with the Mets through the first month of the 1977 season, and was released. He turned down offers from St. Louis and California to serve as a minor league pitching coach because he wanted to remain near his family. He now works as a salesman of business machines in his hometown of Kansas City, Missouri.

Nick Buoniconti played one more season in 1976, then retired to practice law, report football for CBS, and represent the best interests of a dozen or so professional athletes.

A Closing Scene

Mike Current fared better than did the Tampa Bay Buccaneers in the NFL. He played through that disastrous 1976 season, but during the following training camp the team decided it needed more youth on the line, and traded him to Miami. After a difficult training camp ("I retired and unretired three times a day," recalls Current), he settled down as the Dolphins' starting right tackle, received a $15,000 raise, and is now looking forward to making the playoffs in 1978 for the first time in his career.

Index

[*Italic* page numbers indicate photographs.]